The Big Book of New England
CURIOSITIES

Curiosities Series

The Big Book of New England CURIOSITIES

From Orange, CT, to Blue Hill, ME, a Guide to the Quirkiest, Oddest, and Most Unbelievable Stuff You'll See

By Susan Campbell and Bruce Gellerman

With Erik Sherman, Bill Heald, Tim Sample, Steve Bither, Eric Jones, Seth Brown, and Robert F. Wilson

Guilford, Connecticut

The prices, rates, and hours listed in this guidebook were confirmed at press time. We recommend, however, that you call establishments to obtain current information before traveling.

To buy books in quantity for corporate use
or incentives, call **(800) 962–0973**
or e-mail **premiums@GlobePequot.com.**

Photos by the author unless otherwise noted.

Text design: Bret Kerr

Layout artist: Kim Burdick

Project editor: Ellen Urban

Library of Congress Cataloging-in-Publication data is available on file.

ISBN 978-0-7627-5468-7

Printed in the United States of America

10 9 8 7 6 5 4 3 2 1

contents

preface

★ ★

New England is a curious place.

Its six states (all at the very bottom of the list of states in physical size) represent a small corner of a big nation. Yet its influence has always been wildly disproportionate to its size.

In its nearly four centuries of existence, little New England has transformed the larger nation in big ways: by its zealous drive to harness every waterway, plow every field, clear every forest, stack every rock; by its tendency to produce the writers and engineers and politicians and thinkers that set the tone and crafted the arguments that drove America onward, outward, even at times inward.

Yet the rest of the country has always harbored a bit of a grudge against New England, casting it as smug, self-righteous, overly homogenous, even snobbish. In turn, New England has stood its ground at arm's length, gazing at its heavier siblings with an expression both pitying and patient – just as, the high school valedictorian might regard the captain of the high school football team.

Like all over-achievers, New England is used to the niggling jealousies and insecurities of the big jock states. Sure, those other states can run faster, lift more, drink more, and get a date with the prom queen. But just wait a few years and see who's washing whose expensive German convertible.

And yet, for all its intellectual strength, New England is still quite capable of sharing a good joke at its own expense, of smiling good-naturedly and occasionally letting out a hearty laugh. For, Lord knows, it can be a funny place.

So now we pull back the curtain and present the goofy, odd, strange, unusual, zany, funky, head-scratchingly eccentric face of this buttoned-down part of the United States. We've carefully combed through our Curiosities series for each individual New England state for the best and most telling curiosities New England has to offer, which we present to you here in *The Big Book of New England Curiosities*.

—the Editors

1

Connecticut Curiosities

At first glance, *Connecticut might not look too special compared with a lot of other states. It's basically a big rectangle, unlike geographically shapely states like Florida or Italy. Granted, Italy isn't a state, but it's certainly more interesting to look at on a map than a place resembling a big credit card with a tail.*

We Nutmeggers are also saddled with a lack of major league sports franchises. We have no enormous movie studios (yet), no Silicon Valley, and no signature dish (like Texas has chili or California has tofu). New Jersey has Bruce Springsteen, Alaska has Jewel, and Oklahoma has Merle Haggard. Even Hawaii has Don Ho—and they're way out in the middle of the ocean, for crying out loud.

Given this apparent lack of "color," when we were asked to write a book about the crazy, wacky side of Connecticut we were initially skeptical. "Where is the wackiness?" we asked. "Our Connecticut neighbors are pragmatic, sensible New England types. Where's the beef, in terms of outlandish antics?"

Come to find out, the wackiness is around the next corner, in Willimantic, in the form of giant frogs. The beef is found in a beat-up diner that sells gourmet food. Connecticut displays its off-the-wall uniqueness in the creative power that turns a backyard garage into the source of silky horsepower for some of the world's most exotic cars (like Aston-Martins) or the innovative thinking that produced, quite possibly, the nation's first pizza.

★ ★

In these pages you will discover, as we did, that Connecticut harbors strange, unusual, and wonderfully funny people who do some pretty bizarre and fascinating things. Did we uncover wackiness? You bet, but more often than not it is a subtle wackiness that manifests itself in sophisticated ways. Connecticut residents have created submarines—and chronicled political events in ostrich eggs. The first penny was minted inside our borders, and we have the oldest continuously published daily newspaper. We have an incredible history here, and the more you poke around, the wilder it gets.

Poking around, by the way, is the only way to truly see the more unusual treasures that Connecticut has to offer. This is a small-town, nook-and-cranny type of state—a well-populated yet highly private territory where you can easily miss a dinosaur parked in the backyard of a typical suburban dwelling if you're not keeping a wary eye out. Even our geology is interesting, for if a rock isn't engaging enough on its own, someone will paint the sucker so that it literally stops traffic.

We mentioned history, and Connecticut has more than its share. As one of the original thirteen colonies, our revolutionary heritage is found all over the place, and our legends are, well, legend. And in terms of historic hardware, there are many old yet incredibly well-preserved artifacts in this state.

Some of these relics are rather unusual; we tend to cherish some items that less-enlightened individuals might throw away. Fire a cannonball into one of our taverns during a Revolutionary War battle, and we're likely to keep the ordnance for hundreds of years as an alternative home decoration. Our weathervanes last for centuries, even after inebriated soldiers pepper them with bullets. When our Colonial farmers built walls, they lasted to the present day, even though the builders used no mortar of any type.

Ours is a state where Mark Twain once roamed and where he passed his last days on earth. His particular brand of honesty, integrity, humor, and invention fit Connecticut like his trademark white suit.

* *

Wiffle balls—those weird, perforated plastic baseballs that have spared many an urban window from destruction—began life in Connecticut. We have tall, brawny flagpoles and extremely short ferries. Our gardens are unique, our cuisine is remarkable, our oaks are patriotic. We still hand-bottle soda pop and have a parade for boomboxes that will never rival Macy's affair but has a homespun-genuinely-weird quality that dwarfs the aura of even the mightiest helium-filled balloon.

Intrigued? So were we as we traveled around exploring Connecticut's hidden crazier attractions. We now invite you to join us in these pages and explore the singular wonders that make Connecticut unique, entertaining—and even, yes, wacky. A big rectangle? Hah! That rectangle is a canvas depicting a wild, colorful world painted by some of the most talented and quirky artists on the planet. Enjoy!

Kicking the Hollywood Habit
Bethlehem

In the late 1950s, Dolores Hart was a Hollywood starlet. She was a Princess Grace look-alike with a natural screen presence—so natural that her first screen appearance was with Elvis Presley in *Loving You*. In the next six short years, she appeared in ten other films, including another Presley film, *King Creole*, and the classic teen-angst flick *Where the Boys Are*. In that one she was the carefree girl who dove fully clothed into a club's huge fish tank.

Life was good, but Dolores had visited the Abbey of Regina Laudis in Bethlehem on retreat, and she kept finding herself back at the abbey's wooden gate. In 1963 a studio limo once more dropped off Dolores, then twenty-four, with the Benedictines and their Gregorian chant, and after two weeks she knew she would stay. She briefly returned to her worldly life to say good-bye. She told her stunned but supportive fiancé, her incredulous family, and producer Hal Wallis, who could not believe she'd throw away her future for a cloistered life. She has lived the simple life of a nun since.

Mother Dolores, now in her early seventies, is not the only Regina Laudis nun to have turned her back on a successful secular life. There are lawyers and politicians—even a member of royalty—and each nun stays as connected to her past life and profession as her order allows. Mother Dolores is still a member of the Academy of Motion Picture Arts and Sciences and gets videos of first-run movies. By the way, she loved *Dead Man Walking* and was stunned at the rawness of *Saving Private Ryan*.

Where Things Go Bump around the Clock
Cornwall

Near the thriving city of Cornwall is a group of foundation remnants and cellar holes that once was the village of Dudleytown—also known as Village of the Damned.

If that doesn't get your ghostbuster blood flowing, you need to check your pulse.

Legend is that a nineteenth-century curse led to the desertion of this town, located off a little-used path now known as Dark Entry Road. For some reason early settlers ignored that the land was too rocky for cultivation and the area too far removed from a ready water source. Add to those problems the dimness of Dudleytown, which is constantly in the shadows of the surrounding hills.

The legend varies, but boiled down, the town was abandoned after an uncomfortably large number of town residents went insane or succumbed to sudden, violent deaths. One researcher says that the town may have suffered from a kind of collective madness that could be traced to its forebears in England. Some say the early families of the town's inhabitants once tried to usurp the English crown and for their troubles were beheaded and cursed. Others say that since the rocks in the area are lousy with lead, the groundwater must be also. The only thing we know for sure is that by 1899 no one lived in Dudleytown, and the forest moved back in.

★ ★

These days—other than the holes in the ground—all that remains are reported orbs of light that swirl around in the gloom. Hikers swear that birds and forest animals do not enter the boundaries of the hamlet, and, sure enough, the woods thereabouts are eerily silent. Or maybe that's just our imagination. Dudleytown is just south of Colts-foot Mountain. Take Route 7 south from Cornwall Bridge. About 2 miles down the road you'll find Dark Entry Road on the left. Enter at your own risk. "No Parking" signs line both sides of the rural road and the owners don't want visitors.

If These Stones Could Talk

Salisbury

Ruth Shapleigh-Brown is executive director of Connecticut Gravestone Network—a volunteer group that protects historical burial grounds and cemeteries like Dutcher's Burying Ground in Salisbury. She and others travel around the state clearing brush, recording information from stones almost lost to the elements, and making sure the plots are protected from development.

Along with the information on the stones, the network also records the histories of the various burying grounds. Dutcher's was purchased by the town of Salisbury in 1802 from Rulff Dutcher, for one dollar. The earliest graves found here date from 1767, and the latest grave-stone is dated 1881. Carvings on many of the stones are all but eaten away, and people like Shapleigh-Brown discourage "rubbings"—placing thin paper over the stones and then rubbing a pencil across in order to see what the stone once said. Even that tends to wear down the already-fragile brownstones and limestones.

The cemetery is a good example of many of the 2,400 cemeteries scattered around Connecticut. (The last accurate count taken was in 1934, by the Work Projects Administration.) Within Dutcher's, there are the family plots—like those of the Carter family, with matriarch Anna Carter's stone calling her the "relief" of husband Benoni, who

★ ★

is buried next to her. Take a moment to read the stones. Anna Carter must have left suddenly. A poem carved into the foot of her 4-foot-high stone reads:

> When Death is sent from God above
> And calls us from those who dearly love
> He doesn't always warning give
> Dear friends, be careful how you live.

Dutcher's Burying Ground is on Route 44, heading west just past the Housatonic River and up Weatogue Road on your right.

Some of Connecticut's early settlers are buried here.

There's No Such Thing as "Just a Chair"

And don't you think otherwise, bub. For nearly 200 years, the Hitchcock Chair Company turned out distinctive hardwood furniture from an 11,000-square-foot factory in New Hartford. At its peak the company had around one hundred employees.

Initially, founder Lambert Hitchcock (1795–1852) manufactured individual chair parts that he sold as do-it-yourself kits. Later, he sold complete factory-made chairs typically painted black or red with stenciled decoration. The seats were not upholstered but caned.

Today, Hitchcock chairs are included in many a museum's collection of American decorative arts.

Padlocks of the Ancient Ones

Terryville

If you told someone you had traveled a great distance to see a baroque lock, they might ask if you would be likewise interested in viewing a damaged tool box or malfunctioning toaster oven.

But this time we're talking about baroque as in Baroque, the dominant style in Europe around the seventeenth and eighteenth centuries. The Lock Museum is one of those weird and wonderful places where commonplace objects take on a whole new dimension. Did you know that the basic design for the tumbler lock dates back thousands of years? This museum even has an Egyptian lock to show how thieves were deterred back when home security meant you owned a large club or, like Pharaoh, had some particularly well-trained cats.

★ ★

This museum at 230 Main Street (860–589–6359) has probably the world's most comprehensive collection of locks of every size and description, manufactured by such famous names as Mosler, Reese, Slaymaker, Sesamee, and Slage. There are regular padlocks, push-button combination locks, and even an enormous lock from an English castle. Locks don't just mean the external variety, either, for there are plenty of doorknobs with integral locks from such storied venues as the Waldorf Astoria Hotel. These are not just devices designed to keep maids out of your room early in the morning; they're small works of architectural art. In fact, most big hotels like the Waldorf made the lock companies destroy the patterns once they had finished installing the locks in the hotel to ensure that no other building would have the same design. Neat stuff.

Got keys?

Connecticut's state song, "Yankee Doodle," was first sung, according to recent scholarship, during the French and Indian War as a taunt to the ragtag militia. But the lyrics are far older, stretching back to the 1600s. The Dutch may have come up with the nickname "Yankee," the approximate equivalent of "country squire," or somewhere thereabouts. New Englanders hated the song, and singing it could spark a fistfight. But by the battles of Lexington and Concord, the new Americans were singing the song in defiance as the whipped British retreated. The tune so enraged British troops that part of the terms of surrender at Yorktown was that the American bands would not play "Yankee Doodle." When the British troops marched down a column of French and American soldiers, however, they kept their heads turned to the French as an insult to the Americans. Angry, the Marquis de Lafayette ordered the musicians to strike up—you guessed it—"Yankee Doodle."

Say "Bridge!"
West Cornwall

The covered bridge at West Cornwall is one of the state's three picturesque covered bridges (and one of America's maybe 1,000), and it may be the most popular. Every Columbus Day, townspeople hold Covered Bridge Days with fly-fishing demonstrations, samples of local food, and a chance to win stoneware from Cornwall Bridge Pottery. The event attracts people from all over New England—even from Vermont, where they have covered bridges of their own.

In addition to being on the walls and in the scrapbooks of photographers near and far, the bridge has been featured on Connecticut state lottery tickets. Not bad for a bridge built in 1864. By the way, do

★ ★

not be confused with Cornwall Bridge, the town. That's farther south on Route 7. You want West Cornwall, at the intersections of Routes 7 and 128.

This kind of picture-pretty place really does exist in Connecticut. No, really.

It's about Time
Bristol

If you are Quasimodo, or have an aversion to things that tick, buzz, or gong on occasion, you should perhaps avoid the American Clock and Watch Museum at 100 Maple Street in Bristol (860–583–6070, www .clockmuseum.org). There are all manner of timekeeping devices here, and they have all kinds of noisy ways to notify the world that time, in fact, is marching on.

★ ★

But if (unlike the famous hunchback) you're not tormented by "The Bells!" and you've ever been curious about the scope of timekeeping devices and where they all came from, this is your Mecca.

Why are all these clocks and watches here in Bristol, ticking, buzzing, and, on occasion, gonging? Why did literally thousands of timekeeping devices decide to flee their owners and congregate here, in the historic Miles Lewis house?

Simple. Years ago Connecticut was a world hub for watch and clock manufacturing. While this formidable collection has timekeeping devices from all over the world, the bulk of these clocks and watches come not just from New England but from Connecticut itself. For nearly fifty years this museum has been collecting timepieces and now possesses more than 1,400 specimens.

From tiny key watches to a Porky Pig wrist timepiece (for p-p-p-p-punctuality) to massive tower clocks, there's something here for just about anybody who enjoys mechanical devices. The collection is here; all you need is the time.

The Country's Oldest Continuously Operated Amusement Park
Bristol

In 1846, a Bristol scientist conducted what was advertised as "a series of beautiful experiments in electricity," and attracted a crowd at Lake Compounce. The experiments failed, but the crowds inspired the land's owner to set up picnic tables and organize lakeside concerts.

Lake Compounce was born. Over time, a restaurant was built, then a carousel and a ballroom, which hosted the up-and-coming Frank Sinatra. Rides were added, and Lake Compounce reigned supreme in the post–World War II years. Families from all over New England took their little baby boomers for a look at the Cowboy Caravan.

But like many amusement parks, Lake Compounce fell on hard times in the '80s, and sometimes heroic measures were taken to hang on to that "continuously" part of their advertisement.

In recent years, the park has grown and expanded. They've managed to thrive, in fact, and their Boulder Dash roller coaster received

★ ★

the highest rating by the National Amusement Park Historical Association in its first year of its operation.

The park is just off exit 31 on I-84 in Bristol. For more information, visit www.lakecompounce.com.

Perhaps the sign should say open in perpetuity.

But Would You Join a Club That Would Have the Likes of You?
Hartford

As long as there have been people, there have been people who are better than you, or at least think they are. New York has elite clubs. So does Boston.

A Whole Lot of Shakin' Going On

In the mid-eighteenth century a British woman, Ann Lee, founded a Protestant sect known as the Shakers—so called because of their ritualized twitching during worship services. The sect quickly took root in the New World in utopian communities from Kentucky to Ohio to Maine.

Members believed in heaven on earth through an orderly kind of living that included celibacy. Married couples who joined the sect together understood they would live in separate living quarters as brother and sister. Shakers kept the pews packed with converts, the destitute who had no place else to go, and orphans left with the community.

Shakers came to Enfield, north of Hartford, and established a community that at its height boasted five villages—called families—and 260 members, who settled into one hundred stately buildings on prime farmland. This particular group is thought to have been the first manufacturers of packaged seeds in the country. But attracting members to an obscure, sexless group grew too difficult. During World War I, the Enfield community disbanded and its remaining members moved to other Shaker villages. The bulk of the old community now lies on the grounds of a Connecticut prison, but several large, white barnlike buildings remain and can be seen from Shaker Road (Route 220).

Why not Hartford?

By the turn of the nineteenth century, Connecticut's capital had its Hartford Female Beneficent Society, its Hartford Arts Union, and its Sons of Temperance. But it is the Hartford Club that sustains. This

★ ★

oh-so-exclusive enclave was formed in 1873 as a site for "gentlemen who had agreed to form an Association for the promotion of social intercourse, art, and literature." This during the economic Panic of 1873, which Hartford weathered nicely, thank you.

Through the years the place has been home to some famous Connecticut names. The group first met in the old Trumbull House, home of Joseph Trumbull, nephew of a former state governor and a former

The Hartford Club is lowering its standards—
even the likes of you can eat here now.

(inept) governor himself. Later they moved to the former Wadsworth mansion (near the current Wadsworth Atheneum), where George Washington's horse once slept in the barn out back. No kidding.

In 1881 Samuel L. Clemens was elected to the club. He'd first come to Hartford in 1868 to arrange for the publication of his *Innocents Abroad,* and he liked what he saw. He wrote to a friend, "I tell you I have to walk mighty straight. I desire to have the respect of this sterling old Puritan community . . . so I don't dare to smoke after I go to bed, & in fact, I don't dare to do anything that's comfortable and natural." He livened things up just a bit.

If you're not a member, see if you can cadge an invitation to lunch at the club at 46 Prospect. It's loosened its cravat just a tinge.

A Home for Huck

Hartford

It's hard to say whether it most resembles a riverboat or a chocolate factory, but Mark Twain's Hartford home on Farmington Avenue (860–247–0998, www.marktwainhouse.org) is a bizarre structure. Designed by architect Edward Potter (no relation to Harry, as far as we know), the place is a wild, warm, intriguing residence as complex as the man himself. As if mimicking his wild, unruly hair, there are chimneys sprouting everywhere and no fewer than five balconies. A now-defunct local paper, the *Hartford Daily Times,* wrote an apt description of the place in the 1870s:

"Many of the readers of the *Times,* doubtless, have had at least an external view of the structure, which already has acquired something beyond local fame; and such persons, we think, will agree with us in the opinion that it is one of the oddest looking buildings in the state ever designed for a dwelling, if not in the whole country."

Twain and his family lived in the house from 1874 to 1891, and early on, the endless building process wore the famous writer's patience a bit thin. According to Albert Paine's biography, Twain complained:

★ ★

"I have been bullyragged by the builder, by his foreman, by the architect, by the tapestry devil who is to upholster the furniture, by the idiot who is putting down the carpets, by the scoundrel who is setting up the billiard table (and has left the balls in New York), by the wildcat who is sodding the ground and finishing the driveway (after the sun went down), by a book agent, whose body is in the backyard and the coroner notified. Just think of this going on the whole day long, and I loathe details with all my heart!"

There's no home on earth quite like it, and excellent tours are given for a modest fee.

Riverboat meets chocolate factory.

America's Oldest Continuously Published Newspaper

The *Hartford Courant,* which began publication in October 1764, has seen 'em come and seen 'em go – and nowadays it seems they mostly go.

In 1776 the newspaper, like other New England publications of the time, printed the "Declaration of Independence"—on page 4. Back then, news judgment was not a consideration. News was printed as it was received—and often, "news" was little more than reprints of letters or tavern gossip.

In 1806 the newspaper was indicted for criminal libel against the administration of Thomas Jefferson. It's been an interesting history. For more information, call (860) 241–6200, or visit www.courant.com.

Witches? We've Got Witches

Hartford

Salem, Massachusetts, may get the tourists, but Connecticut had its own witch scare before the folks to the north had even dreamed up familiars—or the dunking test.

In 1647, Alyse (or Achsah) Young was hanged at the site of the Old State House on Main Street in Hartford. Another woman, Lydia Gilbert, was tried as a witch in 1653. She was accused of using witchcraft to influence one man to shoot another. The man who shot the gun was fined twenty pounds. Like Alyse Young, Gilbert was hanged.

Others—all women—were tried and hanged as witches. (Despite the common belief, persons convicted of witchcraft were rarely burned in America. They were more often hanged, drowned, or crushed under large rocks—a manner of death that went by the more genteel name of "pressing," as one would a pair of pants.)

Legend is that a portion of Trinity College in Hartford's South End, known as "Gallows Hill," was also once the site of a witch hanging. The same legend holds for Hartford's South Green, located at the juncture of Main and Wethersfield. A Trinity College dance instructor, Judy Dworin, has written and performed a piece about the Connecticut witch trials, called "Burning."

An Onion Grows in Hartford

Hartford

Samuel Colt was one of America's early industrialists. He was also a big blowhard. In 1835 Colt patented the revolving-breech pistol and opened a new factory to manufacture pistols. That venture failed within six years. In 1847 he opened another brownstone factory in Hartford, which he topped with a Russian-influenced blue dome.

Around it, the aggressively self-aggrandizing Colt built what he thought would be a remarkable utopian factory complex that included worker housing and recreational areas. His wife, Elizabeth, organized day care centers. They christened it Coltsville, and historians say it turned Hartford into the "Silicon Valley of the nineteenth century."

But the high-living Samuel died in 1862 and left his wife to keep the business going. She did so assiduously, even through a disastrous 1864 fire that killed one employee and did $33 million in damage—and destroyed the beloved globe. Within two years the factory was rebuilt—this time in brick—and the blue, star-spangled globe, modeled after a church in Moscow, was replaced. The building itself is now under renovation.

Don't you wish you had one on your house?

Pop with Class
New Britain

It's tough to find a soft drink company that doesn't have a major star or two hawking their product on television. It's even harder to find one that makes flavors that a true soda connoisseur can appreciate—tasty concoctions that go beyond the mundane flavors we've allowed to dominate the marketplace.

But Avery's in New Britain (860–340–0830, www.averysoda.com) can take care of your carbonated beverage needs, for they truly hand-craft every bottle of liquid joy they sell. The Avery name has been on

★ ★

soda pop since 1904, and the company still does things in a low-volume way that ensures the kind of quality you can't get from the big soda conglomerates.

Like variety? Avery's has about thirty standard flavors and a special-edition Flavor of the Month. You can actually watch such exotics as Watermelon or Kiwi get bottled, too, as the machinery is right there in the store. Even the bottles are cool, and you can't beat the taste.

To learn more, visit the Web site: www.averysoda.com.

There's some serious soda inside this bottle.

The Southwick Jog

Along Connecticut's northern boundary there is a hitch known as the Southwick Jog—a 6-square-mile piece of Massachusetts that juts into Connecticut along what is otherwise a fairly straight border.

The line was originally drawn in 1642 by Nathaniel Woodward and Solomon Saffrey, two men known for their professionalism and artistry—but who had trouble drawing a straight line. They started southwest of Boston, sailed around Cape Cod, into Long Island Sound, and up the Connecticut River to set their next marker. They were a little south of where they needed to be, and that area—what is now Enfield—was disputed for decades.

You could say that Connecticut won that dispute but lost Southwick. It was said for years that the notch served as a tab, keeping Massachusetts from sliding into the sea. Others say Woodward and Saffrey were frightened by Algonquin Indians as they tried to draw their straight line—or maybe they were tippling, just a bit. Either way, the notch and its Congamond Lakes, which provided power for mills in the area, remain Massachusetts land.

By 1820 Connecticut had conceded the land, although state officials have issued subsequent threats to overtake it. They're kidding, of course. A volunteer organization, Citizens Restoring Congamond, keeps the place looking splendiferous. While there, try the fare at Crabby Joe's.

A House Full of Words
West Hartford

Who among us at some point in their personal history hasn't either perused, studied, thrown, or used for its sheer heftiness (such as a

★ ★

doorstop or gravity clamp when gluing some broken objet d'art) a *Webster's Dictionary*?

I think we have all met up with this formidable volume, but have you ever wondered what kind of mind it would take to tediously record all the words in a given language? We have, and it boggles our minds, to say the least. Here in Connecticut we have the unusual opportunity to gain some insight into the upbringing of Noah Webster, the man who brought the first American dictionary to the world.

The Noah Webster House Museum of West Hartford History (860–521–5362, www.noahwebsterhouse.org) is a beautifully restored peek back into New England history courtesy of the amazing scribe's childhood home. Noah lived here the first sixteen years of his life before

Noah Webster's childhood home was clearly a place of great in-house Scrabble games.

Look, Ma! No Mortar

Lining two-lane country roads and snaking across the horizon of distant hills in eastern Connecticut is a maze of rock walls, many of them built by colonists looking for a creative way to use the rocks they dug up as they plowed their fields.

The rocks—many of them now covered with lace-doily lichen that will eventually break down the rocks and destroy them—were simply stacked atop one another to make a wall. There is no mortar holding them together, but the farmers knew what they were doing. Some of the walls have stood for 200-plus years. Their biggest predator is the contractors who dismantle them to recreate the look of old New England in new housing developments—that, and the aforementioned lichen.

A particularly pretty assortment of rock walls lines fields along Route 169 at the northern border of Canterbury.

heading off to Yale, and thanks to guides dressed in period costume and a variety of artifacts from the era, you get a glimpse into the life of his Connecticut family and maybe some clues as to how he became so patient, well organized, and scholarly. You'll find out that after college Noah became a teacher and became so disgusted that there were so few genuine American textbooks, he started his literary legacy by writing a grammar book that became known as the *Blue Back Speller*. He eventually moved on to the dictionary, and the rest is reference history.

The house is where the words that Noah would later put down on paper first started swirling around in his head. Inhale the ambience,

★ ★

and see if you can detect the faintest whiff of "pernicious," "discombobulated," or any other wild terms that may well have been subtly working their way into the young Webster's psyche. There are some period activities you can engage in, and with a visit to this fine home you gain an appreciation for the life the Webster family and countless other New Englanders experienced on a daily basis.

State nicknames: Constitution State, Provision State (we supplied a lot of the stuff for the army in the Revolutionary War, and don't you forget it), Nutmeg State (not necessarily a good thing), and—keep this one to yourself because it's damn embarrassing—Land of Steady Habits.

The Serious Business of Puppetry
Mansfield

All right, class. Now lift the right arm! No, the right! The right! Don't you know anything?

The folks at the University of Connecticut's puppetry program and the Ballard Institute & Museum of Puppetry take their puppets very seriously. Besides stunning men and women's basketball teams, the school offers the only puppet arts training program in the country where students can earn an FBA, MA, or MFA.

It's not kid's play, either. Alumni have worked on Broadway (*The Lion King*), in Hollywood (you name it), and throughout the world.

The puppet program, part of the drama department, was started in 1968 by Professor Frank Ballard, who'd joined the faculty a few

Most of Ballard's puppets aren't nearly so static.

years earlier. It has expanded now to include classrooms, theaters, and a puppet lab where, twenty-four hours a day, students can build the perfect beast. They are encouraged to do that, in fact, and if you walk through the lab or anywhere near it you might hear the kind of frustrated cries any creator is subject to: "Damn these hands!" "My eyes won't work!" "I can't get her to stand straight!" Puppetry students are encouraged to mount at least one production in their UConn career; puppet classes are open to any UConn student.

The Ballard Institute & Museum of Puppetry is in Willimantic Cottage on Route 44 at the UConn Depot Campus—what was once the Mansfield Training School. Call (860) 486–4605.

★ ★

Here's an old Connecticut custom we think should be revived: bundling. When a young man and a young woman were trying to make a decision whether to marry, the idea of sexual compatibility was not overlooked. Oh, no. The two were allowed—under fairly strict supervision—to spend the evening together. In bed. Fully clothed. Often with a long board between them. Many times they were wrapped tightly in separate blankets (hence, "bundling"). Of course the overseers—usually one or both sets of the young folks' parents—had to sleep eventually. And boards can be removed, as can tightly wrapped blankets—and clothing. Oh, those nutsy, kookie Puritans!

A True Cinematic Survivor
Mansfield

It's a curious thing when an icon of past popular culture stays around when many considered it to be obsolete. A perfect example is the drive-in movie. There are abandoned examples of these outdoor theaters all over this country. What's really weird is when you find one that is not only surviving but growing, expanding, and thriving.

The Mansfield Drive-In and Marketplace on Route 32 in Mansfield (860–423–4441, www.mansfieldmarketplace.com) was originally built in 1954 during what, we think it's safe to say, was the drive-in boom. In 1962 the outdoor theater changed hands and soldiered on weak knees until 1974, when Michael Jungden came in to manage the place. In 1991 he was able to make a down payment on the theater and take over the ownership. Now it's billed as not only a drive-in, but the largest flea market in Connecticut.

★ ★

All during this period, when the fortunes of most other drive-ins were fading away, Jungden kept the place going by making steady improvements and using the facility for flea markets during the off-season. He loves the place and intimately knows every aspect of its construction and operation.

"When I took over in 1974, the place was in pretty bad condition," he explains. "The previous owners pretty much went bankrupt, and things were in bad repair. I worked on it little by little, and the place started doing a little bit better year after year."

In 1985 Jungden put up two additional screens on the property, which made the Mansfield a three-screen drive-in. Three years ago he bought land adjacent to the theater and now has built facilities for an indoor flea market to keep things going no matter what the weather.

What's this? A drive-in movie theater that's not abandoned and overgrown with weeds? There are a lot of kids that have never seen such a thing before.

★ ★

But he attributes the theater's success largely to his long, hard struggle to get first-run movies for his customers. "It took twenty-five years to get things to the point where the film companies will give us what we want when we want it," he says. "And now that there are so many great family films coming out, it's really been great for us."

The nutmeg seed—the part the Colonists craved—is encased in an apricot-sized fruit. It's a flavoring, it's an emetic, it's a hallucinogen. Malcolm X wrote in prison that one hit of nutmeg stirred into cold water had the "kick of three or four reefers." However, he also allowed that the high wasn't all that great. Nevertheless, nutmeg was the first global commodity. It seemed everyone wanted a hit. In fact, the nutmeg was so in demand that dishonest peddlers would substitute grated wood chips to unsuspecting Colonists, so maybe that sobriquet "Nutmeg State" isn't all that complimentary.

Lost in the Dark
Thompson

As you may have noticed, we're really into mazes. We've experienced some pretty cool ones in the state already, and up in Thompson they have not only a truly singular maze, it's actually a member of a franchise of mazes that is spreading through America's cornfields. They're popping up all over, much like selectively hungry locusts eating their way through the kernels to create their own special brand of crop circle.

Located on the spacious Fort Hill Farm on Quaddick Road (860–923–3439, www.cornmaze.com), this maze offers some weird and

★ ★

wonderful variations on your basic cornfield maze, including a theme for the field itself.

But by far our favorite feature of this maze is that you can navigate it at night if you wish, provided you bring your own flashlight on selected nights. This makes the experience all the more surreal, and proves those who will challenge the maze only during daylight hours are wimps who can't truly achieve the level of Maze Master.

If you like a puzzle you can walk around in, have we got a cornfield for you!

It should be noted that Fort Hill Farms has many other attractions just in case the corn maze is not your kettle of vegetables. These include some excellent gardens (called the Quintessentials) that include a Lavender Labyrinth with over 300 of the fragrant plants in a sunken garden. There's something here for just about everybody who likes growing things, for as we mentioned before, this is a very spacious spread.

★ ★

The Fort Hill Maize Quest is a seasonal affair, typically running from mid-August to the end of October.

Would You Like Some Books with That?
Union

Not only do they encourage reading at the table at Traveler Book Restaurant in Union, they give you a free book—and sometimes more than one—with your meal to urge you along.

The restaurant was started in 1970 by Marty Doyle, an avid reader who one day brought a few books to the restaurant to give to a handful of valued customers.

Like any good idea, things got out of hand. Before long, Doyle was handing out a book with every meal. In 1993 Doyle sold the restaurant to first-time restaurateurs Art and Karen Murdock, a husband-and-wife team who knew not to tamper with success. Doyle didn't go far. He moved into the restaurant's basement to run—you guessed it—a bookstore of his own, but the Murdocks are still doling out books with cheeseburgers and turkey sandwiches. They find their wares at over-stocked stores, library book sales, estate sales—and sometimes they even get donations from customers.

On a recent snowy afternoon, a young woman walked past a table of considerably older patrons, clutching four thick books under one arm. "Reading all those?" one of the older diners asked. "You bet!" the young woman replied.

For their book-a-meal policy, Traveler has garnered the attention of the literary world. Hanging on the walls are letters from writers such as William Styron and Dr. Seuss, who approved of the restaurant's marriage of commerce, food, and literature. Customers are free to pick their own volumes.

It should be said, as well, that the food's pretty good. The restaurant specialty is turkey. One year, Art Murdock says, they sold thirteen tons of the stuff. The restaurant is closed twice a year—Christmas and Turkey Day. Otherwise they're open 7:00 a.m. to 8:00 p.m. every day.

★ ★

The Traveler Book Restaurant is at 1257 Buckley Highway (exit 74 off I–84, for you highway types).

Drive-in Time Machine
Bethel

Nostalgia is making a big comeback, and all you have to do to partici-pate in the renewal of classic designs is buy a new car. The new Ford Thunderbird, Chrysler PT Cruiser, and Volkswagen Beetle all hearken back to a simpler, more stylish time (like the 1950s). The question is, as a person concerned with maintaining stylistic continuity, where are you going to take your new retro car that is equally nostalgic?

The Sycamore Drive-In Restaurant, even beyond the neo-retro cars that often hang out in the parking lot, is a veritable time machine, with chrome bar stools and carhops. This is quite probably the oldest

Please don't eat and drive.

drive-in restaurant in America, and to walk through its doors (or order from your car) is to step back to an era when cell phones were found only on Dick Tracy's wrist.

Owner Patrick Austin said his family has owned the Sycamore for little more than a decade, "but the Sycamore has been in continuous operation since 1948. The recipes were handed down as the business was sold from family to family. This includes our root beer, which is a secret recipe, to the steak burgers, where we cut and grind our own fresh beef every day. This is not done much anymore these days, but the tradition here has continued since 1948."

From the decor to the cuisine, and even (amazingly enough) to the prices, this joint is a solid gold blast from the past. Located at 282 Greenwood Avenue (203–748–2716), this is a true drive-in where you can flick your headlights and one of the Sycamore's finest will come to your car and take your order. That goes for folks who drive twenty-first-century automobiles, too. To see (and hear) more, go to: www .sycamoredrivein.com.

Ladies and Gentlemen, Suckers of All Ages
Bridgeport

You can find a lot to like about the Barnum Museum, but our favorite is the display that's a fake of a fake.

Former newspaperman P. T. Barnum quit journalism in 1834 and moved to New York City to become a famous carny, purveyor of hokum, master of nonsense. Perhaps even he didn't know how successful he'd be. He brought the world the FeeJee Mermaid—really, the carcasses of a fish and a monkey rather sloppily sewn together. What he told paying customers, however, was that the wizened, scary figure was an embalmed sea maiden bought near Calcutta by a Boston seaman. Even when people knew the thing was fake, they came to see.

He also brought us the 161-year-old woman (give or take a hundred years), who claimed to have been the nursemaid for George

Washington, whom she called "Georgy." Mostly, though, Barnum brought us the notion that if it isn't real, it can still be entertaining— maybe especially if it isn't real.

The museum was started with $100,000 seed money from the maestro himself in 1891. It was intended to be the Barnum Institute of Science and History, but it, like Barnum, got sidetracked. See the diminutive coach of little person and native son Gen. Tom Thumb and his wife, Lavinia Warren. Don't look for Jumbo, Barnum's famed "Largest Elephant on Earth." At the height of his career, that elephant was hit by a freight train. The remains went to Tufts University, where Jumbo was stuffed and displayed until 1975, when a fire destroyed the carcass. But mostly see the fake FeeJee Maiden. And this is what we like best about it: The modern-day FeeJee Maiden is a fake, too. The original probably burned with the museum in the 1860s. New York artist Stanton Kip Miller made the new fake one for an HBO special. But it looks real. At least, it looks as real as the original fake one did.

The Barnum Museum is at 820 Main Street. Call (203) 331–1104, or visit www.barnum-museum.org.

"Pop" Goes the Culture
Cheshire

Want your kids to grow up safe and strong? Buy them action figures by the dozens. OK, that's an oversimplification. But when Herb and Gloria Barker started allowing free tours through their Barker Character, Comic & Cartoon Museum, they hoped that children would see that there are other, saner ways to spend their time. Like collecting Psychedelic Pezes (there's a whole PEZ Room in the museum), or a vintage Yellow Kid gum dispensing machine. Or a California Raisin board game. (Bet you didn't know Elvis had one, too.)

You name it, the Barkers have collected it. Their museum is a veritable temple to pop culture—Kermit telephones, Superman telephones, one of the Seven Dwarfs telephones (Happy, maybe? Doc?). The museum has recently been expanded, but still has the feel of a very

★ ★

cool toybox. And when you're done looking at the not-for-sale stuff, the for-sale gallery is equally impressive. The art's not bad.

Admission is free. The Barker Character, Comic & Cartoon Museum of Memories is at 1188 Highland Avenue (Route 10). Call (203) 699–3822, or visit www.barkermuseum.com.

Sorry, no pictures inside, but there's
loads of things to snap outside.

Mad as a . . .

Danbury

At its height in the 1880s, Danbury—also known as Hat City—was home to thirty or more hat-making factories. It was, suffice it to say, the hat-making capital of the world, and for a time one lit sign pronounced that "Danbury Crowns Them All."

The process of making a hat included something called "carroting"— or washing animal furs with an orange-colored solution that included mercury nitrate. Over time—and not much time at that—exposure to the compound attacks the nervous system, and leaves the afflicted person with symptoms similar to that of being drunk. For a while, such symptoms were called the "Danbury shakes." You don't hear that phrase much now, but "mad as a hatter" has stuck. (Lewis Carroll borrowed it for Alice in Wonderland.) After labor unions complained in the early 1900s, another process for preparing animal fur—which didn't use a mercury compound—was introduced. As a testament to hats' influence on the town economy, a derby hat adorns the town seal.

The mat hatters of old may be gone, but the mercury, say scientists, has sunk into the sediment. The Danbury Museum & Historical Society operates the John Dodd Hat Shop, built in the late 1700s. For more information, call 203–743–5200, or visit the Web site at www .danburyhistorical.org.

The Hardware Store as Historical Treasure
Danbury

Ah, the neighborhood hardware store. It's not just a vanishing fixture of small town America, or just a place to find that elusive solid-copper toilet valve you've been searching for like it was some sort of plumbers' Ark of the Covenant. No, if you're lucky (or just live in Danbury) your hardware store is a registered National Historical Place.

Meeker's Hardware at 86 White Street (203–748–8017) is such a store; in fact, it's the only hardware store in the country that is certified as a historical treasure. This is largely because it has been in its present location since 1889, and the family (through five generations now) has been taking care of the feed, hardware, and tool needs of the working community for more than a hundred years.

The monument in the front of the store is a part of the building's heritage, for it used to be found on the fourth story facade of the building as it stood until 1896. A fire that year destroyed the top two stories, and the stone was buried in the rubble and wasn't discovered until an excavation of the basement in 1976. The original two stories remain to this day, and despite the aura of historical holiness Meeker's is still a down-home place where you can score that evasive nut or bolt.

"My husband's grandfather built this store in 1883," explains Lucille Meeker, "and it was feed and grain mostly. We still sell hay and birdseed, but when the farms left we evolved almost completely into hardware. We still sell woodstoves, honey, whatever people need, like a general store. You can still buy nails and things by the pound here, too. You go into a modern hardware store and you have to buy them by the package."

From hay to history, Meeker's has what you need.

Art Deco to Go

Between 1934 and 1940, the 37½-mile Merritt Parkway, named for Schuyler Merritt, a state congressman from Stamford, was built at a cost of $22.7 million. It was meant to ease congestion of the heavily traveled U.S. 1, also known as the Boston Post Road.

It did that—but it did more. It also showed travelers that a highway could be beautiful. In addition to what is known as a "ribbon park" that threads alongside the road, the highway was the product of landscapers, sculptors, and architects, among them George L. Dunkelberger, a Highway Department draftsman who designed the sixty-eight bridges that brought the highway national attention.

His Depression-era budget was small, so he used the very pliable concrete to his advantage. Some of the sixty-eight bridges have Gothic touches. There are wings on one in Stratford, and relief sculptures of Native Americans in Norwalk. All carry at least a hint of the Art Deco design popular at the time.

But what is a pretty bridge if you're cruising by at 70 mph? The original speed limit was set at 45 mph—to allow travelers a chance to enjoy the ride and the view.

Strangers at the Station
Danbury

At first glance, the Danbury Railway Museum looks like an appealing little facility that chronicles the history of rail travel in this charming Connecticut city. That's exactly what it is, too.

★ ★

But there's something weird about the place. In fact, you might get a creepy feeling that you've somehow seen it before. Lest you think this is a genuine case of déjà vu, you should know that your strange feeling of unspecified remembrance is cinematically derived (especially if you're a Hitchcock fan).

Today the historic Danbury Station at 120 White Street (203–778–8337, www.danbury.org/drm/museum.htm) may be the location of the Railway Museum, but fifty years ago it was a key location for one of Hitchcock's most memorable films, *Strangers on a Train*.

Can't you just see the murderer strolling from the train?

The year was 1950, and Hitchcock renamed the station Metcalf for the film, which starred Farley Granger and Robert Walker. The train station was critical to the story, as Granger and Walker meet on a train and this chance encounter results in murder with a very original version of blackmail thrown in. Toward the end of the movie, an important scene featuring Walker trying to fish Hitchcock's Maguffin (in this case a cigarette lighter) out of a storm drain was also shot right in front of the station. Hitchcock also carefully chose the garbage placed in the drain for the shot.

America's First Pizza Pie (Probably)
New Haven

All right, at least a handful of restaurants try to lay claim to the title, but we are officially giving it to Frank Pepe's Pizzeria of New Haven, home of the first pizza, ever.

Sure, everyone has his or her favorite, but at Pepe's they've been making pizza for seventy-six years, and they've been making it right. (The shop has a picture of former President Bill Clinton savoring a slice.)

No, we're not restaurant reviewers, but we know a good pie when we eat it. Try the white clam. No, wait. Try the sausage and pepper. No. No. Wait. Try the pepperoni. Or take a bunch of friends, and try them all.

Pepe's is at 157 Wooster Street. Call (203) 865–5762 or visit their Web site at www.pepespizzeria.com.

Dem Bones, Dem Bones
New Haven

Beneath the busy New Haven green lie the bones of long-dead residents of New Haven, unmarked, and—generally—unremarked upon.

The seventeen-acre green—which was purportedly designed by Puritans anxious for a meeting place large enough for all the saved upon the Second Coming—was the town's first burial ground. Unlike today's neat rows of graves, New Haven's departed were placed wherever there was room, and only the wealthier could afford a stone to mark their grave. Sometimes people were buried on top of each other. The

★ ★

cemetery began to fill quickly after the yellow fever epidemic of the mid–1790s, and a new cemetery—Grove Street Cemetery—was commissioned on what was then the edge of town.

The green, which may have held as many as 5,000 final resting places, was still used as a cemetery until 1812, when Center Church was built.

When the church was built, the green's gravestones were moved to the new cemetery on Grove Street. New Haven residents and Yale students stood shoulder-to-shoulder to pass the stones to the new site.

But the graves remain. And the green is still one of the busiest plots in the state, as host to the annual International Festival of Arts and Ideas and concerts throughout the year.

Wait a second... who left the boots?

Have a Pfefferminz!

Orange

Today's lesson, class, is in Austrian history. In 1927 in Austria, an accomplished candyman named Edward Haas III marketed a tiny, compressed peppermint candy—a Pfefferminz. It was meant to be a mint for adult smokers, but when Haas brought the company to New York in 1952, he researched children's growing attachment to the tiny

Favorite characters have dispensed PEZ candies for decades.

candy. Soon after, the company began to sell dispensers from which candy-eaters could gobble them—in an eerie manner, if you think about it. The dispenser head tilts back and out pops a candy.

But there's no accounting for taste and PEZ dispensers are among the most popular of all collectibles. The candy company moved to

★ ★

Connecticut twenty years later, and now even the Orange-based company can't tell you how many dispensers they've dispensed, but here's something you may not know: Dispensers sold before 1989 had no feet, so the dispensers could not stand upright on their own. Some of the rarer of these older models are the Baseball Glove, Batman with black hood and cape, and Captain America. (It's a PEZ rule that no living, real person can be made into a dispenser.)

Whatever the dispenser, the company says more than three billion of the candies—in orange, grape, lemon, and strawberry—are eaten annually in this country alone. Although the candies are made in Orange, the dispensers are made in Austria, Hungary, the Czech Republic, China, and Slovenia. Top sellers are Mickey Mouse (thought to be the first dispenser), Santa Claus, and, inexplicably, Dino of *Flintstones* fame.

Sadly, because PEZ is an FDA-regulated food plant, they don't give tours. Let your imagination wander instead, or visit www.pez.com.

Cannon Balls at Happy Hour
Ridgefield

Picture this: You finally find that special watering hole you've been searching for all your life. The atmosphere is cozy, the bill of fare filling and affordable; best of all, the company is stimulating. Shoot, you've finally found people who share a lot of your views about politics, and you can discuss the issues of the day with a gaggle of sympathetic ears. Then what happens? The British attack and park a cannonball in the wall of your newfound home away from home. Typical.

This is sort of what happened at the Keeler Tavern back during the Battle of Ridgefield in 1777. In those days a place like the tavern was a very important gathering place in the community, as well as an important rest stop for travelers between New York and Boston. Times being the way they were, the British actually had the gall to make the Keeler a military target because of claims that the charming establishment was manufacturing musket balls. (Lest you think these were some type of Happy Hour cocktail snacks, we're talking about the round lead shot that was placed in rifles and fired at those nasty Redcoats.)

Long battle short: The Keeler Tavern survived the attack, and now, more than 200 years later, still wears a small cannonball lodged in a beam on the north side of the house as a badge of honor. A trip to 132 Main Street in Ridgefield can get you a tour of this historic saloon, complete with a docent in period garb and a peek at this rather unique Revolutionary decoration. Call (203) 438–5485 or visit www.keeler tavernmuseum.org for hours.

The Birth of Wiffle Ball
Shelton

At age twelve, Dave Mullany was a pretty good ballplayer, and that was saying something. Everyone in his neighborhood played ball, and games were fiercely played.

The problem, though, was there were rarely enough kids to make up two teams, and there weren't any full-sized baseball diamonds. As the kids got better, their hits went farther—into too many unsuspecting windows, if you were to ask the older neighbors with perhaps less of an appreciation for America's pastime.

To cut down on the broken windows, Mullany and friends improvised. They used a golf club and a plastic ball that wouldn't travel nearly the distance of a regulation baseball—or even a softball. They called a strikeout a "wiff," the approximate English equivalent of the noise a bat makes when it's swung, hard, without hitting a ball.

But that ball was wearing on Dave's young arm, so his father—also named Dave—perforated a plastic ball used in cosmetics packaging. After a lot of trial and error, father and son finally settled on a particular series of eight cuts in the ball, and Wiffle Ball was born. In 1953, the product hit the market. Today, all Wiffles are born in Shelton, along with Wiffle golf balls, Wiffle flying saucers, and Wiffle outerwear.

★ ★

Goodspeed's Folly

East Haddam

In the late 1870s, East Haddam had two ferry landings, one lower down the river than the other. As will happen anywhere, the ferry landing upstream was considered the upscale ferry landing, while the lower landing was for the common folk.

To bring more revenue to the area, shipowner William H. Goodspeed built a tall and gangly wooden structure at the lower landing on the site of his father's grocery store and named it after himself.

The folly still rules.

Construction on the Goodspeed Opera House began in 1876: six stories and a hotel, the Gelston House, nearby. It was and remains the largest wooden structure along the 410 miles of the Connecticut River.

Goodspeed, faithful to his upbringing, included a country store within the building, where operagoers could shop. It was also the post office, steamship arrival point, and office building. The theater opened in October 1877 and would eventually house not only productions and plays but also odd exhibits like the 65-foot, 75-ton embalmed whale that Goodspeed brought in at the then-astonishing cost of $5,000.

The building was high Victorian, and it looks something like a wedding cake sitting on the water. Some said it was overdone. In 1938 one reviewer called it "the most extravagant, the most impossible of all monstrosities disfiguring the river shores." Eventually the state decided to tear it down to make room for a state garage, but historians and preservationists—including former Governor Abraham Ribicoff—helped save the building in 1963, and it's still the home of Broadway revivals, musicals, and other productions. It's come quite a way from being what a recent history of the place called "Goodspeed's Folly."

Come see for yourself. The still-active theater is on Route 82 on the east side of the Connecticut River. Call (860) 873–8668, or visit http:// goodspeed.org for more information.

Some Things Age Rather Well
Guilford

Now here's something you don't see every day: a lovely, rustic, yet almost contemporary-looking house (and a study in stone masonry) that is more than 360 years old.

Holy cow! Makes you wonder what kind of shape the plumbing is in.

Well, since plumbing was something akin to science fiction back in 1639 when the Henry Whitfield House was constructed, you don't have to really concern yourself with it. But this attractive house on 248 Old Whitfield Street in Guilford (203–453–2457) has the distinction of being the oldest house in Connecticut. So when your neighbor

★ ★

complains about his water heater problems and how his system was installed "in the Stone Age," be advised that he is exaggerating; his house is a mere pup compared with the Whitfield. In other words, he should stop complaining.

The Whitfield house is nearly 375 years old. Yikes!

As for the old stone house itself, it's a perfect example of architecture that never goes out of style. When the house was built, the town of Guilford was just getting established and was inhabited mostly by Puritans who were fleeing religious persecution back in Mother England. Henry Whitfield was Guilford's first minister, and the house served for a while as a tiny house of worship as well as a defensive stronghold if needed (thanks to that sturdy stone construction).

★ ★

As you can imagine, the house was home to many, many families after Whitfield left in 1650, until the state acquired the property back in 1900. Today tours are held for the public and the house is stocked with all kinds of interesting furniture and artifacts from Colonial times.

My Dear Watson

Hadlyme

William Gillette was the son of a U.S. senator and was urged onto the stage by Hartford neighbor Samuel Clemens. He wrote plays and trod the boards, as it were, but Gillette was most famous for his portrayal of Sherlock Holmes, then a huge favorite of the playgoing public.

He worked in New York but returned to Connecticut every chance he got. In 1914 he began what would be a $1 million (no chump change then) five-year project of building a castle on the shores of the Connecticut. The building was, for its time, an exercise in modern conveniences and odd shortcuts that only a bachelor living alone could dream up. Chairs were mounted on runners so that diners could push back without scratching the floors. Doors were held shut—even closet doors—by elaborate locks, the workings of which were known only to Gillette. Fieldstones made towers and parapets that looked, from a distance, like melted wax. A small train ran guests throughout the wooded acres.

Gillette died in 1937, childless and no less weird for his maturity. His will directed that Gillette Castle not fall into "possession of some blithering saphead who has no conception of where he is or with what surrounded." The train went to Lake Compounce, America's oldest continuously operating amusement park. All that remains are a few bridges and trestles. The state bought the estate to use for a park in the mid-1940s. Although the castle is often closed for repairs (the place is not watertight, for one thing), visitors (some 300,000 a year) can still get close enough to wonder: Did the sapheads win out in the end?

The castle, on a 184-acre estate, is off Route 9 (heading north) at Route 148. Follow the signs, or call (860) 526–2336.

But Don't You Dare Pet It

Meriden

There's a legend that when hikers make it to the top of West Peak, they may run into an apparition in the shape of a black dog. The dog supposedly never approaches hikers, but hikers know how to communicate with the mangy beast.

The dog supposedly barks without making a sound and leaves no trace of its presence—no footprints, no nothing.

Hikers lucky enough to see the dog once can expect good fortune. The second dog sighting signals bad luck. The third time means death.

A City for Kids

Middletown

At the KidCity Museum at 119 Washington Street in Middletown (860–347–0495, www.kidcitymuseum.com), the only way you get in at a special rate is if you're less than twelve months of age. This policy is

Sure it's a place for kids, but their parents might enjoy this indoor theme park as well.

appropriate, because in some ways the kids are the adults in this city. They get to encounter a variety of rooms including a scaled-down Main Street that allows them to go grocery shopping, and therefore get a glimpse of the adult world years before they will have to deal with the real thing on a daily basis (and all the fun is taken out of it).

KidCity is a volunteer-run nonprofit, the creation of founder Jennifer Alexander and a lot of fine folks who remember what being a kid is all about. The main building itself has an enchanting history, for it started life as the convent for the St. Sebastian Church and used to reside more than a football field's distance away from its present location.

Now an addition has been added and there's enough space for a lot of young 'uns to explore and act out many a fantasy. This is their city, to be sure, but their parents will appreciate the place, too. The sound of so many kids having fun is pretty much worth the price of admission alone.

They Called It Horsepower
Rocky Hill

The Rocky Hill–Glastonbury Ferry is both a holdover and a carryover. This modest little shipping concern has been carrying passengers and other items across the river for so long, it has garnered the unusual distinction of being the oldest continually operating ferry in these United States. If you're taking Route 160 and want to travel from Rocky Hill to Glastonbury (or vice versa) it's still the only way to cross the river.

Back in 1655 the ferry was a log raft pushed along by poles. This was replaced with a strange craft that was powered by a horse on a treadmill. In the 1870s steam power replaced the pony. These days a diesel-powered tug tows the Hollister III—a large, flat barge that can hold three cars—from shore to shore. Just $3 gets you across the river in about four minutes.

★ ★

The horse may be gone, but the ferry lives on.

Our Official State Depression

Rocky Hill

A state is truly measured by the quality and character of its State Fossil. And in Connecticut we have a doozy—a huge, menacing footprint of a meat-eating dinosaur that roamed the state well before the Lady Huskies began their first basketball practice.

It all started when construction worker Edward McCarthy unearthed a chunk of sandstone with his bulldozer back in 1966. He was working on the land for a new state building at 400 West Street in Rocky Hill and in the process discovered a veritable treasure trove of dinosaur footprints that were made during the Jurassic period, about 200 million years ago.

Extinction may not have been such a bad thing.

Once this find was discovered, plans changed abruptly. The state knew it had something more important at this site than a prospective office. Experts were called in, the tracks were carefully preserved, and State Troopers kept watch to discourage renegade paleontologists/souvenir hunters. Dinosaur State Park (860–529–8423, www.dinosaur statepark.org) was opened officially in 1968, and a huge geodesic dome now protects the prints and houses a host of very cool exhibits.

Trivia

Maybe you didn't know it (and maybe you didn't care) but Oxoboxo Lake in New London County is a palindrome, or a word that's spelled the same backward and forward, like pop or ma'am or Able was I ere I saw Elba. Neat, huh?

A Mock Turtle Like No Other
Essex

The Revolutionary War certainly had no shortage of heroes, and Connecticut is filled with tales of bold battles and courageous exploits. In addition to brave deeds, a great deal of innovative thinking also took place here during the Revolution. In one case it meant creating an entirely new form of warfare. Thanks to a couple of dedicated craftsmen, one of the weirdest contraptions ever created has been reborn for new generations to gaze upon and ask, "What the hell is that?"

The "that" is the Turtle, originally built in Saybrook around 1775 by David and Ezra Bushnell. Considered by many to be the world's first operational submarine, this roughly 8-foot-tall craft resembled an enormous tick sitting upright or an equally huge walnut—or, perhaps, a turtle. This submersible housed one operator and was designed to cruise underneath British ships and attach a mine to the hull. Then this strangely housed intruder would light the waterproof fuse and furiously hand-crank the propulsion propeller to escape. After extensive testing in the Connecticut River, the Turtle brought submarine technology to war in New York Harbor, although it was never able to successfully attach a mine to a ship.

But the curious device impressed all who saw it (including, it is said, some inventor-type named Ben Franklin) and was without a doubt the father of undersea warfare, at least in theory. And thanks to the incredible efforts of Joseph Leary and Frederick Friesé in 1976, the Connecticut River Museum at 67 Main Street in Essex (860–767–8269, www.ctrivermuseum.org) has the world's only full-scale, functional Turtle model on display. It's a very weird vessel, to be sure, but you can't help but admire the incredible ingenuity that went into the design all those years ago—or the bravery of the poor soul inside, furiously cranking to safety.

We Give You . . . Flagzilla!

New London

There, up ahead, flying in the breeze, is Flagzilla!

Well, "flying" is probably an overstatement. When you're this big, you more or less "float." And sometimes, you "tangle."

The Coast Guard Academy has impressive public displays through the year, but few are more eye-catching than the sight of their giant flag—affectionately known as "Flagzilla"—floating off the bow of the USCG *Barque Eagle,* the academy's floating classroom.

The ship is impressive even without the flag. The *Eagle,* a favorite, is 295 feet long, has a 4,400–pound anchor on the starboard (right) side, and couples that with a 3,500–pound anchor on the port. It hauls 140 cadets, but has room for 239. To keep the ship moving under sail, cadets are responsible for more than 22,300 square feet of sail and six miles of rigging.

Long may she wave . . . and flap . . . and scare seagulls.

★ ★

It is no small feat to keep the ship afloat. Ironically, it was built in the '30s in Germany and used to train German sailors.

Today, the *Eagle* is the country's largest tall ship to fly the Stars and Stripes—which brings us back to Flagzilla, 30 by 60 feet of cloth, flown during special, in-port occasions. The flag is impressive in size—and depressing to keep untangled from the yardarm, or horizontal timbers of spars mounted on the ship's masts. So it's a very special occasion that will get Flagzilla out in public, and rare indeed that it will be flown at half-mast, where the opportunities for tangling are even greater.

For more information on the *Eagle,* visit www.cga.edu.

The Disneyland of Bookstores
Niantic

You've got to love it when you pull into a parking lot and you're greeted by a big, shaggy, friendly dog. When was the last time that happened to you at a major book chain, hmmm? Most of the bookstores in the malls have no such welcoming parties; in fact, you are often confronted by massive security guards who have no desire to discuss serious literature.

The Book Barn at 41 West Main Street in Niantic (860–739–5715, www.bookbarnniantic.com) is not just different from such cold, impersonal places. It's a different world altogether, which you realize not only after the canine greets you but also as you walk toward the barn itself and see that it's not just a bookstore (for used and rare, out-of-print books) but more of a book village. In satellite buildings arranged in a little town outside, there's even a pen with sheep and goats and small sheds where different types of used books are bought and sold.

"We're unique, and part of this was driven simply by the geography," explains owner Randi White. "When we started here in the basement of the barn in 1988, we just rented the room where we sold books. We kept renting more and more of the barn and then other buildings on the property; it seemed that we'd expand every four years or so, and we almost put ourselves out of business! But it's always

You may come for the literature, but you'll stay for the atmosphere.

worked out in the end, and now we own the buildings. Our business continues to grow, and now I've got twelve employees."

The barn itself is cozy (and well stocked with all manner of literature and the odd content feline), and the employees Randi mentioned are as enthusiastic and devoted to the book trade as he is. All in all it's an unusually cool place to roam around—and you don't even have to be looking for a book.

A Cast of Thousands
Norwich

John Slater was the Bill Gates of his time. He operated mills in Jewett City and Hopeville, Connecticut, and he directed many other companies, including the Norwich and New London Steamboat Company. In 1882 he donated $1 million for the education of southern "Freed Men." In 1884, the year of Slater's death, his son William decided to donate a museum in his honor to the Norwich Free Academy.

A principal there at the time, Dr. Robert Porter Keep, was a Greek author of some renown. He suggested that the museum house Greek casts—plaster replicas of all the biggies from the Greek pantheon and elsewhere. The effect is room after room of eerie-white statutes that look as though they've walked off a movie set.

Athena awaits you.

The Slater cast collection is still one of the largest in the country. The museum was built by the CCC during the Depression and has an impressive slate roof and many marble columns. The Slater Museum, which is part of the Norwich Free Academy campus, is at 108 Crescent Avenue (Route 2) in Norwich; exit 81E off I–395. For hours call (860) 887–2506.

America's Oldest Government Lighthouse
Stonington

In 1823 ships at sea were warned away from Stonington's rocky coast by a large light atop a 30-foot tower. The light was actually ten oil lamps and parabolic reflectors to increase their brightness. But sea and wind beat the tower, and in 1840 it was dismantled and reassembled at what is now 7 Water Street in Stonington Borough, with a larger structure that included living quarters for the lighthouse keeper. The light stayed active until 1889, when a new light was built on an equally new breakwater built to protect Stonington Harbor.

This beacon still beckons.

The Stonington Historical Society opened the Old Lighthouse Museum in the old lighthouse in 1925; today the museum houses everything Stonington, including an impressive collection of Stonington stoneware made in or around the village between 1780 and 1834.

Visitors who climb up the stone steps to the tower can get a view of three states, if you count Connecticut. Call ahead at (860) 535–1440, or visit the Web site at www.stoningtonhistory.org.

2

Massachusetts Curiosities

After working on *a book like this for a while, you no longer get embarrassed by asking such questions as, "Excuse me, do you know where Mary's little lamb is?" or "Are Jumbo the Elephant's ashes kept in a jar of plain or crunchy peanut butter?" or "Where can I find the world's largest thermometer collection?" Yes, those around you still look at you cross-eyed, but you no longer mind: It just goes with the territory of being curious about Massachusetts, as curious a place as ever there was. After all, it got its start in part by Puritans who couldn't stand intolerance and European persecution, and who thus fled to a new land where they could have the freedom to persecute and be intolerant of everyone else. Upon reaching Cape Cod, one of the first acts of the morally upright Pilgrims was to steal corn that Indians had stored for the winter. After finally coming to their last stop—which they still thought was somewhere in Virginia—the Pilgrims set up the first public utility, a grain mill. (You can thank them for hundreds of years of misbillings and poor customer service.) And you thought they survived that first winter on turkey? We're lucky we're not munching on a giant loaf of corn bread for Thanksgiving.*

You might think it easy to distill Massachusetts into a combination of Puritanism, rocky soil, and history—an image set in native granite: predictable, solid, inflexible. We thought the same when each of us moved here decades ago. And, like us, you are in for a surprise. Massachusetts is a contradictory land, full of unusual people, places, objects, ideas, and

★ ★

cranky misfits. Talk about ornery: The settlers couldn't even form a state, and instead chose to create a commonwealth.

Perhaps political unrest and opposing the usual order of things was a healthy release for the residents, because all you have to do is look at what happened when there wasn't some government to overthrow, action to protest, or election to contest. A colonial daredevil decided to challenge puritanical Bostonians by flying from atop the Old North Church—more than 150 years before the Wright brothers. The city leaders' reaction? You'd think that they'd be thrilled at the technical marvel. Nope. They got annoyed and banned flying. And what can you say of a place where people build giant sea horses and large granite towers, for the sole purpose of marketing? Or where a golf course includes an eighteenth-century grave or a monument to modern rock-etry? Speaking of graves, you don't have to dig far to find some very curious final resting places. Massachusetts is the last stop for Jumbo, Mother Goose, and Mary Baker Eddy (founder of the Christian Science Church). It's also the birthplace of Mary's little lamb, one of the Peter Rabbits (ah, the cotton tales of literary controversy), the Cat in the Hat, and the ubiquitous Kilroy. Here you will find what might be the coun-try's oldest example of graffiti; an ancient bowling ball found in a privy; a place that always remembers the Maine; and museums dedicated to collections of dirt, shovels, and burnt food.

So, come meet the pirates and the healers, the artists and the ward heelers. See the house made of rolled-up newspapers, and the giant neon flag. Visit museums of plastic and of sanitary plumbing. Catch magic shows, ax murders, and lighthouse hauntings. Experience brightly painted gingerbread cottages on an island and entire towns smothered by a manmade lake. Just stifle your laughter, as the folks here can get touchy.

Massachusetts: You've got to love it. Or else.

★ ★

Trivia

Can You Top This?

You would expect a statehouse to be crowned by a symbol of the state, but in the case of Massachusetts, you'd be wrong. Atop the magnificent gold dome, atop Massachusetts's magnificent statehouse, atop posh Beacon Hill, is a gilded pine cone. The white pine cone and tassel is the state flower of Maine. When this section of the statehouse was completed in 1798, Maine was a district of the Commonwealth of Massachusetts. Maine didn't gain its independence from Massachusetts until 1820, as part of the Missouri Compromise. So Maine may be gone but the pine cone remains.

Top that.

Fighting Joe Hooker
Boston

A statue of Maj. Gen. Joseph "Fighting Joe" Hooker, on his mighty steed, stands in front of the entrance to the Massachusetts State House. One shudders to think what the statue might have looked like, considering what Hooker is best known for: lending his last name to the oldest profession.

Joe Hooker was a favorite son of Massachusetts. He commanded the Army of the Potomac during the Civil War, but Fighting Joe's men were a rowdy bunch, and Hooker's headquarters was a den of iniquity. The encampment was said to be a combination barroom and brothel. Hooker allowed women who followed his troops to set up their tents nearby. Hence, the phrase "Hooker's Division" became the popular equivalent for prostitutes.

There is some evidence that the term "hooker" was used before the Civil War, but the story of Fighting Joe clearly was responsible for its common use today.

Maj. Gen. Joseph Hooker lost his major battle at Chancellorsville even though he had twice as many troops as General Lee. We remember him for his activities off the battlefield.

The Sacred Cod and Holy Mackerel
Boston

Suspended over the entrance to the Massachusetts House of Representatives chamber is something you won't find hanging over any other deliberative body in the world: a codfish. And it's not just any codfish. It's the Sacred Cod Fish. Measuring 4 feet 11 inches, the pine carved fish is a constant reminder of the importance of the fishing industry to the state's early history. The Pilgrims and Indians feasted on cod along with turkey that first Thanksgiving, and it was the state's first export. We even named the Cape after the cod.

The Sacred Cod.

The fish that currently holds the place of honor above the legislative body's entry is actually the third-generation cod. The first was destroyed in a fire in 1747; the second, during the Revolutionary War. The current one has been hanging around since 1787, moved from the old statehouse to the new House chamber in 1895. It has hung there ever since, with one notable exception. In 1933 pranksters from the *Harvard Lampoon* "cod-napped" the state's seafood symbol by cutting the line holding it aloft, and they made off with their prize catch. Lawmakers were outraged. The state police were called in to investigate. The Charles River was dredged. Days later an anonymous tip led to the revered fish's recovery, and it was hung 6 inches higher to prevent it from being stolen again.

★ ★

Those who say something very fishy is going on in the Massachu-setts State House have a basis for their claim. In 1974 the cod was elevated to the status of official state fish. Not to be outdone by the lower house, the Senate has in its chamber a wrought-iron chandelier with a fish in its design. It's called the Holy Mackerel.

The Holy Mackerel.

The Massachusetts State House is on Beacon Hill overlooking Boston Common on Beacon Street. Self-taught architect Charles Bulfinch designed the building, which was constructed between 1795 and 1797 on a pasture owned by John Hancock. Although it may look high now, the hill is 50 feet lower than its original height, as land from the hills was used to fill in Boston's Back Bay. The gilded dome, first made of wood shingles, is topped by a lantern and a pinecone (the latter is a symbol of the forests of Massachusetts). The fish are indoors.

Trivia

Oy, You Should Only Live So Long and Prosper

Mr. Spock from the TV series STAR TREK© comes from Vulcan via Boston. Leonard Nimoy, aka Spock, grew up in an Orthodox Jewish household in Boston. His religious background played a pivotal role in developing his Vulcan character.

According to Nimoy, the idea for the Vulcan salute, where four fingers of each hand are split, comes from a boyhood lesson he learned at temple. The gesture creates the Hebrew letter shin, representing the first letter of the Almighty and the word peace. Nimoy proposed the hand signal when the producers of the show were trying to come up with a salute for his character.

Red Sox, Red Seat

Boston

Boston's crown jewel, Fenway Park, is the oldest stadium in Major League Baseball. The first season was in 1912 and since then, the ballpark has been steeped in history and tradition. In left field is the Green Monster: Built in 1937, the 37-foot high wall was painted green in 1947 to cover ads that graced the outfield fence.

Good luck getting any seat, let alone the red one.

★ ★

Fenway has the lowest seating capacity in the Majors. Depending on who's doing the counting, the seating capacity is 34,898. All of them are painted green except for one. Seat 21 in Row 37 of Section 42 in the right field bleachers is painted red. It's where, on June 9, 1946, Sox slugger Ted Williams hit the longest homer in Fenway history, a 502-foot blast that bonked a snoozing fan, Joseph Boucher on the bean. Serves him right, turns out Boucher was a Yankee fan.

Fenway Park is off of Kenmore Square at 4 Yawkey Way.

Once Upon a Midnight Frogpondium

Although Edgar Allan Poe pondered weak and weary and died in Baltimore, the master of the macabre was born in Boston in 1809. Orphaned as a child, Poe lived in Boston only a short time, returning briefly in 1827 when he enlisted in the U.S. Army under the name Edgar A. Perry. While Poe was in Boston his first book of poems, *Tamerlane and Other Poems*, was published, written anonymously "by a Bostonian." Poe had a love-hate relationship with Boston and may have been reluctant to have his name attached to the city of his birth; he often referred to Boston as "Frogpondium" after the frog pond on the Common.

Perhaps appropriately, Poe's exact birthplace is in dispute. Some put it at 33 Hollis Street; others say it was on Carver Street, which is now called Charles Street South. To avoid the dispute, the plaque honoring Poe is near 176 Boylston Street.

The Running of the Brides

Filene's Basement's notorious bridal gown event has been likened to the running of the bulls at Pamplona. But according to the store's PR person, Pat Boudrot, some years it's more like a prize fight, as brides-to-be go head to head in an attempt to grab a designer wedding gown at a bargain-basement $249.

Some of the women arrive with retinues that include their moms and matrons of honor, ready to do battle. Boudrot says they come wearing boxing gloves and chomping on mouth guards. It's a knock-down, no-holds- or clothes-barred fight to the finish as the gals make a mad dash for the dresses, stripping themselves and the racks bare in just seconds. The record, witnessed by a CBS news camera team, is just 36 seconds. It's a scene that makes the floor of the New York Stock Exchange look like, well, a walk down the aisle.

Filene's Basement first emptied its warehouse of designer gowns for the one-day sale in 1947. Since then, on at least five occasions, starry-eyed women, with their sights set on a "baaaahhhgain," have broken down the doors to the store before they were opened.

The objects of their affections are dresses that come from manufacturers' overstocks, canceled store orders, and, of course, canceled weddings. The gowns may retail for up to $10,000 and sell for as low as $199 on this one lucky day. One memorable gown featured a peacock hand-painted in pastels; another had a map of the world laid out in Mercator projection on the skirt.

Brides strip the racks and themselves bare at Filene's Basement Bridal Gown Sale.

★ ★

You Definitely Save on Wall-to-Wall Carpet

Boston

Jennifer Simonic; her husband, Spence Welton; their daughter; and their dog and cat live at 44 Hull Street in Boston's North End. This 200-year-old, four-story town house has been beautifully restored, but it is easy to miss. The house is just 10 feet 5 inches wide. The home is so narrow that the front door is located on the side. The ceilings are 6 feet 4 inches high. (Spence Welton is 6 feet 1 inch tall.)

The house at 44 Hull Street in Boston is the skinniest house in the city, and perhaps in the entire commonwealth.

* *

The Skinny House, as it is called, is the narrowest home in Boston—
if not the entire commonwealth. Legend has it that the house was
built out of spite to block the view of neighbors behind it. Admittedly,
that's a pretty thin story. More likely it is the last of a series of similar
homes built in the area around 1800. At one time eleven people lived
in the house. Ironically, the Skinny House has a spacious, 1,000-square-
foot backyard, one of the largest in the densely populated North End.

The Skinny House is located directly opposite Copp's Hill Burying
Ground. The house number is on the side.

You Need This Museum Like a Hole in the Head
Boston

The Warren Anatomical Museum is the kind of place to which Alfred
Hitchcock might have brought a first date. The museum is fascinating
in a macabre sort of way, and not without humor, with a vast collection of medical instruments, photos, anatomical models, machines,
gadgets, specimens, body parts, and medical memorabilia. In all, more
than 13,000 artifacts detail the evolution of modern medical science
from the nineteenth century. You'll be astonished by how far medicine
has come in such a short period of time . . . and perhaps be unnerved
by just how primitive it was until not too long ago.

Dr. John Collin Warren started collecting unusual anatomical specimens in 1799, when he was just twelve years old. In 1848 he hung up
his stethoscope (there are scores of models on display) and resigned
his Harvard professorship, donating his world-class collection of weird
artifacts to the medical school. His own skeleton is now part of the
collection.

On display is the phrenological collection of Dr. Johann Gaspar
Spurzheim, who studied skull bumps for clues about personality and
brain function. In 1832 the famed German doctor died unexpectedly
in Boston while on a lecture tour. His body is buried in Mount Auburn
Cemetery in Cambridge, but his unusually large skull is on display at
the Warren Museum.

★ ★

The most popular exhibit is the skull of Phineas Gage. An on-the-job accident sent a thirteen-pound steel bar flying through Gage's cheek into his brain. Unexpectedly, Gage survived. His memory was intact, but his personality took a turn for the worse. He became mean and lost his social constraints. Scientists studied Gage's skull for clues about personality. Seems they needed just such an accident, like a hole in the head, to discover the inner workings of the brain.

The Warren Anatomical Museum Exhibition Gallery is on the fifth floor of the Countway Library of Medicine, 10 Shattuck Street; (617) 432–6196.

Spurzheim's tomb is at the intersection of Fountain and Lawn Avenues, left sides, adjacent to the road in Mount Auburn Cemetery, Mount Auburn Street, Cambridge. Watch out for the bumps in the road.

Curiosity of the Month
Boston

When Jeremy Belknap founded the Massachusetts Historical Society in 1791, he asked the public to submit unusual contributions to the organization's collection. Since then, the Society's "curiosity collection" has grown to hold some very unusual artifacts, including a five-dollar bill featuring Santa Claus, issued in 1850 by the Howard Banking Company (it was legal tender back then); a letter from Boston native Benjamin Franklin describing his attempt to electrocute a turkey; and a World Series medal from the 1912 Boston Red Sox. Little is known about the medal, but it is obviously very rare. After 1918 the Red Sox did not win the World Series again until 2004.

The Massachusetts Historical Society is at 1154 Boylston Street, (617) 536–1608. The society maintains an "object of the month" online showcase of some of its more unusual artifacts at www.mass hist.org/welcome.

★ ✳ ★ ✳ ★ ✳ ★ ✳ ★ ✳ ★ ✳ ★ ✳ ★ ✳ ★ ✳ ★ ✳ ★ ✳ ★ ✳ ★ ✳ ★ ✳ ★ ✳

Trivia

"The British are coming. Open wide. The British are coming. Bite down."

Trying to get sleepy colonists awake and aware that the British were coming must have been like pulling teeth for Paul Revere. It's a good thing, then, that our alarmist, patriotic midnight rider wasn't only a highly skilled silversmith but talented in the art of oral health and hygiene as well. On August 20, 1770, five years before his midnight ride, Revere took out this ad in the *Boston Gazette* and *Country Journal*:

Paul Revere Takes this Method of returning his most sincere Thanks to the Gentlemen and Ladies who have employed him in the care of their Teeth. He would now inform them and all others, who are so unfortunate as to lose their Teeth by accident or otherways, that he still continues the Business of a Dentist, and flatters himself that from the Experience he has had these Two Years (in which Time he has fixt some Hundreds of Teeth) that he can fix them as well as any Surgeon-Dentist who ever came from London. He fixes them in such a Manner that they are not only an Ornament, but of real Use in Speaking and Eating. He cleanses the Teeth and will wait on any Gentleman or Lady at their Lodgings. He may be spoke with at his Shop opposite Dr. Clark's at the North End.

George Washington's Pheasants under Glass

Cambridge

Harvard's Museum of Natural History is an eclectic and eccentric collection of stuffed stuff, embalmed animals, and mounted fossils. It includes a dodo, giant tapeworms, a thirty-five-million-year-old bee, the world's largest frog, and the only known Kronosaurus, a 42-foot-long prehistoric marine reptile. The museum is also home to the Ware Collection of Blaschka Glass Models of Plants. The unique collection of lifelike plants made out of glass was the life's work and passion of Leopold Blaschka and his son Rudolph. Over 3,000 plants represent more than 800 species.

A pair of George Washington's pheasants reside in a glass corner case, a gift to the founding father from the Marquis de Lafayette. When the pheasants died, a taxidermist had them stuffed and mounted. The birds must have overheard a foul- (or is it fowl?) mouthed visitor, because they were recently put on indefinite loan to a museum in Philadelphia.

The museum, at 26 Oxford Street in Cambridge, belongs in a museum. It's a nineteenth-century throwback to the days when museums had rich wood paneling on the walls, high ceilings, and white frosted globe lights. Set aside a couple of hours to see all of the exhibits, and be sure to stop by what may be the most curious oddity in the entire museum: the antique wooden telephone booth on the second-floor staircase. It may be the last of its kind in Cambridge, if not in all of Massachusetts, and it still works.

For Solving Really Big Problems
Cambridge

It's only fitting and proper that the nation's numero uno school for nerds—MIT—is the home to one of the world's largest collections of that icon of nerdom: the slide rule.

In 2005, after months of intense negotiations, the MIT museum became the permanent repository of the Keuffel & Esser Company Slide Rule Collection. The New Jersey firm was the largest producer of the antiquated calculators in the United States. Among the more than 600 historic slip slicks are a rare three-sided brass rule and giant 2.5-meter-long models used for demonstration purposes.

Only at MIT does one make an appointment to see a slide rule.

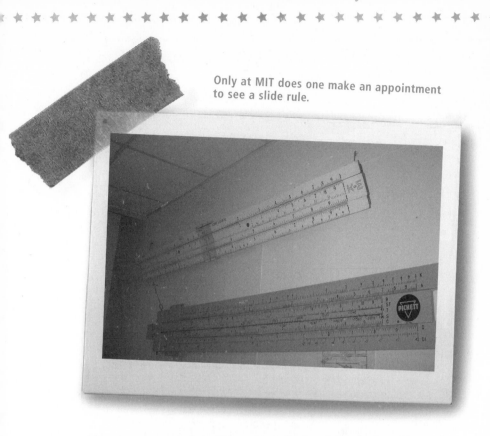

Museum curator Deborah Douglas calls the slide rule the most important technology of the twentieth century that historians have not studied yet. Not far from the museum MIT engineers used slide rules to design the first lunar lander.

The slide rule collection is currently housed in the basement of the museum and can be see by special appointment. Bring a pocket protector and you'll fit right in.

For further information call (617) 253–4444 or visit http://web.mit.edu/museum.

Who Said Grime Doesn't Pay?

Cambridge

Since 1977, Elizabeth Magliozzi's sons have been driving radio listeners nuts and sending them reaching for their dials. Her boys, Tom and

Ray, better known as Click and Clack of the weekly show *Car Talk,* are a public-radio phenomenon. These days they have two million listeners a week, from Sweden to Sheboygan. The gregarious grease monkeys are a mega-industry perpetually trying to unload their books, records, T-shirts, and whatever else they can get away with on their shameless e-commerce Web site. The entire shenanigans come out of *Car Talk's* dumpy offices high above Harvard Square in Cambridge, aka "our fair city," and can be found above the Curious George store at the intersection of Massachusetts Avenue and JFK Street.

Whatever you do, don't drive like these brothers.

Car Talk Plaza, appropriately located above
the Curious George shop in Harvard Square,
is the intergalactic headquarters of public
radio grease monkeys Click and Clack.

Harvard University's Famous Overachieving Non-Grads
Cambridge

Some of the most distinguished people in the world have earned diplomas from Harvard University, including seven U.S. presidents, poet T. S. Eliot, authors Norman Mailer and John Updike, educator W. E. B. DuBois, jurist Oliver Wendell Holmes, Senator Elizabeth Dole, and many more household names.

And then there is the list of equally distinguished Harvard students who walked the same hallowed halls but never graduated. Among those who dropped out of Harvard or were otherwise "excused" are

Hasty, Not Tasty, Pudding

Harvard University's Hasty Pudding club was founded in 1790 as a secret social society. The club is named after a traditional American porridge made with milk and corn, which is required to be served at every meeting. Membership in the Pudding is selective and includes five U.S. presidents (John Adams, John Quincy Adams, Teddy Roosevelt, FDR, and JFK).

In 1881 the club formed The Hasty Pudding Theatricals club and, today, is the nation's oldest theater company. For the past few decades male members of the organization have dressed up in drag and awarded man and woman of the year awards—a hasty pudding pot. Recipient John Wayne showed up in Harvard Square in an M-113 armored personnel carrier. Other winners of the pot include John Travolta, Bob Hope, and Samuel L. Jackson. Female winners include Katherine Hepburn, Mamie Eisenhower, Jane Fonda, and Cher.

actor Matt Damon; poets Robert Lowell, Robert Frost, and Ogden Nash; and Edwin Land, inventor of the Polaroid camera and holder of more than 500 patents. R. Buckminster Fuller dropped out twice—once during midterms so he could take a dancer and her entire chorus to dinner. William Randolph Hearst got the boot after sending personally inscribed chamber pots to his professors while they were considering his academic probation, and bazillionaire Bill Gates left Harvard in his junior year to devote his energies to a fledgling start-up.

Pop singer Bonnie Raitt never made it through. Neither did folk singer Pete Seeger, although he was honored years later with the Harvard Arts Medal, telling the crowd that he "was tempted to accept [it] on behalf of all Harvard dropouts."

Dead Pet in Dedham

Dedham

Founded in 1907 Pine Ridge Cemetery for Small Animals is the oldest continuously operated pet cemetery in the country. It's run by the Animal Rescue League of Boston.

The bucolic twenty-eight-acre site is the final resting place for over ten thousand animals including many celebrity pets. Among the notables are horses from Boston Police Department's mounted unit and Lizzie Borden's beloved bowsers: Donald Stuart, Royal Nelson, and Laddie Miller. Oddly Borden's dogs' tombstone is an exact replica of the one belonging to her parents in Falls River, Massachusetts.

Polar explorer Richard Byrd's terrier Igloo is also buried in the cemetery. A pinkish stone chiseled in the shape of an iceberg with the carved inscription IGLOO MARKS THE SPOT. Byrd's faithful companion accompanied him on expeditions to both the Arctic and Antarctic.

For information contact the Pine Ridge Animal Center, 238 Pine Street, (781) 326–0729.

Doctor Death

Watertown

Part of the permanent collection at the Armenian Library and Museum of America in Watertown, Massachusetts, are pictures painted by Dr. Jack Kevorkian. Known to many as "Doctor Death," Kevorkian is a controversial physician who promotes assisted suicide and has been jailed for practicing what he preaches. Kevorkian is also an oil painter of some note, and being an ethnic Armenian, he has donated a number of his works to the Armenian Library and Museum. Two of his oils, *Very Still Life* and *Genocide,* are hanging in the museum at 65 Main Street, Watertown. For more information, call (617) 926–2562.

Dr. Jack Kevorkian's *Very Still Life* hangs in the Armenian Library and Museum in Watertown.

The Massachusetts Vikings

Three public monuments in eastern Massachusetts lay claim that it was Viking Leif Eriksson in 1000, not Christopher Columbus in 1492, who was the first European to step foot on North America. The monuments were built by Eben Norton Horsford, a Harvard professor of chemistry turned amateur archaeologist who was convinced that "Leif the Lucky" was the first European in the New World.

Professor Horsford made a fortune in the mid-nineteenth century selling "Horsford's Cream of Tartar Substitute," a new-formula baking powder, and used the money to fund excavations in Cambridge, Weston, and Watertown. According to Horsford, Eriksson landed on Cape Cod, sailed up the Charles River, and built a house in what is now Cambridge. Horsford said he found some buried Norse artifacts near the intersection of Memorial Drive, Mount Auburn Street, and Gerry's Landing Road. He built a small monument there marking the spot.

Farther upstream stands Norumbega Tower. Horsford built the structure in 1889 to commemorate the site on which he believed the Vikings had constructed the

A Greasy Pole and a Tough Italian
Gloucester

Since 1931, Gloucester's Italian-American fishing community has paid homage to the patron saint of fishing by holding its annual Saint Peter's Fiesta. Here, commercial fishing is a way of life and, too often, death. Gloucester was the hailing port of the *Andrea Gail,* which encountered the *Perfect Storm*.

legendary Norse settlement of the same name. A summary of Horsford's theory is engraved on a plaque on the tower. To see it, take Route 128 to Route 30 West to River Road North.

The third monument to Horsford's fanciful theory is located at Charlesgate East on Commonwealth Avenue, near Kenmore Square in Boston. It was unveiled in 1887 and depicts Leif the Lucky on a pedestal scanning the distant horizon. The back of the memorial is inscribed: LEIF THE DISCOVERER SON OF ERIK WHO SAILED FROM ICELAND AND LANDED ON THIS CONTINENT AD 1000.

Horsford's theories of Vikings in Cambridge were later debunked as just bunk, and he's considered a crackpot today. But recent scientific analysis of a controversial parchment drawing, the so-called Vinland Map, and an accompanying manuscript called "The Tartar Relation" seem to suggest that maybe the chemist was onto something archaeological after all.

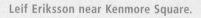

Leif Eriksson near Kenmore Square.

According to Alphonse Millefoglie, vice president of the Fiesta Committee, the celebration's most unusual event is the Greasy Pole Contest. A heavily greased, 45-foot telephone pole is extended over the water, 200 feet off Pavilion Beach. Contestants must wiggle and squirm their way along the pole and capture a red flag nailed to the end. The winner then swims back to the beach. All the other contestants lift the victorious pole walker onto their shoulders and parade around the town.

The fiesta is a five-day event held on the June weekend closest to the Feast of Saint Peter. It's a time for prayers, food, a parade, food, sporting events, and food . . . sometimes a knuckle sandwich. For more information, visit www.stpetersfiesta.org.

The greasy pole is a permanent fixture and can be seen year-round. It's offshore, in the harbor right behind the Cape Ann Chamber of Commerce on Commercial Street.

Each year contestants squirm along this greased pole to capture a red flag.

On the Road On a Roll
Lowell

As literary lore has it, Lowell's legendary writer Jack Kerouac wrote his classic novel *On the Road* in a three-week typing marathon. To capture the essence of living in the moment, Kerouac taped sheets of paper together, enabling him to write uninterrupted. His inspiration, fueled by coffee and Benzedrine, drove him to write a 120-foot long manuscript.

Kerouac was born in Lowell on March 12, 1922 and is considered one of the pioneers of modern fiction. He lived in Lowell for the first seventeen years of his life and returned to the city later in life. The city holds the annual Lowell Celebrates Kerouac one weekend in October.

In 2001 James Irsay, owner of the Indianapolis Colts, purchased the original scroll for $2.4 million. The National Park Service visitor center at 246 Market Street in Lowell has a daily screening of the film *Lowell Blues* about native son Jack Kerouac.

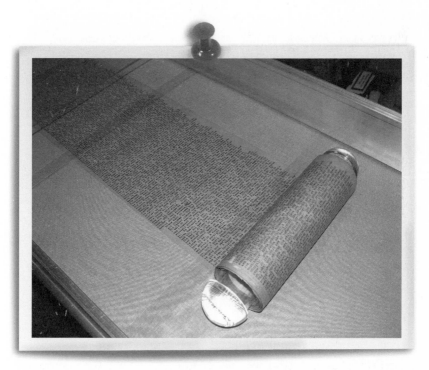

The National Park Service has an exhibit of Kerouac's life and times in Lowell.

★ ★

Billions of Sweet Nothings

Revere

Back in the 1920s there were at least thirty-two candy manufacturers in the Boston area churning out sweet stuff by the megaton. One
is still going strong. The New England Confectionery Company, or
NECCO, recently celebrated its 150th anniversary, making it the oldest
continuously operating candy company in the United States.

Until 2003 NECCO was located in a huge building next to the MIT
campus in Cambridge. It was the largest factory in the world whose
entire space was devoted to candy production. The company has since
moved to Revere, north of Boston.

NECCO is literally a sweetheart of a company. Besides its signature
Necco Wafers, it produces eight billion Sweethearts Conversation
Hearts a year. They're the chalky-tasting, heart-shaped candies bearing
saccharine sayings such as "Kiss Me," "Be True," and "Be Mine."

The Valentine's Day amore mottos have been updated in recent
years to include "Girl Power," "Swing Time," and "Got Love." For a
minimum order of $7,600, you can even have a custom-made cupid-
saying printed on the hearts. You will have a whole lot of loving to go
around. That's about 1.6 million candy hearts.

Extra! Extra! Read All About It!

Rockport

At 52 Pigeon Hill Street in Rockport is an unusual home you not only
can read about; you can actually read the home itself.

The house and most of the furnishings are built out of old newspapers. Elis F. Stenman constructed the house as a hobby. Perhaps
his talent for paper construction had something to do with being a
mechanical engineer who built machines to make paper clips. Certainly
he had a passion for newspapers. He read three a day.

In 1922 Stenman started experimenting with newspapers as insula-
tion for the cottage he was constructing. The material proved so strong

that he decided to varnish it. The outer walls are 215 pages thick, and the roof is lined with newspapers but has a wood outer shell. It took Stenman two years to build the house and eighteen years to construct the clock, chairs, tables, and piano that furnish it. Although the fireplace is made of bricks, the mantelpiece is built from the magazine sections of Sunday newspapers.

The Paper House is located at 52 Pigeon Hill Street in Pigeon Cove in Rockport. Take Route 127 to Pigeon Cove; after the Yankee Clipper Inn, take the second left onto Curtis Street and then turn left onto Pigeon Hill Street. On Curtis Street you will see handwritten signs on telephone poles directing you to the house. Of course, they're written on paper.

Visitors are on the honor system to make a contribution. To read an interview with Elis Stenman, go to www.rockportusa.com/paperhouse.

The Paper House is black and white and read all over.

★ ★

Bewitched, Bothered, and Bewildered

Salem

Salem, Massachusetts takes its witches very seriously. In 1692 fourteen women and five men were hanged and two dogs were executed for being witches. Another man, 80 year old Giles Corey, was crushed to death under heavy stones for refusing to enter a plea.

Today, Salem is Halloween Central year-round and witches and things of the occult are big business, attracting hundreds of thousands of tourists a year. The city even has an official witch. In the 1970s then governor Michael Dukakis bestowed upon Laurie Cabot the state's Patriots Award and named her the official witch of Salem. Recipients of the Patriots Award have the privilege of grazing cows on Boston Common and wearing a tri-cornered hat.

Sam watches over Lappin Park.

Cabot, an ordained High Priestess of Celtic descent, founder of the Witches League for Public Awareness, opened the first witch shop in America and currently owns the store The Cat, The Crow and The Crown.

Seems Salem is a place steeped in historic, real, and fictional witches. One of the newest attractions is the statue of Samantha, that nose-twitching witch from the goofy 1960s sitcom *Bewitched*. While the program ran for just eight seasons and just two shows took place in Salem, in 2005 executives of that rerun cable network TV Land decided the city was the perfect place for a 9-foot statue honoring the show starring the late actress Elizabeth Montgomery.

For a more moving monument, visit the Salem Witch Trials Memorial near the Charter Street Old Burying Point, the second oldest cemetery in the country. The monument, dedicated in 1992, consists of twenty large granite stones and a low wall. The names of those who died during the witch hunt are inscribed in the stones.

The *Bewitched* statue is in Lappin Park at the corner of Washington and Essex Streets. The Charter Street Cemetery is one block south of the park off where Washington turns into Hawthorne Boulevard. The Cat, The Crow and The Crown is located at 63R Pickering Wharf, Salem, Massachusetts (978-744-6274).

A Hatchet Job

Fall River

Forget television movie re-creations of sensational crimes or even reality shows. If you have an ax to grind with secondhand titillation, you might find a trip to the Lizzie Borden Bed and Breakfast Museum intriguing. This was the site of the double-hatchet murder of Andrew J. and Abby Borden and the trial of their spinster daughter, Lizzie. Legal authorities not only charged Lizzie with the murder of each parent, but they also accused her of an additional charge of killing both of them—sort of a double double-homicide.

Lizzie was tried and eventually acquitted—whether fair or not we couldn't say, as that would be splitting hairs. But much of the

★ ★

defense's success seemed to lie in excluding testimony Borden gave during the inquest that contradicted what she said at the trial, as well as having certain other testimony labeled inadmissible. Oh, and there was that mysterious man who had been hanging around the Borden home. No matter about the verdict, though, as the town didn't forgive her. That rhyme about "giving her mother forty whacks and when she was done giving her father forty-one" had to hurt, and it was untrue—Mom got nineteen and Dad, only eleven.

The old Borden house is now a bed-and-breakfast.

Now, thanks to the time-honored commercial tool of exploiting the macabre, you can experience the Borden house up close and personal

★ ★

by spending the night in the very dwelling that was the site of the deeds. You can even have a suite that includes Lizzie's room. The meal portion is actually similar, so we read, to the ones the Borden parents had the morning of that . . . uh . . . unfortunate incident: bananas and johnnycakes, washed down with coffee and sugar cookies.

There are tours of the house on weekends in May and June, and daily in July and August, but the hours vary. For more information, go to www.lizzie-borden.com or call (508) 675–7333. To reach that (hopefully not) final resting place, go to 92 Second Street.

It's a Small World
Middleborough

The lesser things in life are usually those that qualify for small talk, and these days, the public is interested in bigger and better. However, today's small was the mid-nineteenth century's big. Mercy Lavinia Warren Bump, born in Middleborough, was more—or is it less?—than diminutive. At 32 inches tall, she was one of the two most famous little people in the country. (The other was her husband, Charles Sherwood Stratton, otherwise known as "General" Tom Thumb.)

Lavinia had a sister who was also only 32 inches tall. Her other sister was normal size, and all four of her brothers grew to over six feet. Yet she gained a level of fame that towered over that of her siblings. She spent a few years working on a relative's steamboat show on the Mississippi, then was hired by P. T. Barnum when she was 21 and dubbed "the Little Queen of Beauty." Although we're sure she was attractive, to be fair, there probably weren't a lot of contenders to the crown.

Her future husband already worked for the master showman, and it would seem destiny that the two should marry, or at least form a conglomerate of their interests. Barnum turned the engagement announcement into a money-maker, putting the future bride on display for tens of thousands of people. The wedding, in 1863, was a major event in New York City, with more than 2,000 guests.

★ ★

After her husband's death, Lavinia lived in retirement until her marriage to Count Primo Magri, an Italian dwarf. She lived until the age of sixty-four and is buried in South Amenia, New York. But some of the personal effects of both Lavinia and Charles are on display in the Middleborough Historical Museum, which has the world's largest collection of Tom Thumb memorabilia, including his 12-inch walking stick. The collection is behind the town police station, on Jackson Street. Call ahead (508-947-1969) for the hours, though the management has been known to set up appointments at other times.

Cable Entertainment
Orleans

Sociologists and economists would argue that the telecommunications industry leaves a mark on society. We have learned that this is literally true. Just check the French Cable Station Museum, which celebrates what was a straightforward business investment of the day. Despite the reputation Yankees have of being taciturn and uncommunicative, Massachusetts became a hub of firsts in communication. Granted, this was largely because the innovators were from Europe. Alexander Graham Bell, a Scot, invented the telephone in Boston, and although the weather was against him, Italian Guglielmo Marconi looked to Cape Cod to provide a base for the first transatlantic radio broadcast— probably a good excuse to write off a vacation. But what the French Cable Museum commemorates is the time when the French, in 1869, laid their first transatlantic telegraph cable. It ran from the western tip of France to Newfoundland, to Orleans, and finally over to Duxbury. Given the difficulties of ocean travel, this was an impressive engineering feat. It was also a slow one, as the Atlantic Telegraph Company had managed to make a transatlantic hop a few years before. Yet being in second place didn't hinder the cable's usefulness. It was the mechanism by which the United States learned of Charles Lindbergh's successful landing in Paris. News from the French end was cut off in the spring of 1940 with the message "Les Boches sont ici—The

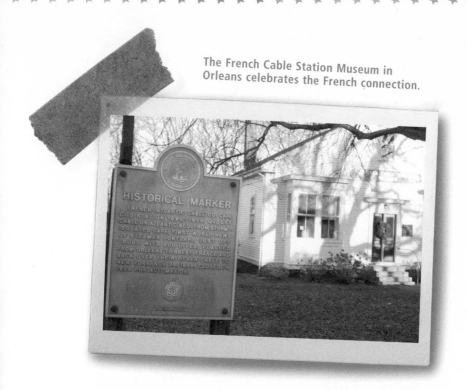

The French Cable Station Museum in Orleans celebrates the French connection.

Germans are here." The sister station in Brest finally resumed transmission—in 1952. (We figure that one of those famous French labor
strikes might have slowed things down after the end of the war.)

The museum is not the only legacy of the cable. To this day, you will
find many Norgeots, Deschamps, and Ozons in local phone directories.
These are the descendants of men who came from a French-owned set
of islands near Newfoundland to work at the station. To check out the
museum, go to 41 South Orleans Road, which is near the intersection
of Cove Road and Route 28. It's open various hours, though not at all
times of the year, so call (508) 240–1735 ahead of time to be sure.

Were the Pilgrims Really Stiffs?

Plymouth

The Pilgrims have a reputation for being unbending—religious,
industrious, and no fun at all. Yet there is stiff, and there is . . . stiff.

★ ★

At the Pilgrim National Wax Museum, you can find representations of the sect that are entirely unmovable. Interest in our national forerunners is hardly unusual, and wax museums are common enough. But how many wax museums are completely devoted to the people who landed at Plymouth Rock? This one is located on Cole's Hill, where the *Mayflower* immigrants secretly buried their dead after their first winter on this continent so that the Wampanoag Indians would not know how their number had dwindled (amusing, as the group would have disappeared had the natives not helped them). Here, though, the dead still live. A series of dioramas show scenes of the Pilgrim's past: being jailed in England, signing the *Mayflower* pact, the first Thanksgiving, the blossoming love of John Alden and Priscilla Mullins. There are twenty-six scenes in all and a total of 180 figures. That's a lot of wax. If you get tired of the educational tour, then step outside, cross the street, and take in the salt air of the harbor. Just remember that this is a unique experience. In fact, you might say that no other attraction holds a candle to it. The museum is at 15 Carver Street. You can get more information at (508) 746–6468 or by checking www .falmouthvisitor.com/plymouth_national_wax_museum.htm.

Taken for Granite

Plymouth

The Pilgrims stand tall in American history and imagination, and even taller on a hilltop on Allerton Street—81 feet tall, to be precise. The largest freestanding granite monument in the world, the National Monument to the Forefathers is a massive edifice commemorating the arrival of the *Mayflower* and its occupants and visited by a quarter million people annually. The designer was Boston artist and architect Hammat Billings—the original illustrator of *Uncle Tom's Cabin*—while the sculptor was Joseph Archie, a Spaniard.

The monument, at a cost of $150,000, wasn't finished until 1889, some fifteen years after the death of Billings. But you don't realize just how long it took to erect the monument until you realize that the cornerstone went into place in 1859.

The names of all those who came over on the *Mayflower* are on two plaques, and a front panel reads, "Erected by a grateful people in remembrance of their labors, sacrifices and sufferings for the cause of civil and religious liberty." Hopefully someone remembered to thank whoever made it possible to haul the granite into place. To learn more about the monument, go to www.mass.gov/dcr/stewardship/rmp/downloads/rmpforefathers.pdf.

A Tale of Two Presidents
Quincy

Like father, like son? There is a long tradition of offspring following parents into a line of work, except when it comes to being president of the United States. The Bushes managed it, but before them the only case was that of John Adams and his son, John Quincy Adams. There are a number of similarities between the Adamses and Bushes, such as both the fathers serving only one term and the sons taking office after losing the popular vote in a disputed election. But the presidents Adams were far closer, at least physically, in their origins and ends. They were born within 75 yards of each other in the same house, and both are buried, along with their wives, at the United First Parish in Quincy, also called the Church of the Presidents. The church keeps the Adams crypt open to visitors and is actually part of the Adams National Historical Park, although it receives no public funding. The rest of the park includes the birthplace of the presidents as well as the Stone Library, which includes the entire book collection of John Quincy Adams. During the season, April 19 to November 10, there are guided tours of the homes. Go to the visitor center in the Galleria at Presidents Place for the first-come, first-served, first in the hearts of their—sorry, wrong president—tours. There is validated parking and a free trolley between the center and the historic homes about every thirty minutes on the quarter hour. For more information call (617) 770–1175 or visit www.nps.gov/adam.

Kilroy Was in Quincy

Anyone whose parents lived through World War II has likely heard of Kilroy. Like an armed forces Mary and her lamb, anywhere the military went, the mysterious man was sure to go. But unlike the nursery rhyme, Kilroy was a pioneer, not a follower. Wherever GIs went, the bet was more than even money that they would find written on a wall, a monument, or even a latrine that "Kilroy was here," often accompanied by a cartoon face peering over a wall. It got to be a race among soldiers and sailors to see if they could chalk the presence in a spot before others.

What might have surprised most of those GIs was that there actually was a Kilroy: James J. Kilroy, to be exact. The man worked at the Fore River Shipyard in Quincy, once a major building facility. He was an inspector, seeing how many holes riveters would fill in a day. To avoid double-counting by some worker trying to make the job rosier, Kilroy would mark his passage by writing "Kilroy was here" with a yellow crayon. Once a ship was finished and sent overseas, the expansive presence of Kilroy continued as it sailed around the world. Kilroy eventually got around in a big way: The name has supposedly been found on Mount Everest, the torch of the Statue of Liberty, the underside of the Arc de Triomphe, a girder on the George Washington Bridge, and in the dust on the moon.

Although Kilroy is no longer there, you can see the shipyard and the United States Naval Shipbuilding Museum, which is housed on the old USS *Salem* at 739 Washington Street. For information and hours call (617) 479–7900 or visit www.uss-salem.org.

Belly Confusing
Wellfleet

The Wellfleet town clock confuses the uninitiated. When its bell rings four times, it is 6:00 in the morning . . . unless it is 10:00 a.m., 2:00

p.m., or the middle of the night. No, the mechanism is not broken. Wellfleet has the only town clock that rings on ship's time. It's a complex system in which the day is broken into watches and then subdivided into hours marked by anywhere from one to eight bells. You can see and hear the time at 200 Main Street.

The First Congregational Church in Wellfleet is believed to have the only town clock that rings on ship's time.

. . . Seven, Six, Five, Fore!

Auburn

Halfway between the tee and the green on the ninth fairway of the Pakachoag Golf Course in the town of Auburn is a unique hazard: a stone marker commemorating the flight of the first successfully launched liquid-fueled rocket. Robert Goddard, a physics professor at nearby Worcester Polytechnic Institute, set off his 10-foot rocket on March 16, 1926, on what was then his aunt's farm. Goddard's gas- and liquid-oxygen powered missile, nicknamed "Nell," soared 41 feet into the heavens before landing in a frozen cabbage patch. The home-town newspaper's headline the next day read: "Moon rocket misses target by 238,799½ miles."

The successful, if not stratosphere-breaking, launch earned Goddard the title of "Father of Modern Rocketry," and today road signs leading into Worcester proudly honor the hometown scientist.

Quite a different reception from the one the *New York Times* gave Goddard in 1929. The prestigious newspaper proclaimed him a crackpot who lacked "the knowledge ladled out daily in high schools." Everyone knew, reported the *Times,* that space travel as theorized by Goddard was impossible because without atmosphere to push against, a rocket could not move. Despite Goddard's certainty that Newton's law of action and reaction was with him, the article sent the scientist into a funk from which, despite his aeronautical achievements, he never really did recover. In 1969, after the first lunar landing, the *New York Times* published a correction.

You can find the Goddard Library at 90 Main Street, Worcester, at (508) 793–7711, or at www.clarku.edu/research/goddard.

World's Biggest Garage Sale
Brimfield

Are you an inveterate collector? Is that being kind? Do friends and family more often use the term "pack rat"? If so, you will be in rat . . . uh, hog heaven three times a year at the Brimfield Fair. The fair is the work of a number of event producers, all of whom have their own staked-out spots. On a Tuesday through Sunday in late spring, summer, and early fall, 5,000 or more antiques dealers from all over the country converge here, lining a mile of Route 20. Add bargain-hunting crowds and you have something modern in the midst of the old treasures—a traffic jam.

Planning an outing through Brimfield on a show day is something like planning the Normandy invasion. If you are a serious shopper, do not—we repeat, do not—decide to "wing it." Go to www.brimfield .com and check out the pre-show schedule. Also, come prepared. You'll want a backpack to carry your swag. And, another must, don't claim to be with the Internal Revenue Service; cash is by far the preferred currency. Another piece of advice: These dealers have paid good money to attend, and show organizers aren't inclined to offer refunds, no matter what the weather, so if it rains, quickly find an umbrella. Don't put off a trip until the last hours, as dealers often wrap up early. If you're so inclined, it's okay to buy some new things while you are there; they'll probably be antiques by the time you finally get out of traffic.

Syn(thetic) City, USA

Leominster

Fifteen years before Dustin Hoffman received unsolicited career advice in the 1967 movie *The Graduate,* Brownie Wise was cleaning up in plastics. Brownie Wise was a marketing genius who built an empire out of bowls that burped. Wise teamed up with Earl Silas Tupper, the inventor of the bowls that bear his name, and their work earned them a place in plastics history. Today a Tupperware party is held somewhere in the world every two and a half seconds, and 90 percent of American homes own at least one piece of the flexible containers.

The story of Tupperware is just one of the plastic fantastic tales told at the National Plastics Center and Museum in Leominster. From bulletproof "glass" and Styrofoam cups to Saran wrap and soda bottles, the past, present, and future of plastics is presented at the museum.

The museum that pays homage to plastics and polymers is aptly placed. In Leominster nearly half the companies are involved in the plastics industry. You could say the pioneering plastic city got its roots as the comb capital of the world. In 1770 Obidiah Hill moved to Leominster and began making combs by hand out of natural materials. By 1885 there were twenty-five comb companies in the city. As the demand increased and the supply of horn, tortoise shell, and ivory became scarce, the hunt for a replacement material began. A hundred years later, when celluloid (the first semi-synthetic material) was developed, one of its first uses was in making combs. Unfortunately, celluloid was highly flammable. For the next thirty years it caused many a bad hair day, until a safer plastic was invented.

Among those honored in the museum's Plastic Hall of Fame are John Wesley Hyatt, "the grandfather of plastics," and Roy Plunkett, the inventor of Teflon. But you won't find Dustin Hoffman among the notables, even though he has made his career in celluloid. Inexplicably, another notable exclusion to the Plastic Hall of Fame is Don Featherstone, creator of the pink plastic flamingo.

The National Plastics Center and Museum is located on Derwin Street off Route 117. For the museum's hours of operation, call (978) 537–9529 or visit www.plasticsmuseum.org/museum.html.

Ironically, they only accept cash at the museum—no plastic.

Nowheresville, USA
Podunk

Yes, Virginia, there is a Podunk. The place, whose name is usually analogous with Nowheresville, is an unincorporated town of about 6 square miles located in East Brookfield, about 15 miles west of Worcester. About a hundred families live there. Podunk is the Indian word for bog or swamp. And this town is podunky.

The town includes the Podunk Gift Barn and the Podunk Cemetery. To visit Podunk, permanently or otherwise, from Route 9/West Main Street in East Brookfield (hey, we said it was Nowheresville), travel south on Philip Quinn Memorial Highway. The road turns into Podunk Pike. Where the Pike intersects Adams Street and Adams Road, just before the cemetery, a sign welcomes you to Podunk.

The One and Only Ewe
Sterling and Sudbury

For the past two centuries, the towns of Sterling, Massachusetts, and Newport, New Hampshire, have been locking horns over a critical civic matter. Did Mary really have a little lamb, or are she and her mutton just a myth? At stake in the historic debate is a claim to fame, if not fortune.

The lamb statue in Sterling.

Sterling says that in 1815, when Mary Sawyer Tyler lived in the town, she had a little lamb named Nathaniel and it did indeed follow her to school one day. A visitor from Harvard University reportedly witnessed the entire event and penned the poem.

Supporting Sterling's version of things are reports that seventy-three years later Ms. Tyler announced that she was the Mary. She used her fame to solicit donations to restore Boston's Old South Meeting House by selling wool from unraveled socks made from the lamb's fleece.

You can find a statue of the scholarly Nathaniel in the Sterling town square. There is also an entire room in the town's historical society dedicated to his memorable trip to school. Descendants of Ms. Mary Sawyer Tyler still dress up as Mary, and her lamb dutifully follows in the town's annual parade.

★ ★

Folks 70 miles away in Newport, New Hampshire, say they have evidence that makes mincemeat out of Sterling's claim to Mary's fame. They say there was no Mary, no lamb, and no school. It seems that Newport poet and abolitionist Mary Hale made up the catchy little ditty and published it in 1830. Newport's claim is supported by the *Oxford Book of Nursery Rhymes,* which lists Hale as the author but notes the historical controversy.

To complicate the lamb's tale, the little red schoolhouse to which Mary allegedly went is in Sudbury, Massachusetts, not Sterling. Reportedly, Henry Ford discovered a barn built out of wood from the original school in Sterling, had it disassembled, and then rebuilt the one-room schoolhouse in Sudbury. Ewe figure it out.

A statue of Nathaniel, the lamb whose fleece was white as snow, can be found in Sterling's town square on Route 62.

The red schoolhouse in Sudbury.

The Little Red School House in Sudbury is located on Wayside Inn Road off Route 20 South on the grounds of the Wayside Inn. It's open from May 15 to October 15, Wednesday through Sunday, 11:30 a.m. to 5:00 p.m. But to make sure school is in session and you're not tardy, call (978) 443–1776.

You Say It Your Way, I'll Say It Mine
Webster

Webster Lake, in the town of Webster, is also known as Lake Chargoggagoggmanchauggagoggchaubunagungamaugg. And contrary to popular opinion, the lake with the longest name in the United States does not mean "You fish on your side, I fish on my side, nobody fishes in the middle." The real meaning of the elongated word is derived from the local Indian name that means "Englishmen at Manchaug at the fishing place at the boundary." The Englishman in this particular instance was one Samuel Slater, who built a mill near the lake, near the village where the Monuhchogok Indians lived.

Lake Chargoggagoggmanchauggagoggchaubunagungamaugg is more than 1,400 acres in size and composed of three lakes joined by narrow channels. You'll probably find large-mouth bass there. Very large-mouth bass.

A Fly-by-Weekend Museum
Winchendon

The Top Fun Aviation Toy Museum is all about the Wright stuff. It is the only museum in the world devoted to aviation-related toys. Its mission is to "give children's dreams the Wright wings." Here, on the first floor of the Old Murdock School, kids will find noteworthy (if not airworthy) toys, from hot-air balloons to spacecraft. There are flying toys from around the world made with metal, plastic, and wood. There are cast-iron statues of Bugs Bunny in his plane, and Olive Oyl soars in a die-cast model. A helicopter and an airplane made by children in Burkina Faso were fashioned from Dutch milk tins. Covering the entire wall of one room is an "On-the-Wall Airport" offering a pilot's-eye view of the ground and the feeling that you're flying overhead.

For hours and directions call (978) 297–4337 or visit www.topfun
aviation.com. Check ahead, as the museum is currently looking for
new digs. Or would that be hangars?

The Poop on Indoor Plumbing
Worcester

The curators of the American Sanitary Plumbing Museum have been
the butt of countless jokes, so don't even try to pull their chain.
Despite the obvious potty humor that goes along with the subject matter, the institution is a serious effort to pay tribute to the devices that
made cities livable and prevented countless deaths from disease. On
display in the museum's two floors are toilets dating to the nineteenth
century, along with sinks, bathtubs, and tools of the toilet trade.

The museum also puts to rest many myths about sanitary plumbing. For example, you'll be relieved to know that Sir Thomas Crapper
did not invent the toilet. (He did have a hand in making some of the
innards of the tank.) As his name graced many a toilet, it became
equated with its function.

When you've just gotta go, you'll find the museum at 39 Piedmont
Street. You can take the toilet tour Tuesday and Thursday from 10:00
a.m. to 2:00 p.m. The museum is closed in July and August.

Rags to Riches
Dalton

There are people who dream of wading through piles of money. We
can relate, but short of either being employed by the U.S. Mint or
being adopted by Bill Gates, the closest you might get is the Crane
Museum of Papermaking. While you won't see the finished product,
you can learn a great deal about the paper that our money is printed
on. Crane sold paper to Paul Revere in 1775, who printed the first
paper money in what was then the Colonies, and it has regularly
provided stock for American currency since 1842. In 1844 Crane

developed a technique for weaving silk threads in banknotes to help deter counterfeiters; more recently it has patented the technique of putting in those identifying security threads. Even though the company knows where the money is, Crane also produces stationery and paper for digital printing.

Instead of using wood pulp like most mills, Crane continues to produce papers with high rag content for strength and beauty. And you thought cotton was just for blue jeans. You can learn about how the company has historically made paper and see old paper molds and other educational displays at the museum in Crane's Old Stone Mill, built in 1844 on 30 South Street. It's open early June to mid October; call (413) 684–6481, or go to www.crane.com/navcontent.aspx?name=museum. Oh, and as for that banknote paper—sorry, but no samples.

The Crane Museum of Papermaking traces the history of American papermaking from rags to riches.

Grave Rubbers
Greenfield

Does history leave you cold? Not as cold as the subjects of this organization's focus. The Association for Gravestone Studies thinks that much of history is written in stone—headstones. They see important information—from genealogy and religious history to changing fashions in art and literature—locked into these stone memorials.

Any of the association's 1,200-plus members can check with the central registry for their gravestone information. The association has a lending library of reference volumes and an online store with instructions on how to do research on the occupant of a particular grave.

This organization hopes to rub you the right way.

The association also offers cemetery guides, calendars, note cards with images of gravestones in the snow (be careful whom you send these to), and even software for recording details of gravestones. Information kits give you the practical instructions on how to do everything from making gravestone rubbings to understanding symbols on the stones to learning techniques for analyzing cemetery data. For more information call (413) 772–0836 or go to www.gravestonestudies.org.

On Balance

Lanesborough

Keeping on your toes will be easy after a visit to Balance Rock. This massive piece of limestone, 25 feet by 15 feet by 10 feet and weighing some 165 tons, perches delicately on another rock 3 feet above the ground. You'd think it was a shaky position, and it is—touch the rock and it shivers—but it hasn't come down yet.

This wasn't some invention by a tipsy architect, but rather a natural result of glacial action. That might explain why stories about the boulder go back centuries. In the 1800s it was owned by the Hubert family, who welcomed those who came to gawk. Then a traveling band of rascals who asked to see the rock promptly set up shop and tried to charge others a dime each for the view. Grove Hubert, the family member in charge at the time, was angry enough to try to rock the rock. Luckily, he learned that oxen do little when it comes to moving large chunks of mineral.

Eventually the state purchased the property and planted tens of thousands of trees to make it an inviting park. There are some other interesting rocks here, too: a rock that looks like a whale, one with a series of cracks that look like a cross, and a pair of twin rocks.

On balance, we know it's only a rock that doesn't roll, but we like it. See the stone at Balance Rock State Park on Balance Rock Road in the northwest corner of Pittsfield State Forest. For more information visit www.mass.gov/dcr/parks/western/pitt.htm.

★ ★

Lost Its Marble
North Adams

If you can take slang literally, then North Adams must be one of the craziest places in Massachusetts, having lost a lot of its marble. No, not marbles—we're talking about white marble, the stuff used in hearth-stones and fireplace mantels and cemeteries. For more than a century, the area now called Natural Bridge State Park was the leading source for the material used throughout Massachusetts.

The famous author Nathaniel Hawthorne wrote in 1838 that parts of North Adams seemed gloomy and stern to him. Well, of course, Nat; we're talking the essence of fancy headstones here. The marble owes its quality in part to its chemical makeup: 98 percent calcium carbonate, otherwise known as limestone or natural chalk (or the antacid pills you chew after a bad burrito). Not only is the material beautiful and suited for building, but the dust and chips left after slicing slabs were also put into toothpaste, putty, and soap.

From 1837 to 1947 the mill literally ground out all these products, eventually shipping 400,000 pounds of stone a day. Then came a fire, which put the mill out of business and left the place as quiet as a mausoleum. A man by the name of Edward Elder purchased the upscale rock pit and he ran it as a tourist attraction until his death in the mid 1980s. His widow sold the site to the Massachusetts Department of Environmental Management, which turned it into a park.

One of the interesting features is a natural marble bridge. (Hence the name.) For more information see www.mass.gov/dcr/parks/western/nbdg.htm, or call either (413) 663–6392 (May to October) or (413) 663-6312 (November to April). To cross to Natural Bridge State Park, drive north on Route 8 half a mile from downtown North Adams.

Fee, Fie, Foe, Foot
South Hadley

Many youngsters are interested in dinosaurs, and for a few, the fascination never ends. In the case of the Nash family, you might say that

★ ★

dinosaurs became an obsession that turned into a vocation. The business used to be called Nash Dino Land, but when the founder, Carlton Nash, died, his son, Kornell, changed the name to the Nash Dinosaur Track Quarry.

Dinosaur tracks go back a long time but it was in 1802 that people found the first prehistoric footprints in the South Hadley area. For some reason, during the Jurassic period the roaming lizards were ill-bred, walking through the local mud flats and never wiping their feet. Such is the way of the world that one man's mud hole can be another man's income. Growing up in the area, Carlton Nash was fascinated with dinosaurs. Right after high school he began prowling the local woods, hoping to unearth a cache of footprints. He found one in 1933, but it took him six years to save enough money to buy the property.

The elder Nash began working his quarry on a predictable schedule: He cut Christmas trees in the fall, worked for the electric company in the spring, and sold dinosaur prints in the summer. By 1950 he was able to make dinosaurs his sole business. His son eventually joined him, and now Kornell spends his time updating displays that are starting to show their age. Much of Kornell's living comes from selling two groups of actual fossil prints: one about 4 to 7 inches, and the other about 12 to 20 inches. Prices start at $50 and go to roughly $1,000, depending on the size of the track and the condition. It must be said that he prices by the foot.

Nash Dinosaur Track Quarry is at Route 116, 39 Aldrich Street in South Hadley; call (413) 467–9566.

Seuss I Am
Springfield

That Dr. Seuss, that Dr. Seuss, you cannot fault that Dr. Seuss. Could he, would he illustrate? Books for kids would seem his fate. And his words were always pat. He could write about a cat. He could top the cat with a hat from the desk at which he sat. Kids would laugh and that was that.

★ ★

Before he earned kids' book fame, young Ted Geisel's job was tame, marketing a corporate name. After this came work more rare, magazines requiring care: *Judge* and *Life* and *Vanity Fair*. Then he got to draw and write; publishers had seen his light, work that was a pure delight. Raves from critics it did woo: Emmys, Oscars, a Pulitzer, too.

Dr. Seuss and the Cat in the Hat sculpture.

★ ★

When he died, his hometown thought, "Celebrate," and so they sought something fun, not overwrought. Artist Lark Grey Dimond-Cates was called in, to craft bronze statues thick and thin. These show Dr. Seuss, cat in tow, Yertle Turtle, Grinch, and Max, Horton's Who and the Lorax. The author had watched the sculptress grow; he was her step-dad, you should know. So drive to State and Chestnut Streets to see some art that can't be beat.

Dunking Do-Its

Springfield

If you think a New England winter is cold, imagine December 1891, when central heating wasn't. Spending time in the outdoors generally meant wearing a heavy coat and hurrying from one location to another. But a body needs exercise, so Dr. Luther H. Gulick decided that the young men at the Springfield YMCA needed some wholesome indoor recreation. He asked the Canadian physician and clergyman James Naismith, who worked for him, to see what he could devise. The answer was a cross between football, soccer, and hockey. Peach baskets went up on the walls, and teams of nine men vied to get a soccer ball into one of them.

Naismith had invented basketball, and the sporting world—and social standing of extremely tall people—would never be the same. The game spread like a fast break, and during World War II the U.S. military introduced it throughout the world. Yet the first pro league actually started in 1898 to look after players' interests and promote a gentler game. Who would have thought that the current professional version with its roughhousing would be the outcome?

The Y of those days is now part of Springfield College, a private institution, founded in 1885 to train people to run YMCAs; it's at 263 Alden Street. But if you really want a basketball fix, head over to the Naismith Memorial Basketball Hall of Fame at 1000 West Columbus Avenue. For more information go to www.hoophall.com or call (413) 781–6500.

★ ★

No Wicked Witch Here
Tyringham

Most of us grew up with fairy tales like the story of Hansel and Gretel, who were enticed by the gingerbread house. They had troubles, but nothing that adding a little heat to the situation couldn't cure. Those visiting Tyringham, however, can feel as cool as a cucumber while visiting the gingerbread house of Sir Henry Kitson. The edifice, which he called Santarella, was his art studio. It featured a whimsical design that made visitors feel as if they were in a storybook. But whimsy can be deceptive. The studio's wavy thatched roof is actually a carefully constructed sculpture, formed from sliced dyed asphalt roof shingles set in stacks more than 1½ feet thick. Heavy chestnut beams hold the estimated eighty tons of weight.

There is a certain degree of irony that Sir Henry, a Brit, was the sculptor of the Puritan Maid in Plymouth. He was also responsible for the Minute Man statue in Lexington, commemorating a war in which, to put it nicely, our side whooped his. (The statue is not to be confused with the Minute Man in Concord, created by Daniel Chester French, whose former house is now a museum in Stockbridge.) Santarella is open from Memorial Day through the end of October and is at 75 Main Road. Not only can you visit the museum and gardens, but there are even overnight guest rooms to rent here—just make sure you have easy access to the oven. Call (413) 243–3260 or go to www.santarella .us for more information.

3

Maine Curiosities

"Curiosities and Oddities" are the rule, rather than the exception, in the state of Maine. We're all quirky characters, and every road in every town has some sort of roadside oddity.

It's difficult because there is a cottage industry in Maine that calls attention to how we, as a state and as a people, are unique and different from the rest of the world. We have to show how our collection of quirky stuff is unique and different from the stuff displayed by the guys in the other cottages.

This isn't exactly a tourist guide. A lot of things listed as curiosities or oddities aren't there any more—except as memories of things that have left a footprint on our collective spirit. You will also see some of the offbeat ways we do things, like deorganizing towns or bowling candle-pins. But even this book is not the final word on the subject. We hope that our collection of Maine oddities will whet your appetite for more of the same. This is just the tip of the iceberg, folks. As long as there are long, cold winters followed by tourist-jammed summers, you can bet that Mainers will continue to create newer, better, and more outland-ish roadside attractions. Why do we do it? Who knows? Maybe it's just to get you to stop and ask directions to the next roadside attraction. Ayuh. That's probably it. We always get a kick out of it when you ask directions.

★ ★

The Telstar Bubble
Andover

The little town of Andover wasn't even on the map until the bubble came. "You'd see Byron and Rumford, but the town of Andover was so small they wouldn't even put it on most maps," said Roger, a guy I happened to meet who grew up in Andover in the 1950s and 1960s. Back then the town was so small that Roger's graduating class of seventeen was the largest in Andover High School history. Everything changed in the early sixties when Andover became the site of TXX1, a tracking antenna for one of the earliest communications satellites, Telstar. America was just entering the space age in those days. The Tornados' song, "Telstar," with its space-age organ and guitar sounds, was the rage. And, with the making of a space bubble, Andover was put on the map.

The engineers at Bell Labs developed the antenna-satellite system, along with government-funded Project Relay, using parts from the Nike, Zeus, and Hercules rocket systems. The engineers needed a location free from the interference of microwave and other transmissions. Andover sat in a natural bowl, and it was thought that the microwaves wouldn't interfere with the operation of the station. A sensitive antenna, or horn, was constructed for the transmission of telephone, television, and data communications between outer space and Andover. The most interesting part of the scheme was "the bubble." Built of treated canvas, the giant bubble was designed to keep the elements off the antenna.

The bubble brought opportunities for local involvement. Local workers made top dollar clearing the land for the bubble. At first, the public was invited inside the bubble to gawk, but the constant traffic had an impact on the atmospheric pressure inside. So the "bubbleites" (as they were called) built a viewing area, a "fishbowl," to observe the antenna horn as it circled on its track following an invisible star. Some folks thought the project was a waste of taxpayer money. Others were certain the government was tracking UFOs.

Border Trivia

Maine is basically diamond-shaped, with four major sides. As we learned in school, it is the only state in the continental United States that has only one other state bordering it. (Maine is also the only state with one syllable—you could look that up.)

According to the Maine Department of Transportation and the International Boundary Commission, Maine's borders look like this:

Border with New Hampshire: 140 miles (but it costs you a buck to get there)

Border with Quebec, Canada: 292 miles

Border with New Brunswick, Canada: 319 miles

Maine coastline (nooks and crannies): 3,460 miles

Other folks took potshots at the bubble with their hunting rifles. David Belanger, who worked at the bubble, said a crew once counted seven bullet holes in the skin of the bubble.

In its heyday, the station employed about ninety people, many of them professionals from New York and other foreign lands. These people built nice homes and brought some money into town. Naturally, they also brought with them their own views of how things should be run locally, which caused some resentment.

By the 1980s the bubble had outlasted its usefulness. Newer forms of satellite dishes better withstood the elements. According to David, it cost $100,000 to heat the bubble, which made it economically unfeasible. In 1985 the bubble was decommissioned. Then it was dismantled. "Al Bancroft, a local resident, tore it down and took the scrap metal to

★ ★

the junkyard," says David. Local people took discarded lights and door-knobs from the site, and some folks actually took chunks of the bubble as souvenirs of the early space age.

Belt Sander Races
Bath

We're sure that plenty of grand schemes have been hatched over a couple of cold brews at the now defunct/always funky Triple R Bar in Bath, but it's unlikely that many of them ever developed beyond the stage of pool table banter at the legendary biker bar. The exception that proves the rule is the Belt Sander Races, which have been held regularly for the past two decades or so on the first Sunday in March at the Bath Elks Lodge. The event is run by the United Bikers of Maine, and all proceeds are donated to the Maine Children's Cancer Program.

Mainers clearly invest more in their belt sanders than in their advertising budgets.

If you're not familiar with belt sander racing, don't feel too bad. According to Mac McCreary of Woolwich, the sport is still in its infancy through growing nationally. The turnout for these races doesn't rival NASCAR crowds (although, come to think of it, the per capita beer consumption just might). On a good year you're apt to find two- or three-dozen competitors each with a half dozen or so loyal "fans" egging 'em on.

McCreary's obviously a big fan of belt sander racing. He says that the inspiration for the event came in the early to mid 1980s. A bunch of local carpenters had stopped by the Triple R for a few beers on the way home from work. Some alchemy involving professional pride, alcohol, and testosterone took place, and a new sport was born. Makes sense to me. We believe that, over the years, these same conditions have contributed to the creation of many innovative recreational pursuits, everything from mud wrestling to cockroach racing.

McCreary says the racers don't really have a sophisticated timing system or anything. Whichever sander smashes into the foam pad first wins. But, he estimates that a fast tool in the stock class would run the track in one and a half to two seconds, whereas a heavily modified unit might easily shave a half second off that time.

This Is Dougie Carter Country

Boothbay Harbor

Douglas "Dougie" Carter of Boothbay Harbor is pretty much everybody's idea of a Maine lobsterman straight out of central casting. He's a big rugged guy with a handsome, weather-beaten, Clint Eastwood-after-a-hard-day-in-the-saddle look about him. Behind his sandpaper-rough, Down East drawl lies a wicked yet deceptively subtle sense of humor.

Most days in the summer you can find Dougie hard at work on the waterfront. He owns his own company, The Sea Pier, a harborside lobster wharf/restaurant and wholesale/retail lobster business located on the east side of Boothbay Harbor just across the street from the

★ ★

Catholic church. I always try to stop in and pick up a fresh story when I'm in town. Here's just one from his vast supply.

One summer afternoon, Dougie was hard at work stacking a pile of brand-new wooden lathe–style lobster traps (the type tourists love to lug home and turn into glass-topped coffee tables and lawn orna- ments) on the wharf. He was approached by a rather citified tourist who obviously thought Mr. Carter had nothing better to do than to while away the afternoon chatting with him.

"Do you s'pose I could buy one of those?" the man asked.

"I imagine," said Dougie.

The Sea Pier is the place where you can find out everything you ever wanted to know about lobster but were afraid to ask.

★ ★

"How much would you charge?"

"Oh," said Dougie, "I could let you have one of these for $75."

The tourist must have thought the price was too steep. Without so much as a thank you, he stuck his nose in the air and turned and walked down the pier, leaving Dougie to his labors. A few minutes later the man was back.

"I found a pile of old traps down on the dock over there," the tourist said. "I was wondering whether you could give me a better price on one of them."

"That's interestin'," said Dougie with a grin. "Matter of fact, I'd be happy to sell you one of those old traps. But I'll have to charge you $150 apiece for 'em." That got the tourist's attention.

"I don't get it!" the man said (never suspecting how true that statement actually was). "Why would you charge me twice as much for an old broken-down trap as you would for one of those brand-new ones?"

"That's easy," said Dougie. "These new traps here belong to me. I don't know who the hell owns them old ones!"

So if you want to meet up with an authentic Maine lobsterman, you need look no farther than The Sea Pier in Boothbay Harbor. And if you decide you might want to impress your girlfriend by dickering over lobster prices with Dougie . . . well, you just go ahead and do that, sport. But, hey, don't say we never warned you.

A Real Canoe Is Priceless
Denmark

To most folks, a canoe is utilitarian but ultimately disposable. It gets dented, its paint fades, and its innards get warped or, in the case of the ubiquitous lightweight aluminum canoe, corroded. That's usually when it's time for a new canoe.

But to some, a canoe is a member of the family, a living memento of moonlit rides on the lake, fishing lessons and fishing trips, and other summer fun of long ago. For them, the damaged family member can

★ ★

go to rehab and reemerge to make more memories. In this case, the rehab facility is in a barn on a dirt road in Denmark—the Smallboat Shop, Linda Whiting and Dan Eaton have the materials, secret recipes, and craftsmanship for renovating your Old Town or Rushton. For some canoes they also have copies of the manufacturing records.

Wood/canvas canoes are descendants of the birch canoes that were used by the Native people of Maine. They became popular in the late 1800s, when a system for mass-producing frame pieces was developed by manufacturers, who then covered them in canvas. The Old Town Canoe Company emerged as a leader in the manufacture of wood/canvas canoes, obtaining many of its techniques from the local Penobscots. According to Dan, wood/canvas canoes reached their height in the 1930s. After the war, aluminum became popular, especially with

Dan and Linda will make your old canoe as good as new!

guides, who found it to be lightweight and more resistant to damage from rocks. And, of course, outboard motors made for a new and more exciting mode of aquatic transportation. But the old wood/canvas canoes still had plenty of life left in them.

A canoe that once served a couple of generations at the summer camp comes to the rehab center at the Smallboat Shop looking faded and weary. It is stripped to its essence, including removing the old canvas and old varnish and storing the original screws. Its tips, decks, and thwarts are restored; a new layer of canvas is applied over the frame; wood ribs are replaced where needed; gunnels are repaired; and don't forget the loving treatment needed for the sponsons, which provide extra flotation on larger canoes. Dan and Linda apply several coats of filler over the newly canvassed frame, which they then rub heartily with a canvas mitten—"a good exercise of a number of hours." The original filler formula called for the use of white lead. Now silica is used, but the recipe is the same as Dan got from Mr. Libby, who got it from Mr. Cyr, who got it from sources ancient and now unknown. Dan also applies a mildew-resistant material to the outside. Five coats of enamel are applied to the outside before the parts are reassembled.

All of the work doesn't come cheap. The price for restoration can run to several thousand dollars, more than the cost of a new fiberglass or aluminum canoe. But if this cost is stretched over a couple of generations, it may be a worthwhile investment.

Chester Greenwood, Ear Protector

Farmington

In most towns, the big celebration is sometime in the summer, when the crowds can gather outdoors in warm weather. Not so in Farmington, where the first day of winter marks the celebration of Chester Greenwood Day. Chester Greenwood (1858–1937) was the renowned inventor of the earmuff, so winter is an appropriate time to celebrate. (Of course, if everyone wears earmuffs, it does make it hard to hear the band.)

Chester Greenwood invented his first pair of "ear protectors" at age fifteen, and he had patented the device by the time he was eighteen. He made the first pair with some pliers and coverings and linings sewed by his grandmother. Ten years later, he developed a spring-and-steel hinge, as well as machinery to manufacture the earmuffs; he continued his improvements so that the protectors could be folded to a compact size.

Chester demonstrated both his product and the process of manufacturing it at the state fair in Lewiston in 1880; he received a medal for his exhibit.

In 1883 the Chester Greenwood Company sold 30,000 pairs of ear protectors; by 1918 the figure had risen to 216,000, and by 1936 400,000 were shipped out. The first muffs were all black velvet, but by 1932 there were brighter colors, including checks and plaids.

Even without the earmuffs, Chester is recognized for some of his inventive and entrepreneurial accomplishments. In the late 1890s, he started the Franklin Telephone & Telegraph Company, and he manufactured all of the equipment. Chester also invented or developed a cotton picker, a "teakettle reinforcement," and a doughnut hook. His patented tempered steel rake sold in great quantities in the late 1930s. His company developed machinery so that other companies could make stuff like rolling pins and tool handles. Believe it or not, Chester also designed and manufactured a better mousetrap, which was in demand by local hotels and inns.

His biography notes that he regularly ran a mile without getting out of breath, that he was a teetotaler, and that he was a regular member of the Odd Fellows.

Sand? You Lookin' for Sand? Step Right Up!
Freeport

If you should begin to tire of the lovely green landscape and the rock-bound coast and you find yourself hankering for a change of pace, we might be able to offer some assistance. As a matter of fact, if you're anywhere near Freeport when boredom strikes, we've got just the spot for you.

There are two names for this roadside attraction. Mostly, folks have referred to it as the Desert of Maine. The more mundane (but probably more technically accurate) name, sometimes used in advertising, is Old Sand Farm. When we were kids (when billboards ruled the earth), there were some pretty eye-catching signs for this peculiar roadside attraction that featured a parched-looking camel, a boiling tropical sun, and a palm tree or two—not exactly lobsters and lighthouses. Actually, those signs bore more than a passing resemblance to the picture on the Camel cigarette pack. At least the artist who painted the billboards had the restraint to lose the pyramids in his version.

So how did a desert end up in Maine? Geologists theorize that the acres of fine beach-like sand arrived about the same time as Maine's famous rocky coast. Ayuh, when all else fails, blame it on a glacier.

This unique geological phenomenon was discovered (uncovered?) back in 1797, when the acreage was purchased by a farmer named William Tuttle. Frankly, I can't imagine Tuttle being all that thrilled to realize that, despite his best efforts, all his topsoil kept blowing away, revealing hundreds of acres of sand just underneath it. C'mon, farming in Maine in the eighteenth century was hard enough. Eventually he gave up, and the farm was purchased by a fellow named Goldrup. Rather than fight the elements, Goldrup did what hundreds of other enterprising Americans have done with their oddities and curiosities: He put up a sign and started charging people to come and gawk. It must have been a pretty good idea. He did that for sixty-five years, and the Desert of Maine is still drawing 'em.

L.L. Bean: "Start Here . . . Come Full Circle!"
Freeport

The L.L. Bean retail store in Freeport is perhaps the mecca of American retail marketing. A veritable shrine to hard work and honest value, "Bean's," as it's known, is open twenty-four hours a day, seven days a

★ ★

week, fifty-two weeks a year. The L.L. Bean mystique draws hundreds of thousands of shoppers annually, and for good reason. High-quality innovative products like the classic Maine Hunting Shoe, backed by a no-questions-asked, money-back-if-you're-not-satisfied policy, have proven to be firm bedrock for a vast retail empire. Over the years the locals have watched in awe as the fame and success of this quintessentially Maine company grew.

We also watched in awe (and perhaps a bit of alarm) as the simple wood frame store in Freeport grew and grew. Of course, success breeds success, and L.L. Bean is nothing if not successful. So, pretty soon the original old wooden building on Main Street in Freeport was replaced by a much larger and more imposing one built of stone and metal (featuring an indoor pond stocked with brook trout). Inevitably,

The modest beginnings of a legendary retail store.

as floor space increased, "green space" outside the structure decreased, until nearly every inch of the surrounding acreage had been paved to provide parking for the increasing tide of eager shoppers.

How ironic is that? Here's a company whose whole success rests on appreciation and preservation of nature, wilderness, and the outdoors, and there's hardly a blade of grass within walking distance of the place.

That all changed in the summer of 1999, when L.L. Bean held a grand opening for its latest addition. Yup, right in the middle of what seems like endless acres of free parking, there is now a "green space." That's right. They ripped up the pavement and replaced it with grass and trees and natural shade . . . right there where grass and trees and natural shade had been in the first place. L.L. Bean advertising features the slogan "Start Here . . . Go Anywhere!" In this case, perhaps the line should read "Start Here . . . Come Full Circle!"

Grave of the Unknown Confederate Soldier
Gray

What can be said about a town named Gray? It is home to the Gray Water District. (Do you really want to drink "gray water"?) It has a Gray Marketplace, not quite a black market, and news items from the town are deemed "Gray Matters."

Perhaps the answer can be found at the Gray Historical Society, on the second floor of the former Pennell Institute. The society's museum features cases of memorabilia from the town, which was incorporated in 1778. It is hosted by active volunteers, Gray ladies, who are anxious to tell the historical legends of the town. One volunteer solemnly stated, "Gray has a colorful history."

Gray is the location of the first woolen mill in the United States. It was a central spot on the Portland–Lewiston Interurban Railroad (some of the rights-of-way from this road run through the fields and forests of Gray). And there is a remnant of the Civil War, located right in the center of town.

★ ★

Gray sent 200 of its sons into action during the war; the Historical Society claims this was the most from any town in the state. Many
boys did not come back alive, including one Lieutenant Colley. His
family sent for his body, but when the casket arrived, it contained the
remains of an unknown man clad in the uniform of a Confederate
soldier. The uniform was, of course, gray. The unknown soldier was
buried in an unmarked plot in Gray Cemetery. Lieutenant Colley's body
came home and was buried nearby. Gray ladies, and the Colley family,

Does it make a Reb "blue" to be
buried in Gray? Whose side was
this guy on anyway?

arranged for a stone to be set up for the unfortunate Reb. It's still there, marked "stranger." In an old black-and-white photo, the grave is adorned by an American flag. On Memorial Day, it has two Confederate flags, donated by the Daughters of the Confederacy. The grave, in Lane H of Gray Cemetery, is something of a shrine for Southern sympathizers. Confederate reenactors encamp near the site, which is some 1,000 miles north of the northernmost Civil War battle site.

There's another Civil War mystery in Gray. The town's 1911 Civil War monument features the standard statue of a soldier. To an untrained eye, the soldier on this monument also looks like a Southerner—maybe it's the hat. But the Gray ladies of the Historical Society say this monument is one of many similar stone soldiers built by a firm in Auburn and still to be found in northern New England towns.

Bertha A. Ott of Greenlawn, New York, wrote to us and reported that she had seen a statue in Kingstree, South Carolina, of a soldier who was supposed to be a Confederate, but who was depicted in a Yankee uniform. The legend in Kingstree is that the real Reb had been sent to New England. We'll have to use our gray matter to figure out where he went.

In the meantime, here's to the red, white, and blue, and the stars and bars—long may they wave o'er the green fields of Gray.

Abbot Vaughn Meader: That's Show Biz, Buddy

Hallowell

Quick, what's the fastest-selling recording in history? Something by The Beatles perhaps? Elvis? Alvin and the Chipmunks? You're not even close. Here's a hint. The album was recorded in New York City in October 1962 by a Maine man, and it sold four million copies in four weeks. How good is that? Well, consider that the previous all-time best-seller, the sound track of *My Fair Lady,* took a full year to sell that many copies. In case you haven't guessed, the record I'm referring to is *The First Family Album,* a parody of the Kennedys' White House life at the height of Camelot.

★ ★

The meteoric rise and precipitous crash of Abbot Vaughn Meader's comedy career is one of the strangest and most gut-wrenching tales in show biz history. Meader, born in Waterville in 1936, was working his political comedy/parody act in New York clubs when he hit pay dirt. He was onstage, fishing for a laugh, when he ad-libbed a bit of Kennedyesque "Let me say this about that" dialogue using his native Maine accent as a basis for the universally recognized Kennedy "Bahston" brogue. The audience went wild.

Meader refined the skit and in October of 1962 (on the same evening that Kennedy went on live TV to give his "Cuban Missile Crisis" speech) Meader recorded his trademark parody album of the Kennedys supposed White House life. The response was huge. Meader spent one dizzying year riding a rocket ship to stardom. Within twelve months the album had sold nearly eight million copies, and Meader seemed destined to become one of the great comedians of the twentieth century.

Meader was in a taxi in Milwaukee on November 22, 1963, when the driver turned and asked, "Did you hear about the president getting shot in Dallas?" Assuming he had simply been recognized by one of his millions of fans, Meader replied, "No. How does it go?" Shortly after that, comedian Lenny Bruce quipped, "They put two graves in Arlington: one for John Kennedy and one for Vaughn Meader."

Meader didn't die that day, but, in many ways, his career did. Despite pleas from his legions of fans, Meader kept his vow never to resurrect the Kennedy parody act. (A grateful Bobby Kennedy wrote Meader a note thanking him for his sensitivity in volunteering to cease doing his JFK impression after the president's death.)

Meader's last years were spent mostly out of the limelight, his time divided between homes in Maine and Florida. He made several more recordings, though none approached the commercial success of *The First Family Album*. Vaughn Meader passed away on October 29, 2004, having learned firsthand that the spotlight of fame can inflict near-fatal burns.

It's OK to Be "From Away"

While visiting Maine, you're likely to hear quite a lot about PFAs (people "from away"). So who are these folks, and why is it so important that they be identified? Well, I don't exactly know how to break this to you, but, basically, if you weren't actually born in the state, you are a PFA. PFAs fall into one of three categories:

1. Tourists: folks who stop by for only a few days, generally during summer.

2. Summer People: The old-fashioned term for these folks was "the summer complaint," but you don't hear that much these days.

3. Transplants: People who have moved to Maine "from away" and now live here year-round.

The biggest problem most folks have involves people in category 3. I mean, they live here year-round, right? They pay taxes here. Their kids go to school here. How come they aren't full-fledged Mainers? This is the part that bugs PFAs the most. I'll get to that in a minute.

Meanwhile, you'll need a little background. Historically, Maine has been a relatively poor, isolated state (we are the only state in the nation that borders only one other state). Winters are long and cold. Summers are marvelous, but brief. We figure it takes a certain toughness to make it here over the long haul (and Mainers definitely care about the Long Haul).

On the other hand, Maine, especially in the summer, has always been a big vacation spot. But keep in mind, while all the visitors are here enjoying "Vacationland," the natives are working. After Labor Day? We're still working. In the middle of the long, dark Maine winter? Ayuh, still working, often at two or three jobs just to make ends meet (which we call "gettin' by"). So perhaps there's a little resentment at work here. The old-timers had a saying: "If you can't take the winters, you don't deserve the summers!"

OK, maybe that explains the attitude regarding "summah folks." But what about those who do move here and stay year-round? Aren't they entitled to full native status? Well, yes and no. Actually, they are. And most of them will admit that they are not subjected to any serious discrimination and are well accepted in the community. So why are they still referred to as being "from away"? I think it's just a matter of Maine pride mixed with a big dose of traditional Yankee contrariness.

Perhaps it boils down to the fact that, by maintaining a strict line based solely on what is generally an accident of birth, Mainers are holding on tenaciously to the one thing that cannot be acquired with all the wealth, power, education, begging, wishing, hoping, or arm twisting: a Maine birth certificate.

The Buzz That Just Won't Go Away

Harpswell

Brett Johnson of Harpswell is nothing if not an astute observer of pop culture. A lifelong entrepreneur, Brett has come up with a uniquely Maine response to the nation's seemingly limitless thirst for strong, hot java. Brett's brew is called Maine Black Fly Roast, and the tagline, "For the buzz that just won't go away," obviously gets people's attention.

"We sell literally tons of it to some wonderful registered Maine guides," says Brett. And, he notes proudly, "We are the 'official coffee' of the Maine Blackfly Breeders Association." Brett sells Maine Black Fly Roast throughout New England, in the Adirondacks, and through mail-order catalogs as well. "L.L. Bean carries our product," says Brett.

For those caffeine lovers who find themselves bungee jumping into the Grand Canyon, driving the Indy 500, or pursuing some other

★ ★

activity not conducive to slurping java from a cup, take heart. Brett has a new product for folks like you. "We call 'em Black Fly Bites," he says. "They're dark chocolate–covered coffee beans you can chew anywhere, anytime."

Mmmm, be sure to bring some along the next time you're planning a quick jog to the top of Mount Katahdin.

The Worumbo Mill
Lisbon Falls

In its heyday, in the first part of the twentieth century, the locally owned Worumbo Mill manufactured woolen products. Trainloads of fine wool from around the country would arrive at the mill to be dyed, spun, and woven into woolen blankets and woolen fabrics for clothing. Fabrics made by the Worumbo Mill were recognized around the world for their high quality.

The mill was the biggest employer in the village of Lisbon Falls, where the homes clustered on nearby hillsides housed some French Canadians, some Yankees, and many Slovaks, who contributed to the culture of the town (ask about the Upper Slovak Club and the Lower Slovak Club). There was a turkey at Christmas; there was a summer picnic and a baseball team; and the wages were, arguably, enough to live on. But the textile industry was unstable. In the late 1950s the owners of the mill sold out to J. P. Stevens Company, which closed the mill in the1960s and moved its textile operations down south.

A series of owners, with assistance from the town, tried, with only minimal success, to keep the mill going. Finally, Herman Miller, who owned other textile mills in the area, acquired the mill and its machinery. It was then that Worumbo came into its own. This worldwide center of spinning fine fabrics from many lands became the home of, you guessed it, polyester. The same looms that once wove fine vicuña coats for the powerful and well-to-do now warped and woofed their way into powder blue leisure suits donned at gatherings of mere common folk.

Generic Towns

A lot of us have places in our homes or offices that we call "unorganized territory." But the biggest contiguous unorganized territory east of the Mississippi River is in the state of Maine. It's called the Unorganized Territory, strangely enough, and it comprises about half of the state's geography, mostly in the north and west. Less than 1 percent of Maine's population lives in this area, but it's where you will find most of the state's trees, moose, unspoiled waterfront, and endangered species.

The territory consists of "townships" and "plantations." The townships were laid out in grids, or ranges, by surveyors sitting in warm, cozy offices back when Maine was part of Massachusetts. If you look at the northwest corner of the state, you will see towns with names like "T8 R5 WELS," which translates into Township 8, Range 5, West of the East Line of the State. Other ranges have names like Bingham's Kennebec Purchase, Eastern Division, Northern Division, East and West of the Kennebec River. In addition to being numbered, some townships have "town names," like Upper Cupsuptic, which is T4 R4 WBKP (Township 4, Range 4, West of Bingham's Kennebec Purchase).

When the townships were laid out, some were given to schools or colleges as a means of raising money. So we can find the Hopkins Academy Grant in Penobscot County, the Bowdoin College East and West Grants in Piscataquis County, and the Sandwich Academy Grants (they don't say what kind of sandwiches were made—perhaps a pine-cone rollup?).

When the surveyor's range ran out of neat-looking, square townships on his map, the little piece left over was called a Gore, so we have Misery Gore, Moxie Gore, Powers Gore, and a score more of gores galore. A large number of coastal islands are not part of any town; their few isolated inhabitants are also part of the Unorganized Territory.

What makes these townships "unorganized?" For one thing, nobody lives there to speak of, and governments are just not practical. Some of the unorganized townships were once towns, but they faded away and became "deorganized." The little town of Madrid, in Franklin County, became a township just a few years back. Benedicta, in Aroostook County, deorganized in 1987. Not all of the townships are contiguous; sometimes an unorganized town will sit as an island amid organized municipalities.

When there are enough people to sort of organize a town, but not enough to run the darn thing, the intermediate level of government is called a "plantation." These organizations have some town officers and a town meeting, but many of their functions are taken over by the state or county.

The land in the Unorganized Territory is owned in large sections, sometimes hundreds of thousands of acres. The big landowners were, up until a few years ago, paper companies and companies that harvested wood to sell to the paper companies. Some companies own or have owned entire 36-square-mile townships. Lately, some of the larger holdings have been split up, and the land has been sold to individuals or to companies that want to develop recreational property. (Some people own just a quarter of an acre for their hunting camps.) Other new landowners want to preserve the land, perhaps even creating a North Woods National Park.

Just like the desk in my office, don't expect things to get organized any time soon. The overall population has gone down in the unorganized townships and plantations. Towns with marginal existence are giving more serious consideration to joining the ranks of the deorganized. And most Mainers probably enjoy the fact that half of the state is unorganized. They might even ask, "Which half?"

★ ★

In addition to the mixed blends, the hundred-year-old looms now spin and weave cotton-based fabric. According to Allan Miller, Herman's nephew, the wool process adds a special texture to the cotton. The mill makes a variety of fabrics and products, including blankets sold in stores around the country.

In the Worumbo Mill Outlet store, you will see, in addition to the fabrics and products, spools and cogs from the old looms and an account book from the early 1900s. You will also see, along the walls of the store, large photographs of the men, women, and children proudly standing at their machines and asking, across the chasm of time, "What the hell is polyester?"

The Umbrella Cover Museum
Peaks Island

Everyday objects have stories to tell. Just bring your imagination to any yard sale and you will find items with history—the chest of drawers with the bullet hole, the teapot with the chipped spout, the dog-eared

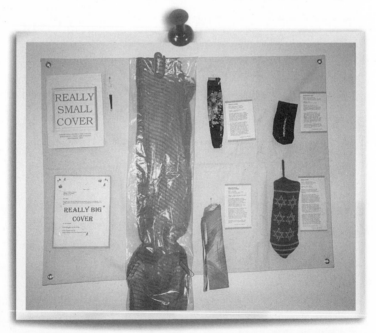

The Umbrella Cover Museum boasts covers from around the world. Here's an interesting place to spend a rainy day.

★ ★

paperback with illegible margin notes—if they could talk, we would hear a story. Maybe not an interesting story, but it would be a story.

So it is with umbrella covers—the tube-like sleeves, sometimes called "sheaths" or "pockets," that keep umbrellas neat and tidy. According to Nancy 3. Hoffman, the proprietress of the Umbrella Cover Museum on Peaks Island, "Each cover has a story behind it." The Umbrella Cover Museum is dedicated to "the appreciation of the mundane in everyday life," says Hoffman, who runs the museum out of her home (visits by appointment only; 207–766–4496). Appreciation of umbrella covers is part of the appreciation of the wonder and beauty in the simplest of things.

Hoffman started collecting umbrella covers about 10 years ago, when some friends of hers couldn't bear to throw them out, "because they were too cute." A critical mass of covers developed, and now the museum boasts more than 300, including new handmade covers, particularly admired for their symmetry.

When she's not curating the mundane, Nancy 3. Hoffman plays accordion with the Maine Squeeze and with the Casco Bay Tummlers.

Nancy 3. Hoffman. Yep, that's her middle name.

The Maine Accent

Few aspects of Maine life are more consistently associated with the state than the famous "Down East" accent. Here are a few examples of Maine speech that aren't likely to crop up anywhere other than the Pine Tree State:

ayuh (exclamation). Yes! Don't even try this one. Here's a tip, though. If you hear someone pronounce it "eye-up," they're definitely "from away."

doaw (exclamation). No! The opposite of ayuh.

cunnin' (adj). Cute. This may be applied to inanimate objects, animals, and people. In Maine it would be entirely possible for a cunnin' girl to have a cunnin' puppy dog and live with him in a cunnin' trailer.

spleeny (adj). Oversensitive, whiney, or person who complains too much. "Ain't that kid some spleeny! He fell off the barn roof on Thursday and broke his ankle, and he's still whinin' about it two days later!"

tilt, or roto-tilt (verb). To till the soil. "It was so nice last weekend, I got out the Roto-tilter and tilted the whole five acres out behind that old DeSoto of Hubert's."

In the decades since Roger Miller completely butchered the pronunciation of the city of Bangor, Maine, by referring to it as banger in his 1960s hit single "King of the Road," millions of people across the nation and the world have compounded the error. Please help stop the madness! Mainers refer to Bangor as either BANG-or or the slightly more old-fashioned version, BAN-gore.

Following are some other mispronounced place names along with their correct pronunciations:

Calais = Callus

Madrid = MAD-rid

Vienna = Vye-enna

★ ★

Bowling Alone at the Woodfords Club
Portland

Not much has changed at the Woodfords Club since it was built in 1913. On Friday nights from October to April, men sit in the lobby, have a smoke, and talk about the weather and the news. At 6:30, they shuffle into the dining room, sing "My Country 'Tis of Thee," salute the flag, and sit down to eat. Some members, on a rotating basis, wait on tables. There's always whipped potatoes and yeasty rolls. Sometimes there's meat, sometimes fish. The men wear coats and ties. They eat with determination.

At 7 p.m. on the dot, the president introduces the guests, somebody reads a report on those who are hospitalized or who died, and finally the program is introduced. It might be a musical group or a speaker with slides. If the program presenter has been properly informed, the program ends at 7:30, and the members retire to their evening's entertainment: cribbage in the cribbage room, bridge in the bridge room, pool or billiards in the beautiful pool hall on the second floor, or bowling in the five candlepin alleys in the basement. It's been this way for almost 100 years, and it is unlikely to change much.

Some things have changed, though. The price of dinner has gone from 25 cents to $8 now—still a bargain. The pin boys who once worked in the bowling alleys were replaced by machines. You can't smoke in the dining room, the card rooms, or the pool hall, as you used to do. Woodrow Wilson is no longer president, and women now have the right to vote.

The Woodfords Club was founded as a community organization for men in the Deering and Woodfords areas of Portland. Unlike the Portland Club and the Cumberland Club, it did not have a political (i.e., Republican) requirement. Social distinctions were unimportant. No booze has ever been served, in part due to the club's proximity to a church, and in part because it seems to work out better that way. There is no secret handshake and no ritual requirements, though many members are also in Masonic or other fraternal organizations. If you

★ ★

are a member in good standing for forty years, you become a "life member," and your dues obligation (currently $150 per year) is waived. And, if you are a woman, you are not allowed to become a member.

Where things are as they ever will be.

The Women's Woodfords Club meets on Wednesdays from October to April. Its membership consists of wives, widows, mothers, daughters, sisters, and friends of male members. They have luncheons, fashion shows, a bridge club, and bowling, if they wish. Not much has changed for this club either. There doesn't appear to be any wish to "rock the boat" and mention the fact that Woodrow Wilson isn't president anymore and that women now have the right to vote. Each gender appears to enjoy its own club and its own way of running things.

In its heyday, after World War II and into the 1970s, the Woodfords Club had 500 members, with a waiting list of as much as six years. Families would use the club's pool room and bowling alleys on Saturdays. Bridge, cribbage, pool, and bowling leagues were full to capacity. As members started to die off, the waiting list for new members to replace them shrank. Younger fellows wanted to spend time with their families, including their wives, who worked outside the home during the week. Longtime members who were still living preferred the pleasures of Florida in the wintertime to those of Maine. A few new members trickle in each year, but their number is surpassed by the deaths and resignations of existing members.

Still, the club is trying to keep up to date. It even has a Web site. So, if you want to join, go to www.woodfordsclub.org, where you'll find a link to a downloadable membership application. Print it out, fill it in, and drop it off. Note, however, that listed after "application fee ($10) paid," "Approved by vote of Board of Governors," and "notified of election" are date blanks for you to fill in, all followed by the year, which is still memorialized on the form as "19___."

Think You've Seen "The Last Shaker"? Think Again

Sabbathday Lake

If you were among the millions of PBS viewers who tuned in to the Ken Burns documentary *The Last Shaker* back in 1983, you could have been excused for thinking that the Shakers, a small religious order who have made a big contribution to our modern American way of life, are an extinct breed. I'm pleased to report that nothing could be further from the truth. Far from being the spiritual equivalent of the passenger pigeon, you will find a half-dozen of these delightful folks alive and well and living in the Shaker community at Sabbathday Lake, in New Gloucester.

Here are a few things we learned while visiting the Shakers. First off, we had somehow formed the impression that Shakers were part of the austere, cranky, anti-technology crowd, sort of like the Amish in

Pennsylvania. You know, dressing in black, driving buggies instead of cars, writing with charcoal on the back of shovels by candlelight, and so forth. No way!

The last Shaker? Not likely, bub! The Shakers are alive and well in Maine.

The Shakers are, like, way into technology. As a matter of fact, they've been pretty much on the cutting edge of it since they first came to these shores from Manchester, England, back in 1774 and founded the Sabbathday Lake Community in 1783. In addition to designing and manufacturing the famous Shaker chairs and other furniture, the Shakers invented a lot of other cool stuff we use every day. The flat broom (as opposed to the round one the Wicked Witch of the West rode), the automatic washing machine, and even the dump truck are among the many inventions and innovations thought up by these pious, gentle, ingenious folks. By the way, in case you're thinking this is some kind of "get rich with God" type of religion, forget it: Shakers never bother to patent anything. When they build a better mousetrap, they just give it to the world, their way of saying, "Hey, God loves you!"

Shakers also just love to belt out a tune. Shaker hymns are for the most part lively and upbeat, not unlike the folks who sing them. Their big hit "Simple Gifts," written by Elder Joseph Brackett right at the Sabbathday Lake Community, speaks volumes about their way of life. You know, it's the song that begins, "'Tis a gift to be simple . . ." Since Shakers take a pledge of celibacy, they must rely on converts to keep the community going. Fortunately, there are currently two new novitiates living with the community. I, for one, hope these newcomers decide to take the pledge and join up when the time comes. The way I see it, the world is a lot better place with a few Shakers in it. Let's all hope the last Shaker is many, many lifetimes away.

Goodall Park

Sanford

The national pastime is Maine's passion. Baseball is played in cow pastures (be careful sliding into third base!), in back fields, and behind schools, where fans sit in rickety bleachers at the mercy of the fickle elements of weather. There is probably no more beautiful setting for the game than at Goodall Park in Sanford, a covered field with 786 individual seats and a history that few parks can match.

The park was originally built, in stages, in the early part of the twentieth century by workers at the Goodall Mills, the town's major employer. It was always a covered facility, but there originally were benches or bleachers for the fans. The stands were destroyed by fire in 1997; after receiving enormous community support, the new structure was completed in 1999, at a cost of $1.6 million. Blaine Jack, the park's unofficial historian, says the 786 new, individual seats were fit in the stands by making them an inch narrower than the standard

★ ★

20-inch seats. There are also bench seats for 150 more. Dugouts are actually dug out, and there is a large press box on the third level. With night lighting, Goodall Park is ready for lots of baseball.

The park appears larger than its seating capacity. It's 419 feet to the flag pole in center field, 370 to left, and 295 to right, taking away the right-handed advantage provided by Fenway Park's Green Monster. The fences in the outfield do not have advertising, which provides a somewhat more pristine view of the action. And the field itself is immaculately maintained. Jack said that visiting coaches of collegiate teams have assumed that this was a minor-league professional park.

The seats are 1 inch narrower than the standard. Sit in these and you'll know if you put on a few pounds last winter.

It's the history, though, that makes Goodall Park stand out. The semiprofessional teams of the early twentieth century battled it out here. One special day, the park etched its name forever in Maine baseball history. October 4, 1919, saw a record crowd watch the Sanford Professionals play the Boston Red Sox. As the headline in the *Sanford Tribune* said, the Sanford nine played "gilt-edged baseball," but the visitors prevailed on the strength of a three-run home run by Babe Ruth. The Bambino knocked the ball out of the park. The locals, though losers, were not disappointed: "It was a grand good game to watch," said the *Tribune,* "and many watched it—the biggest paid attendance of the season for the stores and mills were closed for the occasion." When Ruth made an error in the fourth inning, one fan remarked, "G'wan, you lout, get in there and play baseball. What d'yer spose I paid a quarter for your pictures for, anyway?"

Lenny the Chocolate Moose
Scarborough

For reasons I've never fully understood, glimpsing a moose seems to be near the top of a lot of folks' short list of things-to-do-while-we're-in-Maine. Although most natives are apt to have had this experience at least once and can give you suggestions about where and when to look, the likelihood of glimpsing one of these gentle giants in its native habitat is still a long shot.

Fortunately for those visitors with limited time and serious moose-gawking lust, there's always Lenny. Lenny is easy to find, mostly because he never moves. He's inside the Len Libby Store on Route 1 in Scarborough. In the great tradition of roadside attractions everywhere, Lenny is grandly billed as "the world's largest chocolate moose." That assertion will likely go unchallenged if for no other reason than, as far as anybody can tell, Lenny is the world's only life-size chocolate moose. How big is life-size? Pretty darn big—8 feet tall from the soles of his edible hooves to the tip of his luscious chocolate antlers. Standing in a Maine woods diorama, Lenny looks all the world like he's apt to turn around and walk out the back door.

Some Things Will Always Be the Same

Everything in Maine is changing and evolving into a place just like the rest of the country. Maine will see more big-box stores, more TV anchors with blow-dried hair, and fewer locally owned businesses. There will be fewer "curiosities," no doubt. But there are some things that will remain the same about our state and about some of its traditions. We predict the following:

• We'll NEVER need a third lane on the turnpike to Lewiston, even though that city will be in a constant state of improvement.

• There will ALWAYS be work on the bridge between Brunswick and Topsham. The bridge spanning the Androscoggin at the waterfalls (sometimes called the Frank Wood Bridge) has been scraped, painted, repaved, shored up, repainted, and re-renovated for the past sixty years, and even if there is a new bridge, it will always be in need of some maintenance.

• No one from Maine will EVER be elected president of the United States. James G. Blaine, Ed Muskie, and Benjamin Bubar (he ran as a Prohibitionist) all tried and failed. Most of the rest of the people in the United States (especially in the South) don't even know that Maine is a state.

• People from northern and rural Maine will ALWAYS hate and resent Portland, even if it breaks off and floats away into the sea. ("It's just not part of the state," they will say.)

• Old Orchard Beach will ALWAYS be tacky, even if they put condos over the french fry stands. The town fathers try to clean up the image, but if the town didn't resemble a carnival, no one would go there.

Czechoslovakian sculptor Zdeno Mayercak and his assistants labored for a month to shape this startlingly lifelike quadruped from nearly a ton of pure first-quality Len Libby chocolate, the same handmade delicacy they've been turning out since 1926. I have to admit that when you factor in the beautifully painted Maine woods backdrop, the results are darn impressive. Visitors are encouraged to take snapshots. And maybe if your photo's just a bit out of focus, nobody will ever know that this 1,700 pound moose is made of chocolate and is actually standing in a pool of white chocolate.

Would you just hurry up and take the picture? My antlers are starting to melt!

Skowhegan Big Indian
Skowhegan

Maine folks talk about the importance of being a "native Mainer," but the real natives would dispute the title, particularly if applied to

★ ★

someone whose ancestors hadn't arrived in Maine until 1600. From that time until fairly recently, those who were here before 1600 were called Indians. Now the term Native Americans is used. For example, in Freeport, what was the FBI—the Freeport Big Indian—is now the MBNA—Maine's Big Native American. In Skowhegan, it's still the Indian, and a very big one.

The Skowhegan Indian, standing at the intersection of Routes 2 and 201, is 62 feet high and weighs 24,000 pounds. According to the Skowhegan Chamber of Commerce, the Indian was carefully crafted of local white pine by sculptor Bernard Langlais of Cushing using five Native Americans as models. It was a three-year process of planning and assembly, ending in the shipment of the Indian in two pieces. Longtime residents recall the day, in 1969, when the Indian arrived, lying on his back with his big feet up in the air.

Originally, the Indian was to be in a park surrounded by bandstand and other outdoor amenities. But gas stations and businesses now surround the spot where he stands and treetops partially obscure the top of his head. According to Janeice Holmes, executive director of the Skowhegan Area Chamber of Commerce, a lot of people would like to see the Indian closer to the Kennebec River, which would better fit with the theme of the Indian as hunter and fisherman (he's holding a spear and a weir net).

The Indian has lost some of his color, due to natural aging. The chamber raised funds for restoration and preservation in 2002. It raised $20,000, which was spent to test for insects (those ants can be wicked trouble) and to restore the guy wires ("We don't want him to tip over," says Janeice). Full restoration cost is estimated at about $75,000. The restoration crew will try to match the original colors. The Skowhegan Indian was created with attention to detail and color. It is a work of "art," distinct perhaps from other roadside oddities. There are some people, however, for whom all "big art" is in the same category. While everyone agrees that the Indian's larger than life, the beholder will have to decide whether the Skowhegan Indian is art, culture, or cultch.

★ ★

The Prison Store: Shoplifters Will Be Prosecuted Immediately!
Thomaston

Any merchant in America will tell you that shoplifting is a major headache and a tremendous financial burden, particularly for small operations such as gift shops. Interestingly enough, one of the busiest gift shops on the Maine coast, a modest storefront operation on Main Street in Thomaston, has no such problems. Despite the fact that many items are small and easily pocketed, manager Joe Allen assures us that with a half million customers a year, pilferage is simply not a problem.

Perhaps the uniformed guards patrolling the aisles may have something to do with it. Then again, it's possible that the sales staff, a half dozen or so inmates from the Maine State Prison, create a certain "crime doesn't pay" ambience.

Originally, the store was right next door to the prison. But the original prison buildings were razed back in the spring of 2002, and inmates were relocated to a new facility in Warren. The store—and its staff—stayed behind on tourist-friendly coastal Route 1.

The Maine State Prison Showroom, commonly referred to as the "prison store," has done a brisk business in downtown Thomaston since the Great Depression. The merchandise consists of high-quality furniture and handcrafted novelty items built by inmates in the prison workshop. Inmates in the program design their own projects and essentially run a small manufacturing business behind bars. Each is allowed by law to earn a maximum of $10,000 per year. Proceeds often go to make restitution to victims of their crimes or to help support their families on the outside.

A lot of prison store shoppers notice that the original crafts projects tend to have an ironic twist. For example, the name of the wooden schooner model for sale in the showroom window, Freedom's Way, makes it hard to forget exactly where and by whom the vessel was built. Parking for the prison store is located out back. To keep you from blocking the loading ramp, the prisoners made a sign reading LOADING ZONE. PARKED VEHICLES WILL BE TOWED. How can you tell that

★ ★

Need a sign? No problem, Warden.

the sign was made by prisoners? Each word is printed on its own individual license plate! Hey, at least they aren't doing time in New Hampshire, where all the plates stamped out by the inmates read Live Free or Die.

Babb's Bridge

Windham

When we were kids, we went to Babb's Bridge, a covered bridge that spans the Presumpscot River between Windham and Gorham. We jumped off its lower trusses into the Presumpscot. Some brave souls jumped from the roof of the bridge, others jumped in by means of the tire swing on the tree next to it. Cars and trucks would beep their horns as they entered the bridge, then you would hear their tires thunk on the wooden floor and make the same crossing that horse-drawn wagons did more than 150 years ago when the bridge was built. This was as bucolic as you could get, and it was the same river that, as it went downstream, powered mighty paper mills and became a foul sewer as it flowed into the sea.

★ ★

The opportunities for swimming might be gone today, but there's still a covered bridge. By car, or horse, just go north on River Road toward North Windham. About 1½ miles after the intersection with Route 202, turn left at the sign and go about another ½ mile to Babb's Bridge.

There you'll find Babb's Bridge, a replica of the original, which had been built in 1864 using the Howe truss method of construction. Upon entering the structure (beep first to alert oncoming traffic) your wheels touch the wooden floor, which is suspended on a series of "chords," or heavy beam trusses, set parallel to the roadway. You will notice the post-and-beam construction of the timbers supporting the roof. It's cozy in there, like being in an old barn.

There are only eight covered bridges left in Maine where once there were 120, which have washed away or rotted out. Babb's Bridge and the other covered bridges were constructed to keep the rain and snow off the timbers holding up the structure and, in many cases, forming the roadway. This reduced the rot and swelling. The remaining bridges have survived for 150 years, so their coverings actually served their noble purpose.

In 1985 the Maine legislature authorized the Department of Transportation to maintain and preserve covered bridges that weren't part of the state highway system. Babb's Bridge was doing well keeping out natural elements, but it couldn't withstand the onslaught of humans. In 1973 vandals burned the structure. An "exact replica" was constructed on the site and opened in 1976.

Some wonder why tax dollars went to reconstruct a covered bridge, when a steel and asphalt structure would cost less and be more reliable. Perhaps a cost-benefit analysis was performed, showing that tourists will shell out more money when they have these quaint amenities. Or perhaps it was because we like the old covered bridges and we want to keep a few of 'em around. At any rate, Babb's Bridge should be there for another 150 years, if the vandals keep away and the river doesn't rise.

Admit it, sometimes quaint ain't such a bad thing. Don't forget to beep your horn before you drive onto Babb's Bridge.

Maine's Biggest Small Eatery

Wiscasset

Red's Eats, on the western end of the Wiscasset bridge since 1938, is a classic example of the New England Clam Shack school of architecture, and the basic menu is pretty much what you'd expect. Besides burgers and dogs, you've got your french fries, fried onion rings, fried shrimp, fried haddock, fried clams, fried scallops . . . are you beginning to notice a trend here? I haven't checked with the American Heart Association or anything, but it's a safe bet that an average meal at Red's will take care of your maximum daily recommended cholesterol intake for pretty much the rest of the summer.

And they're not resting on their laurels, either. The motto at Red's Eats might as well be "When better artery busters are built, we'll

★ ★

build 'em!" Of course, you can't go wrong with the world-famous-since-1938 "sturdly," a grilled hot dog split down the middle and stuffed with American cheese. But if you don't happen to own a bathroom scale and you're feeling lucky today, why not plunge right into Red's latest creation, the aptly named "puff dog," a split wiener, liberally stuffed with bacon and cheese, then rolled in heavy batter and, you guessed it, deep fried.

Are you tired of paying an arm and a leg for a lobster roll with a couple of ounces of lobster and a quarter pound of iceberg lettuce? You came to the right place. Although you may want to check with your broker before treating the family to lobster rolls at Red's, at least nobody will be complaining about the serving size. A few years back, Red (that's owner Al Gagnon, who died in 2008) started making lobster rolls with "at least," he said, "a whole pound of lobster meat in each one!" And the price? Market price. Maybe a few "sturdlies" would be a more responsible choice, after all. Either way, you'll have fun. Just don't mention this little outing to your cardiologist, OK?

Folks drop by Red's for fried everything.

Follow Your "Drems"

For some reason, the dozen or so miles of coastal Route 1 from the east bank of the Kennebec River in Woolwich to the west bank of the Sheepscott in Wiscasset has, over the years, become a magnet for roadside vendors. It's anybody's guess how this happened, but it probably has something to do with traffic congestion. The Bath bridge and the one in Wiscasset have been notorious summertime bottlenecks. So you might as well accept the fact that you'll be doing a lot of idling, downshifting, and gawking on this particular stretch between any given July 4 and Labor Day.

That's OK. This is Maine, remember? Life in the slow lane? Depending on the time of year, you're going to have plenty of opportunities to stop and purchase a dizzying array of products, from fresh farm produce to homemade handcrafts to discounted designer jeans as you crawl inexorably toward your final destination. Take the right attitude, and this ribbon of bumper to bumper, two-lane Maine blacktop might just be the ultimate cure for road rage. You might as well relax. Ain't NOBODY goin' anywhere fast on this road today.

The stretch of road between Woolwich and Wiscasset is not just noted for bottlenecks. It also has a high number of traffic accidents. The August 13, 2005, *Portland Press Herald* reported that, in an effort to "shrink" the number of accidents, the state DOT hired a psychologist to work with engineers in redesigning the road, taking into account drivers' behavior when faced with the type of road conditions that might lead to accidents. Perhaps the psychologist should be asked, "What do my drems mean?"

if you find yourself stuck in the slow lane . . . . . .
why not stop . . . . . . and pick up a bargain or two!

Now That's What I Call Pie
Machias

Helen's Restaurant on Route 1 in Machias is a roadside oasis not to be missed. More than a landmark eatery, Helen's is a local institution. But just who exactly is this Helen anyway? When did she get started? And, perhaps most perplexing of all, how does Helen or anybody else get away with selling "world famous strawberry pie" in Machias, right smack dab in the epicenter of Maine's wild blueberry crop?

Blueberry pie doesn't get better than this . . . anywhere.

According to the current owners, Gary and Judy Hanscom, the Helen in the restaurant's name was Helen Mugnai. Helen's husband, Larry, opened the original restaurant in 1950. "He started off with an ice cream parlor sort of thing," says Gary. "Then people wanted sandwiches and he did that. By about 1955 he was going full force as a restaurant. Then when the Navy people came and built the Cutler towers [an elaborate, cold-war-era early-warning radar array erected by the U.S. Navy in nearby Cutler], that's when it really took off."

And it's been flying along nicely ever since. The Hanscoms have owned the restaurant since 1988, but Judy began working there back in the mid-seventies. I made my first visit to Helen's in the summer of 1970. Driving along the coastline of Washington County in late August of that year, folks kept handing me the same line wherever I went. "When you get to Machias," they said, "you've got to stop in at Helen's for a piece of that strawberry pie." Naturally, I stopped in.

This was, of course, the "old" Helen's on Main Street a half mile or so south of the "new" Helen's established in 1983. Hey, distinctions like this are critical in small-town Maine. One thing I can tell you for sure is that the "old" Helen's certainly was old! Just walking in the door of the dilapidated wood-frame building, I instantly understood why the fishermen felt so comfortable takin' their supper at Helen's. The warped wooden floor of that old restaurant pitched and rolled almost as dramatically as the swells of the Atlantic. I recall that the food was hearty and plentiful. Here's Gary again: "We got written up in *Life* magazine . . . and Helen's Restaurant has the best blueberry pie in the nation!" He continued, "The gentleman who wrote the article, Michael Sterns is his name, was in the restaurant four or five years ago. He was eatin' and critiquin' only we didn't know it 'til after he left."

Can a Funny Story Save a Life?
Stonington

Stonington, located on the southern tip of Deer Isle, is a picture-book example of a Maine fishing village. I once heard an old-timer remark, "Stonington was the last place on earth that God made. Then the Almighty went and decided to put saltwater around it so it wouldn't freeze up."

I can't comment on that, but I do know that, for better or worse, richer or poorer, in sickness and in health, folks in Stonington have been virtually married to the sea for generations.

A few years back, in response to the tragic deaths at sea of two young island fishermen, Sue Oliver started an organization along with other local women, mostly fishermen's wives (and daughters and sisters, too): the nonprofit Island Fishermen's Wives Association. Of the organization. Sue says, "If a fisherman dies or loses a boat, we try to help out the family." One of the first projects Sue and the other wives completed was a fishermen's memorial on the waterfront. The hope was that when the fishermen passed the monument on their way to work on the open sea, they would be reminded to "be safe, have the right equipment on their boats. . . do the right thing."

One of the group's most popular fund-raisers has been the Fishermen's Wives Storytelling Contest. "We did it in January," says Sue, "so it was all local people. No one comes here in January!" The event, held at the Island Center, was the result of a similar event Sue attended at a waterfront bar in Boothbay Harbor, where she recalls the following:

"This woman got up, and she was telling a story about this guy who'd gone to Nova Scotia to pick up a boat. On his way back, he went below to take a nap, and he took his teeth out and left them to soak in a glass of water." According to the tale, the man's shipmates decided to play a practical joke on him by replacing the water with 90 proof rum. Sue continues, "Then they got worried that the rum would rot the dentures. But they figured 'Hey, the way he drinks, if they're not rotten by now, this won't hurt 'em any!' So when he got up in the morning, he took out the teeth, shook 'em a bit, put 'em in, and made a major face." Examining the glass, the sailor is said to have commented, "It's a shame to waste good rum like that." Whereupon he added a bit of Coke and proceeded to drink his breakfast.

Although that story got a laugh out of Sue, she's dead serious about the work of her organization. "If we can save even one life, it will be more than worth it," she says.

★ ★

True North
Big 20 Township

Quick: What's the northernmost spot in the state of Maine? If you guessed Fort Kent, as in "Kittery to Fort Kent," you would be wrong by at least 50 miles. The northernmost spot is Big 20 Township, and it's one of the most remote areas of the state as well. (Our editors encouraged us to write about areas other than the coast. Well, Big 20 is about as far away from the coast, or any part of Maine, as you can get.)

How far north is it, you ask? Well, it's closer to the North Pole than it is to the equator. At least a quarter of Canada's population lives south of it. And it is farther north than Bismarck, North Dakota, hardly a tropical locale.

It is so remote and far north that it doesn't fit on a regular page of the DeLorme Maine Atlas and Gazetteer. It requires a separate insert. If you look at the insert, you will notice something else: there are no state highways, or even "blue highways," in the entire township. There are only a couple of logging roads, which connect to other logging roads, and eventually they get you to the very end of Route 161 in Dickey, outside of Allagash. If you go north, and across the St. Francis River, you will get to the customs station at Estcourt in Quebec Province.

Big 20 Township is big in geography. It's actually two townships: T20 R11 and R12 WELS, which designates the Unorganized Territory— Township 20 in Ranges 11 and 12 West of the East Line of the State. (Thus, the town is not named after the bowling alley in Scarborough.)

The St. Francis River forms the boundary line of Big 20 Township, as well as that of the state—and of the United States—with the province of Quebec, Canada. This line was established by two gentlemen who never set foot in Big 20 Township: Daniel Webster, who was U.S. secretary of state, and British foreign secretary Lord Ashburton. Their eponymous treaty, signed August 9, 1842, ended the "bloodless" Aroostook War. It gave Canada some land that Mainers claimed, and it gave to the United States some land that Canadians claimed. Along with settling the boundary of Big 20, the Webster-Ashburton Treaty

* *

also settled the U.S.–Canada border out through the Great Lakes to the Lake of the Woods, limited foreign inspection of U.S. ships suspected of carrying slaves in international waters, and gave restitution to the United States for a slave ship that Britain had seized and freed the cargo. Other than those issues, we are sure its most important goal was keeping Big 20 Township in Maine's hands.

There's not much going on in Big 20. Most of the action is right across the border, where there is an Irving Paper Mill. Canadians try to sneak across the border to get cheaper tobacco products, although they might spend so much on gas and car repair that it would be less expensive just to pay the extra cost—or to quit smoking. Fewer than twenty people live in Big 20 year-round.

The biggest activity is timber harvesting, according to Don Cote, a senior enforcement investigator with the Land Use Regulation Commission's local office. Two large timber companies own a substantial amount of the land, with smaller lots owned by camp owners. There once was a gas station and a movie theater right on the boundary with Canada, but they aren't there anymore. There are just a few camps on the lakes that stride the border, but the Canadian sides of the lakes (to the east) are developed, including Beau Lake, where the muskies (not the Ed kind) are plentiful. Cote doesn't expect any major development in Big 20. And neither do we—it's just good to know that this spot is sitting there by itself at the top of the map.

Chain Saw Michelangelo
Hancock

Ray Murphy is the self-proclaimed "World's Original Chain Saw Sculptor," and that's not an idle boast. According to Ray, he personally invented the art form back in 1953, when, as an eleven-year-old boy he used his chain saw to inscribe a series of four-letter words on the woodpile behind his daddy's shed.

If you think maybe Ray is overstating his position in the chain saw sculpting hierarchy, a visit to his bus/chain-saw sculpting museum

★ ★

should convince even the most hard-core skeptic. Inside the 1960 GM model with a million miles on the odometer, most of them put there by Ray himself, you find ample evidence that he is exactly who he says he is: the World's Original (and greatest) Chain Saw Sculptor.

The trouble with fame is that you spend half your time posing for pictures with fans.

As proof of his claims, Ray points out that his work is currently on display in all the Ripley's Believe It or Not! museums worldwide. He is officially listed with Ripley's as the Only Man in the World who can accomplish the following seven mind-boggling feats of chain saw artistry.

Using only a standard-issue, nonmodified chain saw, Ray Murphy can

1. Carve the entire alphabet on a regular number 2 pencil.
2. Carve your name on a belt buckle while you're wearing it.
3. Carve a chair (back, seat, and four legs) out of a block of wood in ten seconds.

4. Carve a sculpture using two chain saws at the same time.

5. Carve two sculptures simultaneously using a chain saw in each hand.

6. Carve his name with a chain saw on the head of a wooden kitchen match without lighting the match.

7. Using only a chain saw, carve the numbers 1 through 10 on a wooden toothpick.

That last one is the topper, what Ray calls "the ultimate." He claims that this is "as near impossible as it gets" and says even he, the World's Original Chain Saw Sculptor, needs two solid weeks of intensive training before attempting it.

Ray has carved more than 50,000 chain saw sculptures so far, and he shows no signs of slowing down. He's a living, breathing, sawdust-blowin'-in-the-wind example of a true Maine roadside attraction.

Come on, honey. It'll look great in the den.

★ ★

Not Exactly Disney World

Mount Katahdin

When he visited Maine's backcountry in 1846, Henry David Thoreau wrote of seeing Mount Katahdin in the distance. His guide said it was four miles away, but it was "as I judged it, and as it proved, nearer fourteen." Later, in a footnote in *The Maine Woods* (1864), Thoreau named the very few white men who were known to have visited "Ktaadn" to date and added: "Besides these, very few, even among backwoodsmen and hunters, have ever climbed it, and it will be a long time before the tide of fashionable travel sets that way."

The moving story of how Percival Baxter acquired the land around the mountain and carefully deeded it to the people of Maine, along with a trust fund to care for it, is told in *Legacy of a Lifetime: The Story of Baxter State Park,* by Dr. John W. Hakola. A continuing theme in Baxter's stewardship was that of maintaining the wilderness nature of the park. The first gift of land in 1931, for example, contained the condition that the land "shall forever be left in the natural wild state, shall forever be kept as a sanctuary for wild beasts and birds, and that no roads or ways for motor vehicles shall hereafter be constructed thereon or therein." Subsequent grants of parcels of land were affected by pressure from neighboring Mainers and from landowners who had sold Baxter the property, so that "in the end, [Baxter] provided for land uses completely counter to his original wilderness concept."

Despite some changes in restrictions, Baxter State Park remains basically unspoiled. Unlike Yellowstone or Acadia National Park, there are restrictions on vehicles and only one vehicle is allowed per campsite. No airplanes, except on Matagamon and Webster Lakes. No radios, TVs, cell phones, chain saws, or generators. Also, no snowmobiles, except on the Perimeter Road and on certain designated trails are allowed and hunting is allowed only in a few townships; fishing is OK, with a license.

Perhaps the biggest surprise is that you can't bring your household pets. This was the same Percival Baxter who found the company of

dogs preferable to that of humans. Those who wanted to camp overnight at the park used to line up at the park office at the first of the
year to gobble up spaces. Now, there are rules about advance reservations within four months of the desired date. See the park Web site for
details (www.baxterstateparkauthority.com).

"The House That Orgasms Built"
Rangeley

Wilhelm Reich was either a "renowned physician/scientist" (according to the Web site of the Wilhelm Reich Museum) or someone whose
ideas had "no status in the scientific community" (according to *The
Skeptics Dictionary* by Robert Todd Carroll; www.skepdic.com).

Reich, an Austrian psychologist who lived from 1897 to 1957,
conducted many of his experiments in Rangeley, Maine. He believed
there exists a certain form of energy that can be detected, measured,
and harnessed. To capitalize on this energy, which he termed "orgone"
in 1942, Reich created and sold orgone "accumulators" and orgone
"shooters." The Food and Drug Administration, which also burned
some of Reich's books, banned these devices in the 1950s. Today, the
Wilhelm Reich Museum features equipment used in his pioneering
experiments as well as Reich's library, personal memorabilia, sculpture,
and paintings.

What is this orgone stuff, anyway? It has something to do with
orgasms. The "renowned scientist" described it as "the ability for total
surrender to the involuntary contractions of the orgasm and the complete discharge of the excitation at the acme of the genital embrace,"
which creates an "orgastic potency." In many places, such talk would
get the authorities steamed up. But in Rangeley, most people probably
couldn't figure out what that meant.

Those who disagreed with Reich, and there were many, were called
"orgastically impotent." So it was just as well that folks in the area
focused on Reich's rooftop observatory, which provides a spectacular
view of the surrounding area.

The Best Fly-Fishing Spot in the State of Maine

Now Everyone Knows the Secret

In the old days information about one's best fishing spots was top-secret. "I'd tell ya the best fishing place I know, but I'd have to shoot ya afterwards." Now, either because of the enhanced audience for fish bragging provided by the Internet or because the secret areas seem to get found anyway, there is at least a public discussion about such top-secret places.

A visit to Fly Fishing in Maine, www.flyfishinginmaine.com, not only offers information about top fishing spots but also records what was caught and what fly was used to do it. Dan Tarkinson of Portland, started the site as a college project. Now, as a nonprofit, it raises funds for conservation projects while sharing fishing information.

Etiquette dictates that you can take someone to your secret spot, but they aren't supposed to show it to someone else. Dan says some folks break the rule and post the location on the Web site. This information can be found among the latest spottings of the topless female fishing group, the Tacky Women Angling Team, and with information about "fly swaps." Armchair anglers can also learn of the potential dangers to native brook trout caused by the introduction of smallmouth bass in Rapid River.

Dan's favorite method of fly fishing is catch 'n' release. "A lot of fishing areas are stocked based on the assumption that the fish will be taken. But this wouldn't be necessary if everyone threw 'em back."

So, what's Dan's favorite fishing spot? Besides the West Bank of the Penobscot, it's the Rapid River near Umbagog Lake and Pond-in-the-River. I'd tell you how to get there, but. . .

★ ★

Reich attempted to demonstrate his "orgonoscope" to Albert Einstein, in Princeton, New Jersey, but when was the last time someone from New Jersey listened to someone from Maine? Reich became a martyr to his ideas. He died in 1957, in Lewisburg Federal Penitentiary, where he was imprisoned for defying the FDA's ban on his products. His tomb, with its dramatic bronze bust, stands in a forest clearing near the museum.

Some of Reich's ideas have not been fully released to the public, such as the "orgone-powered motor," which purportedly ran smoothly. This information is expected to be released sometime in this decade. Meantime, visitors to the museum can see the grounds, the guest cabins, and the scientific gizmos that go along with "the house that orgasms built."

4

New Hampshire Curiosities

Try this: Drive around New Hampshire and ask perfect strangers questions like, "How far to the little church on the boulder?" or "Which way to the giant pumpkin chucker?" Sometimes people respond so quickly it was as if they could read your mind—a sign perhaps that they'd been asked the same question many, many times before. When searching for Willa Cather's grave in Jaffrey Center, we didn't even have to ask: A man saw us wandering the Old Burying Ground in the rain and called out from the road, "You lookin' for Willa?" Other times we would see a person working in the yard and stop to ask directions to, say, a 60-foot-tall intermediate-range nuclear missile on a town green somewhere nearby, and we would chat for a while about the snow, or the rain, or the conditions of the roads as a result of said snow or rain, or, if the conversation took a certain turn, about the drinking and/or hunting and/or junk-collecting habits of a particular neighbor down the road a piece, who certainly didn't remain nameless.

Every now and then, when people heard we were looking for weird, wacky, and offbeat people, places, and events in New Hampshire, they'd ask us to name one or two of our favorites. And each time someone asked, we would have to stop and think as if hearing the question for the first time. Was it the outboard motor museum in Gilmanton? How about Frances Glessner Lee's gory little crime scene dollhouses? Or Larry Davis's 2,850 consecutive daily ascents of Mount Monadnock? Maybe the Giant Pumpkin Regatta in Goffstown where they hollow out 600-pound pumpkins and pilot them down the Piscataquog?

The truth was, just like proud parents, we liked them all, not because they were all equally odd, but because they were all pretty darn . . . curious. And the more we scratched the surface of each little New Hampshire oddity and anomaly, the more interesting and down-right weird each of them became.

These curiosities and the peculiar stories behind them have con-nected us to New Hampshire—its history, its places, and its people—in new and surprising ways. Taken all together, they've made this great Granite State seem more real, more complex, more interesting, and certainly more curious.

Give Me a New Blue Eye and a Ceramic Leg—Stat!

Dover

Patricia Aveni has been doctor, nurse, diagnostic expert, therapist, receptionist, and um, finger replacer at her clinic for over thirty years, and she doesn't show any signs of burnout yet. Maybe that's because it's not often that she has to deal with what cops like to call the "Tough Cases," the little tikes who have been neglected or mistreated or, even worse, forgotten. On the contrary, Aveni says, most patients who end up at her clinic have been "loved to pieces."

Sound a bit macabre? Don't worry. Her clinic at 12 Stark Avenue is the Dover Doll Clinic, and all her patients are dolls—literally. Aveni, a renowned doll expert, is the equivalent of a hotshot doc when it comes to doll repair and restoration, from the simplest outpatient procedure—say, a quick stitch job on some overalls—to the most complicated surgery, like a combination face-lift and double eyeball transplant on a seventy-eight-year-old infant.

What are the most common doll injuries? According to Aveni, older ceramic dolls can have damage to noses, limbs, fingers, toes. And, of course, the older a doll is, the more likely it is to need significant work and the more difficult and delicate that work tends to be. For minor surgeries or major makeovers (for dolls, that is), call Patricia Aveni's Dover Doll Clinic at (603) 742–6818.

A Museum with Wonderfully Low Standards
Dover

Maybe you'll head to Dover's Woodman Institute for its extensive collection of nineteenth-century natural history specimens, from the towering stuffed polar bear, to the cuddly-looking manatee, to the last mountain lion shot and killed in New Hampshire (1847), down to the gaggles of stuffed birds, pinned moths, and pickled reptiles scattered throughout.

Or perhaps you'll come for the human history, including an entire seventeenth-century garrison house, impeccably preserved under a large open-walled shelter; Abraham Lincoln's saddle; and a suit of Japanese medieval armor.

Or you can come for the real curiosities. Check out the 6-foot stuffed iguana, found dead by the side of the road right here in Dover (don't ask), or the two-headed snake suspended in some cloudy preservative in an old-fashioned canning jar. He's hard to spot among his pickled compatriots, from bullfrogs to toads to rattlers, each in its own Ball jar of decades-old . . . juices, but if you bend down close enough to read the handwritten index cards, you'll spot him.

Perhaps the museum's most famous animal oddity is the four-footed chicken—just a baby chick, really, with both front-wheel and what looks to be less functional rear-wheel drive.

But, if you're like me, you'll come for the oddest oddities: the glass display case of botanical curiosities that includes specimens like an ingrown branch (think ingrown toenail in the form of a tree branch); wood growing around a stone; a "natural cloth" that resembles a loosely woven stocking tied at one end, donated by an anonymous collector who harvested it from "some species of palm tree" (the collector didn't sweat the details, so why should we?); a 32-inch-thick wedge of bark from a redwood; and, our personal favorite, a "piece of wood badly eaten by ants," the gift (if you can call it that) of one Mr. E. M. Bailey of Andover, Massachusetts.

The Woodman Institute's great strength is that it accepted such donations, and many more like them, because its directors lacked funds for acquisitions and so never had the luxury of saying no. Established in 1916 to encourage the study of local history, natural history, and art, the Woodman has accepted donations ranging from the original 1675 colonial garrison house, to a blackjack used to kill a local cashier in 1897, to a man-killing Australian clam. The Woodman Institute, located at 182 Central Avenue in Dover, is open Wednesday through Sunday, except holidays. The museum drastically reduces its hours in December and shuts down entirely January through March. Admission is charged. For more information call (603) 742–1038.

A Parade for Those of Us with ADD

Durham

The first thing Mrs. Nobel Peterson gave us was a warning: "Now, if you come this year and just plan to watch from the curb, well, I can guarantee you'll be back next year marching in the parade, and then the year after that you'll be the one cheering the loudest." The parade she's talking about is Durham's Leif Eriksson Day Parade, and her warning to me was based on twenty-four years of experience. "We have people come back every year from all over the country, from Texas to California to Michigan, just to march in our little parade," she said.

Take special note of Mrs. Peterson's phrase "our little parade." The parade isn't very big——there are no floats or marching bands or giant inflated Disney characters—just a large group of people marching down the street. And it just may be the shortest parade route in the world. "We gather in front of the Laundromat around 6:00 a.m., admire each other's Scandinavian flags, practice our cheers, then study the parade route to be sure no one gets lost," she explained to me. "Then at exactly 6:30 a.m. we march 25 feet to Young's Coffee Shop, where we all have breakfast." And that's it. Throw in thirty seconds of singing each Scandinavian national anthem followed by "The Star-Spangled Banner" (in its entirety, of course), a brief Parade of Beautiful Sweaters, and a scripted question-and-answer session about the parade itself—including the questions "Why is the parade so early?" and "What proof is there that Leif Eriksson discovered North America in AD 1000?" in response to which the whole crowd shouts out the answers—and you've got the entire program of Durham's Leif Eriksson Day Parade.

The event takes place each year on the Sunday closest to October 9, the date President Lyndon Johnson declared Leif Eriksson Day way back in 1964. For information or to make reservations, call Mrs. Nobel Peterson at (603) 868–9692.

Exeter's Little Incident
Exeter

The Seacoast's preponderance of UFO sightings is a little vexing for area residents, especially since coastal Graniteers like to believe that they're at least as sane as citizens are in the White Mountains or the Great North Woods. As of August 2005, though, there had been more than 145 reported UFO sightings in the Seacoast's Rockingham County, a figure that makes it the state's undisputed champion of alleged extraterrestrial visitations.

Perhaps the most famous UFO sighting happened the night of September 3, 1965, in and around the town of Exeter. Of the five UFO witnesses that night, two were Exeter police officers: David Hunt and air force veteran Eugene Bertrand. Largely as a result of the patrolmen's credibility, the United States Air Force later acknowledged that the sightings, which have come to be known as the "Incident at Exeter" (the title of John G. Fuller's 1966 best-selling book about the sightings), involved an unidentified flying object.

As the story goes, Norman Muscarello, an eighteen-year-old navy recruit from Exeter, was returning home on foot from his girlfriend's house in Amesbury, Massachusetts, when an object, which he later described as being "as big as a house" with bright red pulsating lights, suddenly appeared in the sky before him. The object silently "wobbled" closer and closer toward Muscarello until, utterly terrified, he dropped into a ditch beside the road. After the UFO backed away and disappeared over the horizon, Muscarello flagged down a vehicle, which took him to the police station, where he told his story to officer Gene Bertrand, who just an hour earlier had interviewed a Seacoaster who claimed she had been chased in her car by a large low-flying object with flashing red lights for a distance of about 12 miles.

Local police and UFOs once met in this field.

Muscarello joined Officer Bertrand in his cruiser and led him back to the Dining family farm where the young man saw the object. After a brief investigation, Bertrand heard Muscarello scream and turned to find what he would later describe as "a huge, shapeless object with five sequentially-pulsating-from-left-to-right bright red lights" slowly rise above a stand of pines. The object seemed to tilt back and forth and float toward them with a motion that reminded Bertrand of a falling leaf. As Officer Bertrand made a hasty retreat toward his cruiser with a petrified Muscarello in tow (poor Norm!), officer David Hunt arrived on the scene. All three then watched as the UFO disappeared in the direction of Hampton, where an object of similar description was allegedly observed just minutes later by an anonymous motorist.

Officials at Pease Air Force Base and at the Pentagon offered various explanations, including glare from airfield lights and nighttime refueling exercises, but both explanations seemed highly unlikely, especially the latter, since Officer Bertrand had been an air force refueling specialist. The mystery remains unsolved to this day, making Exeter's incident one of the few government-certified UFO sightings.

To see the field where the UFO sighting occurred, travel out of Exeter toward Kensington on Route 150 or Amesbury Road. Once you cross the Exeter line, it's about a half mile to the field (now surrounded by a white fence) on the east side of the road where Brewer Road intersects with Amesbury.

The Worst Band You Didn't Know You'd Love

Fremont

The Shaggs, a '60s-era rock act, were three teens from Fremont whose father withdrew them from the local high school, scraped together money for musical instruments and lessons twice a week in Manchester, and designed for his daughters a rigorous daily schedule of morning practice, afternoon mail-order home schooling, more practice, and then dinner. Oh, and to finish out the evening, the girls performed a round of calisthenics and rehearsed one last time.

One would think all that practice and self-sacrifice might turn Helen, Betty, and Dot Wiggin into rock virtuosos, but the fruit of all those jam sessions and leg lifts was far more interesting than mere virtuosity.

Described as "primitive," "raw," "unpolished," and "aboriginal" by their more generous reviewers, the Shaggs inspire in their listeners extremes of either appreciation or disgust. To wit: Frank Zappa reportedly said the Shaggs were better than the Beatles. And Lester Bangs, a music critic for the *Village Voice,* claimed that their harmonies sounded like "three singing nuns who've been sniffing lighter fluid." Their music must be heard to be believed.

The Shaggs started small and, much to their father Austin Wiggin's chagrin, they stayed small. For five years, beginning in 1968 and ending in 1973, the Wiggin sisters played in public almost exclusively at Saturday evening performances in the Fremont Town Hall, where as many as a hundred of their peers gathered to chat, dance, and, on occasion, heckle the sisters on stage. Dot led the group through sets that included a song celebrating parents ("Parents are the ones who are aaalwaays there!" she croons) and a number about Dot's lost cat named Foot Foot.

Austin spent most of his savings on the recording of a Shaggs album in the spring of 1969, *Philosophy of the World.* Neither the girls nor the studio producer felt the group was ready to record, but Austin reportedly said he wanted to "get them while they're hot." The record made no splash. A few years later, Austin brought the girls down to Boston for another recording session, but by 1973 Fremont had put a stop to the Shaggs' town hall performances and the sisters, now in their twenties, were beginning to bristle under their father's strict managerial style. In 1975, when Austin died suddenly of a heart attack at forty-seven, the band died, too.

End of story? Wrong. In the 1970s collectors got hold of copies of *Philosophy of the World,* and over the next three decades the album was rereleased a couple of times. With each rerelease the Shaggs got a little more attention and acquired a whole new crew of puzzled, bemused, but often adoring fans—slowly but surely the Shaggs were becoming an outsider music sensation. After best-selling author Susan Orlean wrote an article titled "Meet the Shaggs" in the *New Yorker* in

★ ★

1999, Tom Cruise's production company optioned the film rights. In 2005, a musical called *The Shaggs: Philosophy of the World* opened off-Broadway after a successful run in Chicago. Really. The Wiggin sisters, who all still live within a dozen miles of Fremont, seemed as surprised by their new fame as their fans, but they're just as sweet and good-natured as ever. Austin would be shocked to learn how long he really had to get the Shaggs while they're hot.

A Fake with a Long Shelf Life

Hampton

Some lucky fakes can get so famous, it doesn't matter that they're phony—no matter what, they'll always be stars. As a case in point, I submit Hampton's Viking rock, best known as Thorvald's Rock. Legend has it that Thorvald's Rock, which now sits on the grounds of the Tuck Museum in a shallow well with iron bars across the mouth to protect the stone from souvenir seekers, once marked the Boar's Head burial site of the Viking explorer Thorvald Eriksson, brother of the more famous Leif Eriksson and son of Erik the Red. Those scratches visible on the rock, legend also has it, are ancient runes.

An unlikely artifact, the Viking rock remains silent.

The legend probably started on July 4, 1902, when Hampton district court judge Charles A. Lamprey published a piece in the local newspaper making the case that a strangely gouged stone on his family's coastal property marked the grave of the Viking explorer Thorvald. According to Viking sagas recorded in medieval Icelandic manuscripts, Thorvald was retracing his brother's discovery of Vinland (what is now known as North America) in 1004 when he found a stunning rock outcropping that reminded him of the fiords back home. He came ashore, skirmished with local Indians, was mortally wounded, and with his last breath requested burial ashore. Those rocks in the legend, Lamprey argued, had to be Boar's Head, the rocky promontory just north of Hampton Beach (even though there are many rocky outcroppings along the 3,000 miles of coastline between here and Canada). And because of the strangely gouged stone on Lamprey's property, it stood to reason (reasons not altogether clear) that the rock marked Thorvald's grave.

Sometime in the 1950s, the rock was moved to make way for new construction. In 1973 local amateur archeologists reportedly searched for Thorvald's remains at the original site and came up empty-handed. Tourists sought out the rock; some even chipped off pieces as souvenirs. Finally, in 1989 Thorvald's Rock was moved to the Tuck Museum where it rests to this day behind bars.

The Tuck Museum is at 40 Park Avenue in Hampton; Thorvald's Rock is on the museum grounds close to Park Avenue. For museum hours and other information call (603) 929–0781.

Pro Sand Castle Builders Compete to Justify Dubious Career Choice
Hampton Beach

Greg Grady's so serious about sand that he's one of only about 250 master sand sculptors worldwide who can make a living "in sand," attending sand-sculpting competitions and creating commissioned sand sculptures for individuals, municipalities, and businesses. "A bunch of

★ ★

us sat around trying to figure out how many of us there were, and we came up with about 250," Grady said. "Now, of course, that's not set in stone, but it's a pretty good estimate." Don't you think it's kind of funny for a sand sculptor to say, "That's not set in stone?"

Grady is the organizer of the Hampton Beach Master Sand-Sculpting Competition, held each year in June. A dozen master sand sculptors have twenty-one hours over a period of three days to create original works of art out of their individual allotments of ten tons of sand and all the water they want. "One of the biggest misconceptions people have," Grady told me, "is that we do something tricky to the sand [to create sculptures]. There are no tricks: just sand and water, that's it." (Only after the sculptures are finished can artists spray them with a 10 percent glue and water solution to help prevent damage.)

Judges choose first- through fifth-place winners based on artistic merit, technical difficulty, and overall design, and, with over $10,000 in prize money, the stakes are high. There's also a people's choice award, so you can vote for your own favorite.

While sand sculpting may sound like a great career, don't quit your day job just yet. There are risks beyond sunstroke and premature wrinkling. In the 2005 competition, one of the sculptures fell only an hour before judging, no laughing matter for the sculptor, Fred Mallet of South Padre Island, Texas, or for Greg Grady. "Ten tons of sand is no joke," he told me. "Someone could get really hurt." Luckily, Fred escaped unharmed, but others aren't so lucky. Grady recalled a competition in Fort Myers when an inebriated spring breaker tried knocking down a competitor's sand sculpture to get a laugh: "He kind of ran and tackled the thing, and then he just lay there, crying. An ambulance came and took him away—I think he dislocated his shoulder." That's one college student who won't miss his GREs to go build castles in the sand.

The Hampton Beach Master Sand-Sculpting Competition is held at the end of each June right on Hampton Beach. For information go to www.hamptonbeach.org or, if you'd like to volunteer at the event, call (603) 926–8718.

★ ★

This Divided House Won't Fall

Portsmouth

Strawbery Banke is the name of both the original settlement that later became the city of Portsmouth and a wonderful museum restoration of an almost 400-year-old ten-acre waterfront neighborhood over on the northeast side of town. In the 1950s the neighborhood was slated for the wrecking ball, proclaimed a slum by city officials, its land taken by eminent domain, its inhabitants forced to find new homes. Luckily, citizens concerned about saving Portsmouth's history formed a non-profit, bought the land back from the city, and founded the Strawbery Banke Museum.

A house with a centuries-long rift.

One of Strawbery Banke's many charms is that it's not a historical re-creation like other colonial museums. Instead, it's composed of more

★ ★

than thirty-five restored buildings, thirty of which sit right on their original foundations. Of course, you'll find old houses at Strawbery Banke, filled with all the antiques you might expect, from lumpy beds to looms. And you'll get to talk to historical re-enactors who never break character, dressed up in full period costume. But one of the most unusual features of the museum is that instead of representing only one distant historical period, the buildings and furnishings trace pivotal moments in the neighborhood's evolution over three centuries.

The strangest example of this historical medley is the Drisco House, a dynamic duplex that is half 1950s and half 1795. Think Dr. Jekyl and Mr. Hyde. At the front of the house on the east side you'll find a re-creation of a shop run by the building's very first inhabitants, the Shapleys, with wares including dried fish, tobacco, and grain. And on the western front half of the house you'll find a 1950s-era living room, intended to show what the home might have looked like when it was last occupied, complete with Howdy Doody on TV, some scary-looking TV dinners, and a Technicolor picture over the mantle of Jesus with his twelve disciples at the Last Supper. Oh yeah, and some mid-twentieth-century American wallpaper that'll really knock your socks off.

The Strawbery Banke Museum is located on Marcy Street in downtown Portsmouth. The museum's so-called self-guiding season, when Strawbery Banke is open seven days a week, runs May through October. The museum's guided tour season begins on the first of November and runs through the end of April, with tours on weekends and during Christmas and Thanksgiving week holidays. Call (603) 433–1100 for hours of operation and tour times.

Mom's Bloody Revenge
Boscawen

There's nothing like attacking a woman's family, burning her house to the ground, and forcing her to march through dismal weather for over 100 miles to make her really, really mad. On March 15, 1697, a group of Abenaki Indians captured Hannah Dustin, along with her midwife,

Mary Neff, and her brand-new baby, at her homestead in the town of
Haverhill, Massachusetts. Her husband and six other children managed
to escape, but Hannah must have presumed that they had either been
captured, too, or killed. According to the account written by Cotton
Mather, the minister who made Hannah's story famous, the Dustin
baby was killed not long after the group was taken captive, its head
dashed against the trunk of a tree.

Yet when Hannah Dustin managed to escape, she carried away with
her not one, not three, not seven, but ten human scalps. Mary Neff
and Samuel Leonardson, an adolescent boy from Worcester who'd

A seventeenth-century woman with
an axe to grind.

been held captive for more than a year, helped Hannah with her bloody midnight work of killing and scalping their sleeping captors, a group of two men, two women, and six children, on an island located at the mouth of the Contoocook River. The three then fled in a canoe down the Merrimack River all the way back to Haverhill.

Erected in 1874 on the very island where Hannah Dustin got her revenge, her monument features a life-size statue of Hannah astride a massive stone pedestal, her right hand clutching a tomahawk and her left hand grasping a bunch of scalps. According to some sources, Hannah's sister, Elizabeth Emerson, was executed just four years earlier, in 1693, for killing her twin babies.

The Hannah Dustin Memorial State Historic Site, with its dramatic statue, is located on an island at the mouth of the Contoocook River just off Route 4 in Boscawen. Take exit 17 off Interstate 93 and follow Route 4 west for about half a mile. The parking area for the memorial is a Park & Ride lot on the left-hand side. Follow the path down the hill and across a railroad trestle to the statue.

Egg-Shaped Stone a Mystery
Concord

Here's something we've only recently discovered: Mystery is 99 percent presentation. And Doug Copeley, registrar at the Museum of New Hampshire History, knows how to present a mystery. Before he shows you the museum's so-called Mystery Stone, he'll take you to the bowels of the building, have you sign an official paper, and then let you peruse the multiple files packed with photographs and documents pertaining to the elaborately carved, greenish black stone that was, according to reports, discovered at the bottom of a post hole in Meredith in 1872.

And what a beautiful Mystery Stone it is. About 4½ inches from top to bottom, smooth, egg-shaped, and covered with carvings that look like strange and ancient glyphs, the stone is unlike any I've ever seen. The largest carving is that of a face running the entire length of one side of the stone, which with its elongated profile, large nose, and wide bulging eyes, reminded me of those huge heads on Easter Island. There are also carvings of an ear of corn, a tepee, what appears to be a number of spears crossed over each other, and most mysterious of all, a group of three figures stacked inside a circle: what looks to be a small winged creature that might represent a hummingbird or a bee, beneath that a long slender figure that might be a hoofed animal leg, then a three-pointed, crown-shaped carving that might symbolize water. Through the center of the stone, from top to bottom, runs a circular tapered hole, as if someone had drilled straight through the rock.

As befits a mystery stone, researchers don't know a whole lot about it. What they do know is that Seneca Ladd purportedly discovered it, encased in clay, in a post hole on a farm in Meredith in 1872. (Frances Ladd Coe donated it to the museum in 1927.) But the mysteries surrounding the stone are many. Who made it? When? Why? What do the symbols carved on its surface mean? We may never know—hence, the stone's name. For a true sense of the stone's mystery, though, it's best to have someone like Doug Copeley to present things just so.

The Museum of New Hampshire History is located in between North Main Street and Storrs Street at 6 Eagle Square in Concord. Admission is charged; free parking is located on Storrs Street. For more information or to set up an appointment to see the Mystery Stone, call (603) 228–6688.

Politically Active Horse Put to Pasture
Gossville

You wouldn't know it by looking at him, but the wooden horse on wheels on Route 4 in Gossville was a lot more political in his youth. According to reports, he was originally built decades ago to protest the United Nations, a body the horse's creators believed was detrimental to freedom and democracy and the American way the world over, maybe even in America. Scattered on the lawn all around the U.N., "Trojan horse" were white crosses marked with the names of various

A wooden horse who's lost his taste for politics.

communist countries, like Latvia and Lithuania. Rest in peace, you nations of the Baltic Republic, the U.N. Trojan horse seemed to say.

While the Gossville Trojan horse was a full-time protester for much of his youth, times change and 10-foot-tall wooden horses on wheels change, too. New owners have purchased the property, and the horse with it, so the Gossville Trojan horse has become more conservative in his old age. He doesn't march in the Old Home Days parade like he used to, or indulge in tirades against the illegitimate authority of international bodies; he doesn't wear his mane long and complain about the Man; he doesn't even have a single mock grave marker at his wheels. Perestroika took the fun out of panicky cold war–inspired protests, and he hasn't been the same horse since.

Some say the Trojan horse has sold out and gone corporate, though there's no evidence he's ever tried to sell anything to anybody. As far as we can tell, he's just mellowed a bit with age. May Gossville's big wooden horse without a company or a cause continue to gaze down on passing motorists for many decades to come.

Gossville's Trojan horse is located on the north side of Route 4 right beside the old Sherwood Inn, less than a half mile east of Route 28.

Heavyweight Ali Finds Home In Automotive Sales
Hooksett

After Stephen Singer, owner of Merchants Automotive Group in Hooksett, gave us a story-filled personal tour of his Muhammad Ali Museum, he left us with a parting gift: a personal-size bag of Muhammad Ali Popcorn with a cartoon picture of the Champ on the front and an expiration date marked April 1992. "It's fourteen-year-old

This is the GREATEST collection of Ali memorabilia.

popcorn," Singer said with a smile, as if popcorn were like wine and improved with age.

Singer brought that same humorous sensibility to his collection of Muhammad Ali memorabilia, and the result is a truly one-of-a-kind museum. Displayed in a hallway leading to dealership offices (Singer's among them), the collection includes everything from a neon kinetic sculpture with a two-dimensional Ali rope-a-doping his way to victory, to a sculpture of the champ's hands made from plaster casts of his fists, to a life-size cartoonlike Ali sculpture getting ready to work an Ali punching bag inside a 4-foot-square ring. He's even got the original X-ray of Muhammad Ali's broken jaw from his fight with Ken Norton, signed not just by Ali but Norton as well. (Seems like a rather sporting way to handle a broken jaw, doesn't it?)

The Merchants Automotive Group dealership with the Ali Museum (there are two dealerships) is located at 1278 Hooksett Road in Hooksett. For information call (603) 669–4100 or (800) AUTO–999.

A Staring Contest with a Migrating Salmon
Manchester

Helen Dalbeck, the director of the Amoskeag Fishways Learning and Visitor's Center, admits that it's sometimes hard for kids to understand that the fish they're watching with rapt attention through the center's underwater viewing windows aren't in a tank. Instead, the American shad, Altlantic salmon, American eels, alewifes, and other fish swimming by are headed up a computer-controlled fish ladder, which allows them to bypass a hydroelectric dam at Amoskeag Falls and migrate farther upriver. Admittedly, the fish ladder pool does resemble an aquarium, with its Plexiglas, metal, and concrete walls, but those fish you see at the Fishways, they're wild ones, just passing through, rambling on, making their long and lonesome way home. And, unlike aquarium fish, they don't want any handouts.

In addition to the underwater viewing windows in the basement, the Amoskeag Fishways Center has some wonderful museum exhibits on everything from watershed threats to electricity generation to the life cycles of migratory fish. The center also offers special environmental education programs, where kids can learn about things such as river wildlife, native crafts, and water-quality issues. And, of course, each spring the Fishways is flooded with visitors hoping to catch a rare glimpse of a ladder-climbing fish, a creature no one ever told you about in school. Where else can you look a wild American shad in the eye while she's migrating? Of course, she'll probably be too preoccupied to chat, but you'll just have to forgive her: She's in the grip of an overpowering biological imperative. Don't you sometimes wish you could have such a great excuse?

The Amoskeag Fishways Learning and Visitor's Center is located at 6 Fletcher Street in downtown Manchester. Take exit 6 off Interstate 293 in Manchester and follow Amoskeag Street east towards

Stand back: Migrating fish at work.

★ ★

the Amoskeag Bridge. The Fishways will be on your right, behind the Ramada Inn, just before you reach the bridge. You also want to call ahead, (603) 626–FISH (3474). For more information go to www .amoskeagfishways.org.

A Hermit Whose Dance Card Was Always Full
Manchester

The Hermit of Mosquito Pond. Doesn't that have a lovely, romantic-sounding ring to it? Charles Alan Lambert was a nineteenth-century hermit who, after a severe disappointment in love in the 1840s, bought forty acres beside Mosquito Pond (now Crystal Lake) in south Manchester and lived there in solitude for the next seventy years. Solitude is a relative term, especially when you've got a name with as much mystical mystique and rugged sex appeal as "The Hermit of Mosquito Pond." It probably wasn't long before Lambert started receiving more visitors than was seemly for a hermit, and as his fame grew, reports say he entertained hundreds of guests over the course of a busy summer season. When he wasn't receiving visitors, the so-called hermit spent his time much the same way any hermit would, according to the *Encyclopedia of New England,* meditating on nature, tending his vegetables, selling plants and herbs to locals, and looking after his large flock of sheep. Like Henry David Thoreau, an even more famous hermit contemporary (who lived just one year, not seventy, alone in the woods), Lambert practiced a rugged self-sufficiency, building his own rather ramshackle house using logs and old lumber from his property and growing most of his own food. And like Thoreau, the Hermit of Mosquito Pond piqued the curiosity of a good many people by calling himself a recluse. The last two years of his long life, the Sisters of Mercy at the House of St. John For Aged Men cared for him. He died there in 1914 and was buried in St. Joseph Cemetery, his grave marked by a plain white tombstone inscribed with the words THE HERMIT.

Crystal Lake is in south Manchester, off Bodwell Road. From Manchester, follow Route 28A (or South Mammoth Road) south to the

Interstate 293/93 overpass. Just after you cross beneath the interchange, take a left onto Bodwell Road and continue until you reach the entrance for Crystal Lake Park. There's a public beach and a fieldstone bathhouse on nineteen acres at the north end of the lake. To visit St. Joseph Cemetery on Donald Street in Manchester, take exit 3 off I–293 and head west on Route 101. Continue straight at the intersection with Route 114, then turn right onto Bedford Road. The first cemetery you come to (on your right) will be New St. Joseph Cemetery. Continue on Donald Street until you come to St. Joseph Cemetery on your left.

For Now, Scientists Concede Victory to Gravity

New Boston

Gravity's one of those laws of nature that's so everyday, so ordinary, you don't really start to work up a good strong resentment toward it until you stop and think about it. That fall your poor old grandmother took last year? Gravity. Your bad back? Gravity. Extremely poor gas mileage in your SUV? Gravity again.

Now that we've identified the problem and stoked our collective righteous indignation, what, oh what, can we do about gravity? For starters, we can head to New Boston and pay homage to a man who devoted his life to fighting gravity the way Smoky the Bear devoted his to fighting forest fires. It was here, in this quiet hamlet, that the business and investment guru Roger W. Babson, perhaps best known for founding Babson College, established the Gravity Research Foundation, an organization dedicated to beating gravity once and for all, or at least bringing it down a peg or two. On a traffic island in the center of town, you'll find a simple granite monument that pays tribute to the group's "active research for anti-gravity and a partial gravity insulator."

Babson, who made millions and helped revolutionize the financial services industry by starting one of the first investment analysis services, established the Gravity Research Foundation in New Boston in 1948. The foundation, which occupied a number of buildings in town, held

★ ★

weeklong conferences on gravity (Igor Sikorsky, the gravity-defying inventor of the helicopter, once attended), sponsored a gravity essay contest, and collected statistics from hospitals regarding "the day and, if possible, the hour, of a fracture" in order to see if a relationship could be established between phases of the moon and rates of injury, and thereby implicate gravity.

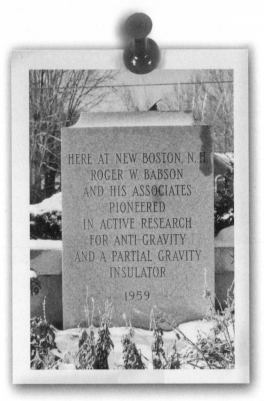

Gravity may not be Enemy No. 1, but
it's certainly not our friend.

Babson's beef against gravity was personal. In an essay titled "Gravity—Our Enemy No. 1," Babson discusses the drowning of his eldest sister in a river in his hometown of Gloucester, Massachusetts. "She was unable to fight gravity," he wrote, "which came up and seized her like a dragon and brought her to the bottom." In spite of Babson's millions, though, the foundation's conferences eventually ceased, the New Boston buildings were sold, and the Gravity Research Foundation seemed to disappear.

But the organization soldiers on, having switched its emphasis from beating gravity to better understanding it. Located in Massachusetts, they offer annual essay awards, with a top prize of $5,000, to physicists doing gravity-related research. The monument to Roger Babson and his Gravity Research Foundation is located in New Boston on the eastern side of the traffic island at the intersection of Routes 13 and 136. For more information on the Gravity Research Foundation, visit www.gravityresearchfoundation.org or email the organization at grideoutjr@aol.com.

America's Got a New Stonehenge

Salem

The folks at America's Stonehenge have done lots of homework on their thirty-acre hilltop maze of stone walls, man-made chambers, and ceremonial stones, said to be perhaps the oldest man-made construction in the United States. While it's said to have been constructed somewhere between 3,500 and 4,000 years ago, an estimate based on radiocarbon dating of charcoal fragments at the site, America's Stonehenge didn't open for business until 1958, when a well-developed roadway system and a burgeoning population of Americans with leisure time and disposable income made it possible for an American Stonehenge to turn a profit.

Originally called the Mystery Hill Caves, the owners changed the name to America's Stonehenge when archeo-astronomers discovered that, like Stonehenge in England, the site functions as an ancient astronomical calendar, with stones marking various solar and lunar events. Researchers also found tablets at the site that contain ancient inscriptions in Oghum, Phoenician, and Iberian Punic. The inscriptions have led some to theorize that America's Stonehenge was built by Celts, Vikings, or Phoenicians who migrated to the North American

Please Return Coffin after Use

New Hampshire folks are famous for knowing how to stretch a dollar and a dime, but sometimes Yankee frugality can get a little out of hand. As a case in point, we offer the story of the Hancock town coffin. For many years, those who died and couldn't afford a coffin in Hancock were graciously offered the use of a nice pine box free of charge, whether they were tramp, pauper, or just plain poor. The only catch was, once the poor and deceased was resting in peace, the coffin had to be returned to storage in the town's tramp house so that it could be offered to the next poor stiff who came along.

Okay, I'm willing to admit it makes good frugal sense to recycle a coffin, especially since its temporary occupant wouldn't really miss it much. But when the Depression ended and the town of Hancock decided to sell their tramp house, and the coffin in it, to the highest bidder, things took a "fowl" turn. Guy Stover, a local poultry farmer looking to expand his operation, bought the tramp house and, setting it up with roosts and nests, turned it into hen housing. And what did the thrifty farmer do with the coffin? He filled it with grain and turned it into a feed box for his hens.

Ruth Johnson, for many years Hancock's town historian, heard that Stover's hens were feeding from the old town coffin, and, frugal reuse though it was, the whole situation didn't sit quite right with her. To rescue the coffin, she had her husband, Willis, make a grain bin and traded Stover the new feed box for the old town coffin. She then presented the coffin to the Hancock Historical Society, where it was finally retired after many brushes with death and a brief stint in the food-service industry. Its third and, hopefully, final incarnation as a museum display is one most anyone would approve.

The Hancock Historical Society Museum is located at 7 Main Street in Hancock. It's open throughout the summer on Wednesday and Saturday afternoons or by appointment. For information call (603) 525–9379.

★ ★

continent, constructed megalithic sites throughout the region (with America's Stonehenge the largest and most elaborate among them), and departed.

One gruesome highlight is a four-and-a-half-ton granite slab with a carved channel running along its outside edges, presumably for blood, known as the "Sacrificial Table." Researchers believe it was once used for ritual sacrifices, whether animal or human is not clear. Maybe there are some details even the America's Stonehenge researchers don't want to get into.

America's Stonehenge is at 105 Haverhill Road in Salem. Take exit 3 east off Interstate 93 and follow Route 111 east for 5 miles to the junction of Island Pond Road and Haverhill Road. Turn right onto Haverhill Road and drive about a mile to the park entrance on the right. For information go to www.stonehengeusa.com or call (603) 893–8300.

Four-thousand-year-old stone chambers! Read all about it!

★ ★

Uncle Sam Was Alive!

Mason

History, like politics, science, and sausage making, is a lot messier than we like to think. The simple story of Mason's claim to fame is that it's the boyhood hometown of one Samuel Wilson, the likely real-life progenitor of Uncle Sam, that striped-pants-and-top-hat-wearing embodiment of national pride. We know this much to be true about Samuel Wilson: From the time he was nine years old until the age of twenty-three, between 1780 and 1793, he lived in a small Cape on Village Road, now painted a beautiful colonial red. At twenty-three, he and his brother walked to Troy, New York, and together started a slaughterhouse and meatpacking operation. Then, at the onset of the War of 1812, the brothers secured a contract with the Army to supply troops with beef and pork.

A national icon once lived here.

★ ★

Now, here's where things get a little tricky. Each version of the story is slightly different. Common to the various tales is the "fact" that the Wilson brothers stamped the letters u.s. onto their crates and barrels of meat bound for the troops. According to one Plymouth State professor, the customary abbreviation for the United States around 1812 was U. States, and the newfangled U.S. abbreviation the Wilsons used caused one of their employees and/or a steamboat passenger and/or soldiers to misconstrue the abbreviation as the initials for Uncle Sam, since it was Samuel Wilson and his men who had slaughtered and packed the meat. But, one might reasonably point out that Samuel Wilson's initials would be S.W. Depending on whom you ask, Uncle was either Samuel Wilson's actual nickname or a common term of affection for an older male authority figure. Pick the explanation you like best.

After that hazy beginning, Uncle Sam got a big boost from illustrator Thomas Nast, who first began drawing him in the mid-nineteenth century. In spite of all we don't know about Samuel Wilson, folks are pretty sure he didn't look anything like the fellow we know today as Uncle Sam. In fact, Nast's earliest drawings didn't even look like our Uncle Sam: In the 1860s he once drew Uncle Sam as a big-bellied, round-cheeked, jovial man carving up a turkey for immigrants gathered around a table. It wasn't until the 1870s that Nast's drawings of Uncle Sam started to bear a curious resemblance to the hollow-cheeked, bearded, top-hot-wearing president Nast so admired, Abraham Lincoln. Samuel Wilson's boyhood home is a quarter mile south of Mason on the west side of Route 123. A green historic marker out front details one version of the story.

War Veteran Horse Buried beside Grandma
Alton

Should a beast of burden be given a town's best eternal digs? Is it fitting for a veteran who saw veterinarians to be buried right beside Grandma Mildred and Uncle Ed? That's the dilemma Alton townsfolk

★ ★

faced when Major George D. Savage expressed the desire to have his Civil War charger Old Tom buried in the town cemetery. A tough question, especially when the man making the request is an influential town citizen, not to mention a certified Civil War hero.

Do you bury a horse 6 feet or 4 feet under?

And as with many a small-town conundrum, Alton kept the peace through compromise. If Major Savage couldn't bury Old Tom inside the cemetery, well then, it wouldn't hurt to let him bury his trusty steed—who, after all, was like a minor member of the major's family— just outside the cemetery walls, now would it? The compromise was acceptable to Major Savage, according to Florence Davis, the part-time curator at Alton's local museum. He buried Old Tom right up next to, but not inside, the cemetery walls.

★ ★

Fast forward 150 years of funerals, and Old Tom now rests in peace deep inside the boundaries of the Alton Cemetery, so deep, in fact, that his grave sits on a little knoll in the dead center of the graveyard. If you go to pay your respects, you'll find Tom's small headstone and large burial plot surrounded by a low white picket fence. Whether intentionally or not, the town of Alton makes a clear case for greater equine equality in the funereal industry. Let's just hope that if the trend catches on, there'll be room for all of us in the graveyards, two legs and four.

Alton's equal equine opportunity cemetery is just south of town on the west side of Route 11.

Big Mortar, No Pestle
Franklin

If you don't think a kitchen implement could make a fine tourist attraction, then you're sadly mistaken. On the northwest corner of the intersection of Central and Dearborn Streets in Franklin, there's a granite boulder with a hollow spot on top that was used first by Abenaki Indians and then by early settlers as a kind of natural mortar, a place

I did, I did see a fish on that rock!

where they could grind their corn into meal for making cakes and breads. For centuries upon centuries, native peoples and the settlers who followed them used this naturally occurring tool to perform the simple but crucial task of preparing the food that nurtured them. Okay, it may not be as exciting as Disneyland, but it still makes for a pretty fascinating detour.

But wait, on the same corner where you'll find the granite boulder with the mortar on top, you'll also find a boulder carved with the faint outline of a fish, a fish that the state historical marker nearby tells me is a shad. The state historical marker also makes the harder-to-verify claim that the shad was the "red man's" favorite fish. As far as I know, the early settlers weren't conducting polls to determine the Abenakis' fish and game preferences, but maybe the proof is in the carving.

You can find the mortar and the shad at the northwest corner of Routes 3 and 11 in Franklin. The green state historical marker is clearly visible at the corner.

Fixer-Upper Castle w/Lake View
Gilford

If one fine summer morning, as the sun rises over the Ossipees, you should find yourself riding in a boat on the remarkably clear waters of Lake Winnipesaukee, look over to the western shore around Belknap Point, just southeast of Weirs Beach. If you raise your eyes to the top of Lockes Hill, you'll see a wide clearing in the northern hardwoods, and in that clearing you'll swear you spy an honest-to-goodness medieval castle hovering above the lake like a vision. The towering gray granite walls, the castle's high battlements with their gap-toothed merlons and crenels, might make you feel as if you'd been transported to the Scottish Highlands or the Rhine Valley.

You haven't. However much the building looks like a medieval ruin, it's neither. Benjamin Ames Kimball, a turn-of-the-century entrepreneur of the Concord and Montreal Railroad, built the castle—reportedly an exact replica of one he saw along the banks of Germany's Rhine

River—for the then quite lordly sum of $50,000. It took a hundred Italian stonemasons two years (1897–99) to build the castle, and during the months of construction Kimball housed them all on the Lady of the Lake, a tourist vessel he owned that once plied the waters of Winnipesaukee. To say Kimball spared no expense in the castle's construction may be an understatement: He even extended a railroad spur to the base of Lockes Hill so he could commute to Concord in his own private railcar.

Kimball Castle stayed in the family until the early 1960s, when it was bequeathed to a local nonprofit. Since that time, the castle has been in a legal limbo that's included land conservation attempts, multiple ownership transfers, and other shenanigans complicated enough to make your head hurt. The end result is that, though the castle had fallen into serious disrepair, the current owners have made much-needed improvements and are trying to sell it to hotel or resort developers. Kimball Castle is at 59 Lockes Hill Road in Gilford. From Laconia, take Route 11 northeast past the airport. After Sawyers Ice Cream on the right, go approximately 1 mile. Just past the blinking yellow light, take a right onto Lockes Hill Road, go to the very top, and the castle will be up a rise on your right. It's privately owned, so be sure to ask permission before investigating. And if you're interested in buying it, visit www.kimballcastle.com.

That's a Big Rock Alright
Madison

The Madison Boulder may be less famous than the Grand Canyon—undeservedly so, of course—but it's a no less mind-blowing manifestation of the awe-inspiring forces of nature at work, if you look at it just so.

First, any boulder visitor should know that the Madison Boulder holds a continental record: at 87 feet long and 37 feet high, it is the largest known "glacial erratic" on the continent, a land area that must literally be littered with glacial erratics. Don't know what a glacial

Going Postal on Lake Winnipesaukee

The 74-foot *Sophie C* may be the oldest floating post office in the country, but the kids on Bear Island don't run to greet it with such gusto just to fetch the mail: In addition to delivering more than 25,000 letters and packages over the summer season to residents of a dozen islands on the north end of Lake Winnipesaukee, the vessel also sells boatloads of ice cream to hungry kids and campers at select ports of call. Owned and operated by the folks who run the bigger and more famous tour boat, the M/S *Mount Washington,* the 125-passenger *Sophie C*—carrying on a tradition started in 1892—has been delivering Lake Winnipesaukee mail to Loon, Beaver, Three Mile, and Bear Islands, among others, since 1969. The U.S. government contracts the vessel as an independent rural route carrier for the town of Laconia, but by a special act of Congress in 1916 the *Sophie C* also has the right to cancel mail, making it the oldest official boat post office in the country. Jim Morash, the *Sophie C*'s captain, said that stamp collectors come from all over the country for the rare red postage cancellation stamp that reads Lake Winnipesaukee.

You're welcome to accompany the captain and the mail clerk on their watery rounds Monday through Saturday, rain or shine. Two-hour trips depart from Weirs Beach twice a day, one at 11:00 a.m. and one at 2:00 p.m., with mail stops that include the private Beaver Island where Klondike the dog comes out to greet the mail boat, a couple of YMCA summer camps, and Bear Island with its rush of dairy-starved kids.

erratic is? Basically, it's a rock that ends up somewhere it doesn't belong as a result of a move there by a glacier. Thus, it becomes labeled an "erratic" by the scientific community, an oddball, a geological freak—oh, the cruelty of labels. No matter, this glacial erratic, as big as an average apartment building and weighing just shy of a million pounds, according to one estimate, was once picked up by a 5,000-foot-thick sheet of ice and carried miles and miles to where it now rests, in a fine patch of woods just off Route 113 in Madison.

From Conway follow Route 16 south to Route 113 south, then travel 3 miles and watch for the sign for the Madison Boulder Natural Area. Take a right onto Boulder Road, and follow it to the end. The Madison Boulder sits in the woods just beyond the parking area.

It just sits there for millennia and geologists still call this boulder erratic.

★ ★

The Castle That Shoes Built

Moultonborough

It wasn't until the 1960s that Thomas and Olive Plant's mountaintop estate on a promontory high above Lake Winnipesaukee, came to be known as "Castle in the Clouds," but it's fitting that the name was changed from its original name. The Plants, who built the estate between 1913 and 1914 on a world-class lake-view parcel that would grow to 6,300 acres, named their home "Lucknow," perhaps as a reminder of the great good fortune they had in possessing wealth enough, and then some, to build it. (It also happens to be the name of a town in India where Plant thought he might build his estate.)

When this Castle in the Clouds isn't in the clouds, the view is world-class.

But by the time of his death in 1941, this rags-to-riches French-Canadian entrepreneur and former owner of what was reported to be the world's largest shoe company—was flat broke in the sixteen-room, eight-bath "Lucknow," reduced to borrowing from friends. Plant had invested heavily in Russian bonds just before the 1917 Revolution, in sugar just before its post–World War I collapse, and in bad land deals throughout the 1920s. After he died, Olive watched creditors auction off everything she and her husband once owned. Their castle, and everything else they owned, vanished into the clouds.

Yet their loss is our gain, because 5,500 acres, seven mountains, miles of hiking trails, and the Plants' mansion itself are all at our disposal, thanks to the Lakes Region Conservation Trust and the Castle Preservation Society, which now own and manage the property. The acreage remains surprisingly rugged and unspoiled, making for great nature hikes. But the true gem is the house. An example of the Arts and Crafts style, it features granite quarried from surrounding mountains, massive hand-hewn beams, a Spanish tile roof, and English leaded doors. And the view out the back door of Lake Winnipesaukee and the White Mountains is one of the most spectacular sights I've now had the good luck to see.

The mansion is open May through mid October. From Moltonborough, take Route 109 south to Route 171 and proceed east toward Tuftonboro until you see the sign for the main entrance to Castle in the Clouds. Trail parking is available on Route 171, just east of Severance Road. Trail use is free and access is year-round. Call (603) 476–2352 for more information or visit the Web site at www.castle intheclouds.org.

This Arch Was Supposed to Be for Tilton

Northfield

Charles Tilton, nineteenth-century millionaire merchant, had a thing about statues. It seems he couldn't stop building them all over town. The most famous among the five objets d'art that yet remain in the towns of Northfield and Tilton is called Tilton's Arch, a towering 55-foot vanity monument supposedly patterned after the Arch of Titus in Rome, dedicated to none other than Charles Tilton himself. And you thought your vanity plates were cool.

Of course, everyone should know by now that when you make a bold statement with statuary, you run the risk of looking a little foolish.

Local lore has it that Tilton planned to be buried under the five-and-a-half-story granite monument (now called by some "Tilton's folly"), but that when the section of the Tilton town on which the monument rested became part of Northfield, Charles refused to be buried there. The four other Tilton–commissioned monuments around town are

A monument to a man with
a thing for bold statuary.

★ ★

allegorical statues of America (depicted as an Indian princess), Europe, and Asia, as well as a zinc statue of Chief Squantum. None serves as gravestone for Charles. He ended up being buried elbow to elbow with the rest of Tilton's nineteenth-century citizens, right in Park Cemetery, beneath a sizable but not colossal monument.

Park Cemetery is on Route 3 about a half mile south of the center of Tilton; Charles's grave is to the back. The arch is in Northfield, just up the hill from Tilton. From downtown Tilton follow Bridge Street across the Winnipesaukee River, take a left onto Elm Street, and then a quick right onto Summer. The entrance to the park will be just up the hill on your right.

Ye Olde Crutch Factory
Rumney

For decades and decades, your sprained ankle, twisted knee, or broken foot was Rumney's good news, since once you got done screaming, you'd be in dire need of a Rumney specialty: crutches. In fact, Rumney was for a while the largest manufacturer of wooden crutches in the world, with a handful of mills along Stinson Brook turning out thousands of pairs of crutches a week during World War I.

One might assume that since Rumney has long been the crutch capital of the world, the town might pay homage either to crutches themselves or to the injuries that require them. But in Rumney, you'll find no Crutch Memorial. You won't even find a good Crutch Festival.

Thankfully, the Rumney Historical Society Museum, located on Buffalo Road in the old town hall, displays a sizable sampling of Rumney-made wooden crutches and crutch memorabilia. And the president of the historical society, Roger Daniels, is more than happy to make disparaging comments about aluminum crutches, the competition that knocked the last remaining Rumney crutch factory (Kelly Manufacturing) off its feet back in 2002. "I wouldn't give two cents for those aluminum ones," Roger said. "You know what I call them? Lightning rods."

★ ★

The Rumney Historical Society Museum is open Saturday from 10:00 a.m. to 2:00 p.m., Memorial Day through Labor Day. To see the old Kelly Manufacturing crutch factory, head north out of town on Stinson Lake Road for about 200 yards, then take the first right onto Water Street; the crutch factory, a red building with a couple of old crutches nailed to the siding, will be down a rise on your left.

Church in Your Bathing Suit

Squam Lake

We all know it's a little harder to make it to church when the weather's fine and you're spending time at the lake. But here's a church recommendation that'll make an hour spent in prayer on a heavenly summer Sunday seem a lot more appealing. Parking at the dock is limited, though, so get there early.

Once home to the nation's first boys' residential summer camp, Chocorua Island on Squam Lake now functions as an outdoor chapel and island devoted exclusively to worship and prayer. In 1903, over a decade after the camp closed down, former campers and others established the Chocorua Chapel Association for the purpose of holding summer religious services on the island. The island's owner eventually donated it to the association in 1928, and since that time the nonprofit group has provided a unique place of worship and religious celebration for local residents and visitors alike.

Each Sunday at 10:30 a.m. from late June through the beginning of September, clergy of various Protestant denominations, many of whom are summer residents in the area, lead services at the island's outdoor chapel. Worshippers arrive by powerboat, by sail, by kayak, and by canoe, and then they gather in front of the stone altar, a large rough wooden crucifix behind it, to pray together under the open sky. If you want to park your boat at the dock, be sure to get there before 10:00 a.m.—if you arrive later, you'll have to anchor at a mooring offshore and get picked up by the association's water taxi. Canoers, kayakers, rowers, and other self-propellers, though, can just pull their boats up on shore.

Chocorua Island Chapel is located just west of the holy center of Big Squam Lake. For information about Sunday services, including which pastor (and which denomination) is on deck for the next service, call (603) 968–3313 or visit www.churchisland.org. To inquire about private services, including baptisms and weddings, call (603) 968–7931.

The Toys Have Taken Over
Wakefield

The Museum of Childhood of Wakefield has a doll overpopulation problem: The small white Cape is literally stuffed to the rafters with over 5,000 of the smiling, glassy-eyed, immaculately dressed little munchkins, as well as nearly sixty furnished dollhouses. But if you can squeeze your way past the nineteenth-century porcelain dolls, the Cabbage Patch Kids, and Barbie and Ken, you'll find lots of less-well-known childhood playthings tucked away in nooks and crannies throughout the house.

A house where the toy chest has exploded.

The place is chock-full of miniature trains, planes, and automobiles; push toys, pull toys, and wind-up toys; music boxes; and hobby horses; and a whole room full of bears (even the walls are covered with bears). My personal favorite, though, was the walnut-shell and acorn-head skier, with the pointy bottom of the acorn serving as her button nose and the acorn cap her dashing little hat. Was that the way Barbie looked 500 years ago? (Maybe back then she was making girls feel bad for not having heads shaped more like acorns.) There's even a fully appointed nineteenth-century one-room schoolhouse out back, no toys included, just to remind you that childhood has never been all fun and games.

The Museum of Childhood of Wakefield is located at 2784 Wakefield Road, just north of the village center. It's open from mid June through Labor Day. For information call (603) 522–8073.

Local World-Record Wooden Bridge: Too Big for Its Own Trusses?

Cornish

The longest covered wooden bridge in the United States, and the longest double-span wooden bridge in the world stretches 460 feet from Cornish, New Hampshire, to Windsor, Vermont, across the Connecticut River. You might think that, by rights, only half the bridge belongs in this chapter since, presumably, only half the bridge rests in the state of New Hampshire and, ergo, only half qualifies as a bona fide New Hampshire curiosity. Well, New Hampshire had good lawyers in a neighborly border dispute with Vermont, and the boundary between the two states was established at the low-water mark on the Vermont side of the Connecticut River. Both the river and the world's longest double-span wooden bridge are ours. Mostly.

Built in 1866 by carpenter/engineers Bela Fletcher and James Tasker, the Cornish-Windsor Bridge, as it's none too creatively called, is composed of two spans measuring 208 feet apiece. Fletcher and Tasker employed something called the Towne Lattice truss, which means that the long sidewall supports, or trusses, from which the roadway is suspended, look like giant lattices made of crisscrossed pine timbers. Operated as a toll bridge until June 1, 1943, and still open to interstate traffic, the bridge has undergone a number of repairs and renovations over the last 140 years including a $4.5 million reconstruction in the late 1980s. I'm sure Vermont reminded us of the fact that the bridge is mostly in New Hampshire when that bill came due . . .

The bridge is well worth the money. When you see her from the banks of the Connecticut, she looks just like a covered bridge only longer—a stretch covered bridge, a slender reminder of another century connecting two states. The Cornish-Windsor Bridge is located in Cornish, just across the Connecticut River from Windsor, Vermont, on Route 12A.

A long wooden bridge that's almost all New Hampshire's.

★ ★

There's Low-Grade Uranium Ore in That There Pit!
Grafton

If you're interested in starting a small uranium collection—strictly for household use, of course—the Ruggles Mine in Grafton could be your best local bet. While you won't gather enough of the heavy element to fuel your own household reactor, you might find some very slightly radioactive, completely safe uranium-containing minerals, like gummite and autunite, that you can chisel carefully from the walls (watch for sparks) of the oldest mica, feldspar, beryl, and uranium mine in the United States. What better way to impress your friends than with uranium you mined on vacation?

Sam Ruggles discovered mica on what's now called Isinglass Mountain (isinglass is the name given to mica in the form of thin semitransparent sheets) in 1803, and people have been tapping at the rocks there ever since, in search of mica for everything from heat-resistant windows to nail polish; feldspar for fine china and other ceramics; beryl for space-age metals; uranium for all the glowing wonders that a radioactive element can offer; and, most recently, souvenirs for the kids.

A century and a half of mining has transformed the mountainside into a stunning and strangely beautiful landscape, a huge man-made canyon whose sheer walls of quartz and feldspar are riddled with towering arches, darkened passageways, and caves so perfectly shaped that they look straight out of the comic strip *B.C.* The best part is, visitors are encouraged to make the open pit a little bigger by mining for their own minerals, whether they be slightly radioactive or just plain pretty, such as quartz, amethyst, mica, garnet, and a whole host of other minerals.

The Ruggles Mine is located in Grafton just off Route 4. Take Route 4 to Grafton Center, then at the sign for Ruggles Mine, turn left onto Riddle Hill Road and follow the signs. For information call (603) 523–4275 or visit www.rugglesmine.com. Admission is charged.

Supreme Court Says You Don't Have to Live Free or Die

New Hampshire's "Live Free or Die" slogan can seem downright uncompromising, especially when put beside less-strident state slogans. Tennessee's, for example, is "Sounds Good To Me," which is about as friendly and agreeable as a Labrador retriever. And someone seemed to mix up their adjectives in Idaho's food-obsessed slogan: "Great Potatoes. Tasty Destinations."

For one George Maynard, formerly of Lebanon but now a resident of Connecticut (the "Full of Surprises" state), "Live Free or Die" was a little too uncompromising. In 1974, four years after the somewhat macabre command started appearing on New Hampshire license plates, Maynard took the liberty of covering up the words "Live Free or Die" on his car's plates with red reflective tape. A devout Jehovah's Witness, he found the statement objectionable because according to his faith, life was more sacred than freedom. Kids in the neighborhood reportedly kept pulling off the tape when George wasn't looking, so he eventually had to cut the words "or Die" off his license plate entirely.

Local police in Lebanon didn't take kindly to George getting artsy-craftsy with his car tags, though, and he was given numerous citations, small fines, and even a jail sentence of fifteen days. The irony of a man being jailed for covering up the words "Live Free or Die" was not lost on journalists, and the case attracted quite a bit of attention. After he got out of jail, the ACLU offered to represent Maynard in a federal lawsuit. In March of 1975, ACLU lawyers filed a suit against Neal Wooley, Lebanon's chief of police, and the State of New Hampshire for violating Maynard's First Amendment rights to free speech. In its 6–3 ruling in Maynard's favor, the Supreme Court wrote that "Whatever else may be said about the motto 'Live Free or Die,' it expresses philosophical and political ideas. Plaintiffs' desire not to be aligned with these ideas falls within the ambit of the First Amendment." Thanks to George Maynard, all Granite Staters now have the freedom not to Live Free or Die.

Is That a Quaking Bog You're Standing On, or Are You Just Afraid of Me?

New London

The first thing you should know about the Philbrick-Cricenti Bog is that it isn't a true bog. An honest-to-goodness, 100 percent genuine bog should not have an outlet. The Philbrick-Cricenti Bog most definitely has an outlet. Still, Philbrick-Cricenti is an ecological wonder thousands of years in the making, so it deserves some grudging respect. Home to such botanical curiosities as the insect-eating pitcher plant, bogs were once stagnant glacial ponds whose waters turned highly acidic over thousands of years. Arctic plants uniquely suited to the nutrient-poor, low-pH environment, including sphagnum moss, sedge, and leather leaf, grow slowly around the edges of the pond and then, century by century, creep across its surface, forming a mat of tangled mossy growth that can one day cover the pond entirely.

Danger: This bog has been known to swallow horses and not even burp.

At the Philbrick-Cricenti Bog, deer, cows, and even a horse have reportedly wandered out onto the mat of vegetation and fallen through, never to be hunted, milked, or ridden again. More troubling still, the animals' remains are probably well-preserved under the sphagnum, since the water's high acidity inhibits the growth of bacteria and other microorganisms that aid in decomposition. That's why bog mats eventually thicken enough to support spruce trees and even people— as the moss, sedge, and other plants die, they don't decompose entirely but instead form layer upon layer of peat.

Visitors should take care to stay on the wooden boardwalks at Philbrick-Cricenti, though, since the bog mat varies in age and thickness, with some boardwalk loops taking visitors through areas that were open water only 150 years ago. On the appropriately named Quaking Loop, which passes over a relatively young portion of the mat, the boardwalk quivers beneath your footsteps as if a living thing. And if even the idea of walking the Bog Peril Loop, where at least one horse is known to have perished, starts your knees knocking, you can always blame it on the bog.

The Philbrick-Cricenti Bog is located on Newport Road just a couple of miles outside of New London. Take exit 12 off Interstate 89 and head toward New London on Newport Road. The pull-off area will be on the south side of the road about a half mile before the hospital road. Maps and guide sheets are available at the trailhead.

Make Ice When the Sun Shines (Hopefully)
North Sutton

Before electricity, a cold summer cocktail must have tasted a little sweeter, if for no other reason than the tippler knew what hard and hazardous work went into chilling his glass. In winter, workers scraped lake or river ice using a team of horses and an 8-foot blade to keep it clear of snow. Once the ice was a foot thick, sawyers cut hundreds of 350-pound cakes, loaded them onto horse-drawn sleighs, and drove the 3,000-pound loads over frozen hill and dale to icehouses, where they unloaded the blocks, stacked them neatly in rows, and covered them with 6 inches or more of sawdust. Delivering the ice during the summer months was, of course, more work, but at least the ice blocks had shed some major winter pounds. In the nineteenth century, ice from New Hampshire even traveled the world, moving from Wolfeboro to Boston and onward to places like New Orleans and Cairo.

If you'd like to gain hands-on appreciation for the miracle of modern refrigeration, attend Muster Field Farm Museum's annual Natural Ice Harvest Day. Held at the end of January, Ice Day features local sawyers cutting ice using both crosscut handsaws and a gas-powered machine that looks a bit like a miniature Zamboni with an attitude. Try your hand at the handsaw, or sit back and watch as volunteers wrangle ice blocks onto wagons and trucks for the trip to Muster Field Farm's circa-1890 icehouse, where the ice is stacked, covered in sawdust, and stored for summer use.

Muster Field Farm Museum's Natural Ice Harvest Day is held at North Sutton's Kezar Lake at the end of January. The Muster Field Farm Museum is located on Harvey Road in North Sutton just off exit 10 of Interstate 89. For information call (603) 927–4276 or visit www.musterfieldfarm.com.

You Mean, They Didn't Have Cell Phones in 1932?

Warner

If you still don't believe old-timers had it a lot tougher, consider the telephone. For decades, callers hand-cranked their phones, like the 1907 Western Electric Model 317, just to generate a signal to raise the operator on the other end of the line. In some New Hampshire towns, as many as a dozen or more businesses and homes piggybacked on the same party line, with every phone ringing whenever one subscriber received a call. (Different ring combinations signaled to subscribers who should pick up.) Of course, if another party was already on your party line, you could eavesdrop—a nice little side-benefit—but you certainly couldn't make that urgent call. And the town operator, well, she knew more secrets than the local priest.

If such hardships pique your interest in the early days of telephony, you should pay a visit to the New Hampshire Telephone Museum in downtown Warner. The creation of Dick and Paul Violette, former chairman and president/CEO, respectively, of the Merrimack County Telephone Company, the museum includes telephones dating from the earliest models to the cell phone; a replica of the phone Alexander Graham Bell first used on March 10, 1876, a working antique switchboard; samples of telephone cable, some as thick as a man's wrist and containing an ingeniously organized jumble of 600-plus individual color-coded lines.

Introduce your cell phone to his great-great-great grandparents.

The New Hampshire Telephone Museum is located at 22 East Main Street in Warner. Take exit 8 or 9 off Interstate 89 and follow Main Street (Route 103) into downtown Warner. For information including hours, call (603) 456–2234 or go to www.nhtelephonemuseum.com.

Dearly Departed Leg

It's clear that Captain Samuel Jones was pretty attached to his leg, otherwise, why would he have gone to all the trouble and expense of buying a plot in the Washington town cemetery and giving his beloved amputated leg a decent, Christian burial? That's right—Captain Jones buried one of his legs in the Washington cemetery.

Captain Jones chose an unassuming, classic headstone for his dearly departed limb—with a simple eight-pointed star as its only adornment, the stone reads, "Capt. Samuel Jones Leg which was amputated July 7, 1804." What's curious is that the stone bears no epitaph, no tribute from the captain for the leg that he gladly leaned upon for support and balance until that fateful summer day when their connection was severed. Perhaps he said all he wanted to say at the funeral service?

From Route 31 in Washington, head west on Faxen Hill Road. Before the intersection with Millen Pond Road, you'll pass two cemeteries, one on the left and the other on the right side of the road. The cemetery on the left-hand side is where you'll find the grave of Captain Samuel Jones's leg. Also, be sure to look for the large communist gravestone marking the burial site of Fred and Elba Chase. It's the only Soviet-style hammer-and-sickle statuary you're likely to find in the live-free-or-die state.

Would the ghost of a buried leg even be scary?

✦ ✦

There's No Business Like an Old Business
Bath

Dating to 1790 when the first President George was in office, the Brick Store in Bath is said to be America's oldest continually operating general store. If you want proof the place is old, look no further than the counters: Their slanted fronts gave female customers in hoop skirts enough room to sashay up and make their purchases. You'll even find a few nineteenth-century mailboxes from when the store did double duty as post office.

The building is brick, of course, and there's a portico out front with a porch, both fronted by four very tall Doric columns that run from the ground to the roofline. But inside, instead of encountering dry goods and cows udder balm, you'll find loads of cheese, fudge, maple syrup, honey, and meats smoked right on the premises. All the sweets and treats are delicious, but if you want a truly unique foodstuff, purchase one of Patti Page's Pure Maple products. That's right, Oklahoma native Patti Page, who sold over a hundred million albums over the course of her career and had a whole slew of top ten hits in the 1940s and '50s, including "Doggie in the Window" and "Tennessee Waltz", has a line of maple syrups and pancake mixes. She and her husband, Jerry Filiciotto, live half the year in Bath on a farm down the road from the Brick Store and have made syrup and pancake mix products since 1995. Between overseeing tap lines and sap boiling, Patti still finds time to perform all around the country, sometimes twice a day. The Brick Store is an oldie filled with goodies, and Patti Page sings the oldies but still finds time to make the goodies.

The Brick Store is located at 21 Lisbon Road (Route 302) in Bath. Call (603) 747–2074 or (800) 964–2074 or see their Web site at www.thebrickstore.com to learn more.

Dollhouse Scenes for Children of the Damned
Bethlehem

If dollhouses received ratings the way movies do, the ratings board would certainly slap Frances Glessner Lee's dollhouse scenes with an

★ ★

R, maybe even an NC-17, rating. Just to give you a representatively gory example, in one scene a 5-inch woman lies in a bed on her side, bedclothes pulled up to her waist, face obscured by copious amounts of dried blood. On the floor beside the bed, a 6-inch man in blood-soaked blue-striped pajamas lies face down on what looks to be a blood-stained comforter. Rose-colored stains bloom on the carpet at the foot of the bed, a large pool of blood darkens the white bedsheet beside the woman, and just above the 2½-inch bedside table, tiny drops of blood fleck the wallpaper.

What evil deeds transpired in this dollhouse basement?

A Chicago heiress who moved to her family's thousand-acre summer estate in Bethlehem after her divorce in 1914, Frances Glessner Lee developed an interest in forensic science, and in miniature macabre bedrooms, after her brother introduced her to his friend George

Burgess Magrath, a Harvard-trained medical examiner. Magrath's seedy casework, which included murdered prostitutes, homicidal husbands, and suicidal housewives, fascinated the well-to-do Lee, and over the years she became a patroness of forensic science at Harvard, funding a new Department of Legal Medicine there in 1936, and a crime scene expert in her own right.

Concerned that poorly trained police were botching investigations, she developed an educational curriculum for homicide investigators consisting of her own obsessively detailed dollhouse re-creations of real-life murders, suicides, and accidental deaths. Lee referred to these eighteen diabolical dioramas, lovingly handcrafted at her home work-shop in Bethlehem throughout the 1940s and '50s, as the Nutshell Studies of Unexplained Death. With stunning details like miniature potato peelings in the kitchen sink and half-inch pencils that actually write, they were intended to train investigators to look and look again for the smallest clues that would help "Convict the guilty, clear the innocent, and find the truth in a nutshell."

The Glessner estate, known as the Rocks Estate and owned by the Society for the Protection of New Hampshire Forests, houses a couple of Nutshell Studies that were never completed. It's open to the public for hiking and guided tours. But remember parental guidance is suggested.

For information on the Rocks Estate, call (603) 444–6228. To get to the Rocks, located at 113 Glessner Road in Bethlehem, take Interstate 93 to exit 40 and follow Route 302 east for a half mile. Turn right opposite the Exxon station, and follow the signs to the parking area and program center.

Antiques on the Odd Side
Bethlehem

It's best to think of Mt. Agassiz Trading Company as an antiques oddi-torium, a shop of the most curious collectibles, the overstuffed love child of *Antiques Roadshow* and *Ripley's Believe It or Not*.

★ ★

To give you an idea of how eclectic a collection owner Roland Shick has assembled, a partial list of recent items up for sale include: a set of exquisite hand-painted ostrich eggs from an artist in Romania; an antique bear trap; a deer antler carving of two human skeletons; an early twentieth-century New York City hot dog cart; a taxidermy alligator head, with teeth bared; a rat skeleton, nose to tail; a collection of vintage embalming fluid bottles; a fish fossil; a Shredded Wheat box from 1939; and a lamp made entirely out of seashells and tiny Christmas lights.

Interspersed among items for sale are selections from Roland's own collection of antique oddities, including a 1924 Model T Ford moving truck, a 1920s dentist's chair, and a nineteenth-century Patent Magneto-Electric Machine "for the treatment of nervous conditions." The pinnacle of peculiarity in the collection, though, has to be Roland's X-Ray Shoe Fitter, a machine that created an X-ray image of a child's feet in his or her prospective new pair of shoes. The Mt. Agassiz Trading Company, located at 2056 Main Street in downtown Bethlehem, is open June through December. Call Roland at (603) 869–5568 for store hours and information.

A Princess Who Went Out of Her Way to Avoid Peas
Bretton Woods

Famous for hosting the 1944 Bretton Woods International Monetary Conference, which established the World Bank and the International Monetary Fund, the Mount Washington Hotel sets the gold standard for grand hotels in the state.

Joseph Stickney, a Concord native who made his fortune in coal mining and railroads, hired a crew of 250 Italian craftsmen to build the Mount Washington, a majestic red-roofed, Spanish Renaissance–style hotel outfitted with electric lights, a pool, and a private bath in every room. They completed it in 1902, but Stickney only got to enjoy his grand new property for a brief season before dying in December of 1903. His young widow, Carolyn Foster Stickney, became sole

Is it kosher for a princess to have a queen-size bed?

proprietor of the hotel. In 1908 she married a French nobleman, thereby acquiring the title of Princess Clarigny de Lucinge.

Maybe it was the fancy new title, maybe it was the royal treatment, or maybe the Princess formerly known as Carolyn just really loved her own bed. Whatever the case, each year when the Prince and Princess returned from Paris to spend the summer at the Mount Washington Hotel, the Princess's wonderful bed was disassembled, crated up, and shipped across the Atlantic to New Hampshire. And each time she returned to France, the process was repeated in reverse. You can sleep on the Princess's bed, now upgraded to a Queen, in room 314 at the hotel. Also, be sure to check out Babe Ruth's golf locker. The Mount Washington Hotel is located on Route 302 in Bretton Woods. For rates (which include full breakfast and dinner), information and reservations, call (603) 278–1000 or (800) 314–1752 or visit www .mtwashington.com.

The Grandaddy of New Hampshire Curiosities

It wasn't much to look at, just a small, clapboard-sided, two-story house six miles from its nearest neighbor at the base of what would come to be called Mount Willey in Crawford Notch. But a peculiar tragedy brought the Willey house national fame, investing it with an aura of the uncanny that drew first hundreds and then thousands of visitors and making it one of the first, and one of the more bizarre, tourist attractions in the country.

In October 1825, the Willey family of North Conway moved to a house in Crawford Notch and opened a travelers' hostel. Less than a year later, torrential rainstorms caused severe flooding and land-slides. During the evening of August 28, 1826, with the flooded Saco River raging below and the terrifying sounds of landslides echoing throughout the Notch, Samuel and Polly, their five young children, and two hired men fled the Willey house, presumably for the greater safety of a nearby shelter. As the party made their break, they were overwhelmed by a wall of earth, rock, and trees that had originated on the mountain above.

Not a single one survived; three of the children's bodies were never even recovered. Certainly a tragedy, but the irony that helped to generate both nationwide fascination in the fate of the Willey family and loads of White Mountain tourism was the fact that their house remained perfectly intact. According to reports, a ridge of land and a couple of boulders on the hillside behind the Willey place divided the landslide, causing tons of debris to pass on either side of the untouched house.

It was mere weeks before the first visitors came to see the Willey house, with the contents of its rooms just as the family had left them, a kind of macabre freeze-frame of domesticity just before natural disaster came to call. Intellectuals and writers mined the tragedy for meaning, including Nathaniel Hawthorne, whose story "The Ambitious Guest" is based on the Willey tragedy. By 1845 a large hotel directly abutted the Willey house, and tourists paid twelve and a half cents apiece to take a tour.

The site of the Willey house is on Route 302 between Hart's Location and Bretton Woods. The house and hotel burned down in the late nineteenth century, but the Crawford Notch State Park headquarters is located here, as well as a gift shop and restaurant. A boulder marks the site of the house. For information call (603) 374–2272.

The first truly weird tourist attraction in the United States.

★ ★

Baldy Knows Snowshoes

Conway

You might be savvy enough to guess that, with a name like Treffle Bolduc, the eighty-seven-year-old snowshoe maker, snowshoe seller, and snowshoe renter Conway locals call "Baldy" is of Franco-American stock. But what you probably wouldn't guess is that Bolduc once dreamed of being a concert violinist and, at the age of eighteen, headed south to study at the Boston Conservatory of Music. "Things didn't work out," Baldy said. "If it's not meant to be, you can practice awfully hard and not get anywhere."

After stints as a factory worker, ship's welder, and carpenter, Bolduc made a trip to Quebec, where he met Native American craftsmen who helped him learn to build some of the finest white ash snowshoes

Baldy's snowshoes are made for winter walking.

you're likely ever to strap on your feet. Not long after Baldy opened the Kancamagus Snowshoe Center, his small snowshoe shop and museum at the eastern terminus of the Kancamagus Highway.

Baldy's Kancamagus Snowshoe Center is located on the Kancamagus Highway, just a few hundred yards from the intersection of Route 16. For information or to place an order, call (603) 447–5287 or 356–8402.

New Hampshire's Gorgeous Flume
Franconia Notch

A stop on our tour of geological curiosities in Franconia Notch State Park is the Flume Gorge. If you enjoy your visit to this, one of the more wondrous of the state's natural wonders, you can just thank

Good old Jess sure didn't need no stinkin' boardwalks.

★ ★

"Aunt Jess" Guernsey. In 1808, at the spry age of ninety-three, Aunt Jess happened to be doing a little bushwhacking in Franconia Notch in hopes of finding some new fishing holes, as the story goes, when she came upon a stunning 800-foot-long natural gorge at the base of Mount Liberty. At the time Guernsey discovered it, a huge egg-shaped boulder hung suspended between the gorge walls, like a giant stone stopper in a bottleneck, but in 1883 torrential rains caused a small landslide that swept it away.

Today there's a visitor center, bus service to the footpath, guided tours, and a boardwalk that follows the course of Flume Brook through the gorge. Its sheer granite walls, separated by as little as 10 feet in places, rise as high as eight stories above the boardwalk.

The Flume is open May through October; admission is charged. For information call the Flume Gorge & Visitor Center at (603) 745–8391.

And You Thought Our Weather Was Bad?

Haverhill

Even though Portsmouth sits at about the same latitude as the French Riviera, we have no Riviera, no warm turquoise sea, and certainly no Cannes Film Festival. The many reasons behind our miserable weather run the gamut from our mountainous terrain to the fact that the Polar Jet Stream runs, more often than not, right through our living room. One weather-related source claimed that New England's all-time high temperature of 107 degrees Fahrenheit is actually higher than the record highs for both Miami and Atlanta, while our all-time low of 50 below zero is colder than the record low for International Falls, MN. But the Museum of American Weather might give the local climate an even worse rap than it deserves. With exhibits devoted to monstrously bad weather—like the Blizzard of 1888, when a massive nor'easter stalled over Block Island, RI, and dumped over 4 feet of snow in places like Middletown, Connecticut, killing hundreds; the Vermont Flood on November 3–4, 1927, when over 9 inches of rain fell in twenty-four hours, causing severe flash flooding and killing eighty-four; and the Great Hurricane of 1938, which had 121-mile-per-hour winds, downed

275 million trees, and caused almost $2 billion in damage in today's dollars—the Museum of American Weather is a showcase of the most dramatic meteorological miseries New Englanders have had to endure over the last 200 years.

The Museum of American Weather is located on Haverhill's South Common. For information call (603) 989–3167.

More Candy Than You Can Count(er)

Littleton

The Guinness-certified longest candy counter in the world at Chutters in Littleton is just a touch shy of 112 feet. Ask Chutters' candy buyer Rodney "The Candy Man" Bengtson how long the candy counter is, though, and you just might detect in his voice a hint of resentment toward the yardstick sticklers at the *Guinness Book of World Records*.

Heaven is not being able to see the end of the candy counter.

"The candy counter is 111 feet and ¾ inches," Rodney told me. "They wouldn't give us the last ¼ inch because of the molding."

With three tiers of candy counter stretching from the very front to the way back of the store, the Candy Man's charged with filling somewhere between 600 and 700 glass jars with just about every kind of confection you could imagine. You've heard of gummi worms and gummi bears, but what about gummi sharks, lobsters, frogs, and gummi turtles? And if it's edible accessories you're looking for, Chutters has necklaces, watches, rings, and bracelets—all candy. According to calculations, Chutters also has around thirty jars of penny candy, about twenty-five kinds of licorice, lollipops ranging from a three-pound sucker to the venerable Tootsie Roll pop, and virtually every traditional candy bar known to mankind in rows of jars toward the back. If you want to see real talent, watch one of the girls at the register speed-count a bag of 200 or so penny candies. Come to think of it, they should probably invite the folks from Guinness back, since Chutters could very well have the fastest candy counter in the world, as well as the longest.

Chutters General Store is at 41 Main Street in downtown Littleton. For information or orders call (603) 444–5787.

How to Bury a Horse without Heavy Lifting
Littleton

The marker at Littleton's Eli Wallace Horse Cemetery, a small fenced-in enclosure that contains stones for three Wallace family horses, white-washes the facts a bit. Yes, Maud and Molly, the matched pair of bay Morgan horses Eli bought as a gift for his bride, Myra, on her twenty-ninth birthday—"the only children . . . [the couple] would have," the marker says—both died thirty long years later in 1919. And yes, the horses were buried in their roomy graves like Egyptians, surrounded by all their earthly effects: their harnesses, bridles, blankets, and feedboxes.

Before Maud and Molly, old and infirm, were laid away, or put down, Eli Wallace dug two deep holes with earthen ramps leading down, and then guided his beloved horses, outfitted in their harnesses, into their respective graves. From there a local veterinarian, Dr. A. F. Hill, kindly took over, firing the two shots that dispatched the old girls.

A cemetery where humans aren't allowed.

Depressing, right? It gets worse. Myra Wallace died a year later, leaving Eli all alone. In his grief he wrote and published a booklet about his life with Myra, Maud, and Molly titled, *When They Were Here,* handing out copies around town. (The Littleton Historical Society has the only two known copies that remain.) When Eli learned that Maggie, the local butcher's horse, was going to be cashed in, he offered to buy her; instead, the butcher gave Maggie to him as a gift, and she remained with Eli—a source of consolation, we can imagine—until he died on April 1, 1929.

The longest set of instructions in Eli's will concerned arrangements for the perpetual care of the cemetery that contained his beloved girls—Maggie would join Maud and Molly after Eli's death. He bequeathed a third of his estate and forty acres to the Littleton Hospital in exchange for care of the horse cemetery, but over the decades

★ ★

the hospital forgot its obligations and the cemetery was left abandoned and overgrown. It was only a few years ago that the Littleton
Historical Society, along with the help of Dr. Richard Hill, the son of
Maud and Molly's gun-wielding veterinarian, restored the cemetery to
its proper condition. The Eli Wallace Horse Cemetery is in the center
of Littleton. From Cottage Street, take a right onto Mount Eustis Road
(you'll see a green sign for the horse cemetery) and head under I–93;
the cemetery will be on your left. The Littleton Historical Society's
museum is located at 1 Cottage Street and is open Wednesdays, May
through November. For more information call (603) 444–5816 or
444–6586.

Isn't It About Time to Fire the Grounds Crew?
North Conway

Without fail, in early September of each year at North Conway's
Hog Coliseum, the field conditions are abysmal. No matter what the
weather's been like in the Mount Washington Valley, the field of play
is virtually unplayable, covered in 14 to 18 inches of soupy, café au
lait–colored mud. With such a woeful performance record, you'd think
the grounds crew would have been fired years ago. Yet folks thank
them each year for a job well done.

That's because they've properly prepped Hog Coliseum for North
Conway's annual Mud Bowl, a three-day-long double-elimination mud
football tournament featuring thirteen touch mud football matches, a
Saturday-morning Tournament of Mud parade, a Saturday-night Mud
Bowl Ball at North Conway's Cranmore Mountain Resort, and, the
grimy highlight, Sunday's World Mud Bowl championship game. Eight
gritty teams from as far away as Maine and Massachusetts, and the
Muddas of Amherst, New Hampshire, a record sixteen-time champion—slip, slosh, and slog their way through soupy field conditions at
Hog Coliseum. And while it's all in good clean fun, with 100 percent
of proceeds going to charity, I can assure you the boys take the games
seriously.

A couple feet of mud? Field conditions are just perfect.

The Mud Bowl takes place each year on the first weekend after Labor Day, in the world-renowned Hog Coliseum, located just off Main Street in North Conway. For more information call the Mount Washington Valley Chamber of Commerce at (800) 337–3364.

A Well-Armed Town Green
Warren

Why settle for a little old Civil War cannon on your town green when you can have, say, a World War II–era tank? And why settle for a little old outdated tank when you can have a retired 60-foot-tall Cold War–era medium-range nuclear missile, the same basic model that delivered a nuclear bomb 38 miles into the atmosphere for the first live nuclear missile test in U.S. history, sent the first American satellite into orbit, and carried Alan B. Shepard, originally of Derry, on his historic suborbital space flight on May 5, 1961?

★ ★

Don't mess with Warren.

Such may have been the thoughts of Warren native Ted Asselin when he asked his superiors at the U.S. Army's Redstone Arsenal in Huntsville, Alabama, if he could take home one of those retired nuclear missiles lying in that field over there, since no one seemed to be using them.

First deployed in 1958, the Redstone was a highly accurate surface-to-surface missile capable of shooting into space everything from a 1-megaton thermonuclear warhead to 3.75 megatons of TNT to a chimpanzee named Ham to a New Hampshire–born jet pilot turned Mercury Project astronaut named Alan B. Shepard.

Using a borrowed semitractor and 60-foot trailer, Asselin drove the missile 1,300 miles to Warren, receiving a fine in Ohio for not having a permit to transport a decommissioned nuclear missile across state lines. Getting the missile to stand upright in the launch position on Warren's quaint town green was a whole different challenge, but the Redstone was dedicated on Warren's Old Home Day, July 4, 1971, before a crowd of 5,000.

The Redstone missile is standing right on the common in the center of Warren, just off Route 25. Next to the missile is the Warren Historical Society, open Sunday afternoons, where you can find a letter from Alan Shepard and pictures of the missile's installation.

Doomsday Disappointments

It seems a peculiar source of disappointment, but when the world didn't end between March 21, 1843, and March 21, 1844, as William Miller of Poultney had predicted, he was gravely disappointed. Then, when one of his estimated 50,000 expectant followers came up with a second date for the Second Coming of October 22, 1844, Miller said, "If Christ does not come . . . I shall feel twice the disappointment I did in the spring." Miller's high hopes for total destruction were twice-dashed, along with those of his followers, among them a splinter group of Miller-believing Baptists from Sugar Hill who gathered in the town cemetery to await their dilatory maker.

William Miller hadn't always been so easily disappointed by the continuation of life on planet Earth. In fact, in his early adulthood he seemed to be a pretty normal nineteenth-century guy, a War of 1812 veteran, farmer and justice of the peace. But by thirty-four he had joined a Baptist church and become obsessed with marshalling biblical evidence to accurately predict the end of the world. Miller shared his findings with pastor Isaac Fuller, who was so impressed that he encouraged Miller to spread the "good" news. Miller published numerous articles and a book, journeying around New England to address crowds and founding periodicals to communicate with a growing number of 1843 doomsday believers referred to as Millerites.

Although there's no record of Miller visiting Sugar Hill, a significant number of Free-Will Baptists in town were Miller believers. After disagreements with fellow Baptists, the Sugar Hill Millerites built their own small church in town and started getting their affairs in order for the end of the world. On the appointed day, October 22, 1844, the Sugar Hill Millerites gathered in the cemetery on the hill at the western end of town, cast their eyes toward heaven, and waited.

One eyewitness account claims that the group looked "very cold and very gloomy" as the sun began to set.

The Sugar Hill Cemetery is on a hill overlooking Main Street at the west end of town.

★ ★

So Just How Good a Lumberjack Are You?

Berlin

If you want to be a lumberjack, you may want to test your chopping, sawing, axe-chucking, logrolling, and chain-sawing mettle in the annual Lumberjack Festival and Competition at Berlin's Northern Forest Heritage Park, a three-acre re-creation of a circa-1900 New Hampshire logging camp. Competitions include the axe throw; the Jack and Jill crosscut (with a male lumberjack at one end of the saw and a female lumberjack at the other); the open chain saw class, a competition in which "anything goes"; and, of course, the logrolling competition. First, a professional logroller shows onlookers how it's done, and then anyone who's feeling brave and well-balanced can give it a whirl.

Caution: Rolling logs.

The Northern Forest Heritage Park is located at 961 Main Street, on the west bank of the Androscoggin River in downtown Berlin. The park is open Memorial Day through October, Tuesday through Saturday, from 11:00 a.m. to 6:00 p.m. You can roll a log at the Lumberjack Festival and Competition in early October of each year. For more information call (603) 752–7202.

Overeager Night Owls Post Nation's First Election Results
Dixville Notch

Drive west on Route 26 from Errol to Colebrook, and you'll soon cruise through Dixville Notch, a beautiful and narrow mountain pass flanked by Dixville Peak and Sanguinary Mountain. After one final turn, the valley opens up and there, beneath a tall ledge of gray granite, a grand old building materializes, a shimmering wedding cake of a hotel reflected in perfect detail in the dark, still waters of the pond at its doorstep.

The hotel in the notch where folks get first votes.

This is the Balsams, a large hotel and 15,000-acre wilderness resort, one of the few remaining grand hotels in the state. And since 1960 it's here that the nation's first presidential election votes have been cast, counted, and posted for the whole world to see. Every presidential

★ ★

primary and presidential election eve for the last four decades, all the eligible voters in Dixville Notch gather before midnight in the Balsams' second-floor Ballot Room and vote. At precisely the stroke of midnight, the Dixville Notchers cast their votes. Polls close at 12:01 a.m., and in fifteen minutes the votes are tallied and the results broadcast to the world.

Since New Hampshire holds the first presidential primaries in the nation, the Dixville Notch primary vote often makes headlines in election-day newspapers around the country. Notch voters are of a Republican persuasion, and they can be counted on to choose their Republican candidates presciently: During every primary election since 1968, the Republican presidential candidate who received the most Dixville Notch votes went on to win his party's presidential nomination.

The Balsams Grand Resort Hotel is located at 1000 Cold Spring Road in Dixville Notch, just off Route 26, midway between Errol and Colebrook. For information call (603) 255–3400.

The Couple That Gets Alien-Abducted Together Stays Together
Lancaster

Recounted in the 1966 book *The Interrupted Journey* by John Fuller and later turned into the 1975 made-for-TV movie *The UFO Incident,* Betty and Barney Hill's alleged abduction by aliens while driving home to Portsmouth through the northern White Mountains on the night of September 19, 1961, is considered by many UFO-ologists to be the grandsire of all alien-abduction and close-encounter tales. It's got classic dramatic elements any *X-Files* fan would appreciate: Late evening, early fall, deserted country road in the mountains. A bright light appears on the horizon, moving closer and closer to the couple driving toward home. Barney stops the vehicle, exits it, and takes a closer look at the light with binoculars, only to rush back to the car screaming in utter terror. The couple's minds fall under the influence of the aliens, and they're brought on board a disc-shaped craft and examined. Afterwards, they're released, unharmed and almost totally unaware of the fact that anything unusual has transpired, except for maybe a little soreness in the umbilicus and a lingering sense that things aren't quite right in the world.

The Hills reported their UFO sighting to Pease Air Force Base officials the day after the incident, but it wasn't until months later, after they sought help for anxiety and stress-related problems from Dr. Benjamin Simon, a Boston psychiatrist and hypnotherapy expert, that they recalled they'd also been abducted and examined that evening by 4- to 5-foot-tall aliens whom Betty described as "rugged, not skinny guys."

Under hypnotherapy, they recalled specific details of their abduction and examination, including the fact that the aliens had a minor freakout when they found they were able to remove Barney's teeth (he had dentures). Betty, a social worker, seemed far less afraid of the aliens and even asked the aliens where they were from. The aliens showed her a star chart, which Betty drew after one particularly fruitful hypnotherapy session with Dr. Simon. (According to some reports, investigators years later produced a match between Betty's map and a cluster of newly discovered stars near Zeta Reticuli.)

Ever since the publication of John Fuller's book, believers and skeptics have been arguing back and forth about the validity of Betty and Barney Hill's abduction tales. But Betty, who gave talks on UFOs and on her abduction for decades, was always a believer. Up until just a few months before her death on October 17, 2004, at the age of eighty-four, she reported that aliens were paying frequent visits to the seacoast area around her home and making good use of a landing spot she had found in Kingston.

A Museum to Make Kermit Proud
North Stratford

Here's a museum for the herpetoculturist in you. While herpetoculture might sound like a chronic disease, it's merely the name for the hobby of collecting amphibians or reptiles, which together make up the animal group called herps. A boa constrictor is a herp, and a bullfrog is a herp, too. But just because they're members of the same group doesn't necessarily mean they'd be fast friends.

That's probably why as herpetoculturists themselves, Carol Hawley and Francis McMilleon only collect frogs. But what their collection lacks in breadth, they more than make up for in depth. You won't find the living, breathing kind of frog at the Foolish Frog Gift Shop and Museum, but you will find just about every other variety of frog you can imagine, and many more you couldn't imagine, even in your most twisted herpetoculturist dreams. They've spent decades traveling the world collecting frogs of every color, shape, size, occupation, hobby, and religious affiliation.

There are, according to experts, over 300 different species of common frogs and over 400 species of common toads (which, though we call them toads, are actually frogs), but those experts have never been to see the extraordinarily varied population of frogs in Stratford.

Up on the slope-ceiling second floor of the couple's home, you'll find a shop filled with whimsical frogs for sale, many of which Francis handcrafted himself, including a wonderfully sturdy-looking wooden hobby frog just waiting for a kid to come and ride him. Just beyond the shop is a bedroom-cum-frog-museum filled with many bug-eyed green critters. "We've got 10,000 frogs," Francis told me, "but we don't have room enough to display them all." Surrounded by throngs of their own kind, the frogs don't seem to mind one bit.

The Foolish Frog Gift Shop and Museum is open by chance or appointment, so be sure to call ahead at (603) 636–9843. It's located on the east side of Route 3 about 7 miles south of North Stratford.

Dude, Let's Go Roll Some Snow
Pittsburg

Prior to the era of the snowplow, managing all the snow that accumulates on North Country roadways was a whole different affair. You couldn't really push it—not enough horsepower—and you certainly couldn't shovel it—not enough shovelers—but you could, if you had the right equipment, squash it down a bit. And that's just what the old-timers did.

Enter the curious-looking contraption in Pittsburg's town park right on Route 3, where the town has chosen to display an old-fashioned snow roller. Think of it as a giant horse-drawn rolling pin for snow. The driver sat above the 5- or 6-foot-tall wooden roller on a seat attached to an axle-mounted frame, and a team of horses pulled the roller and its driver over hill and over dale, flattening the snow as they went. And once the snow was rolled over, residents could get out and about in their horse-drawn sleighs.

Don't be too jealous of the old-timers, though—they didn't get out of shoveling entirely. Instead of shoveling snow off the road, they had to shovel it on—right onto the roadways of covered bridges so that sleighs could pass. And yet another reason why jealousy might be misplaced: After a whole winter of packing down foot upon foot of snow over dirt roads, the old timers must have had a ball when the spring thaw finally came. And we think we've got it bad during mud season.

Pittsburg's snow roller is located in the town park on the west side of Route 3. They've placed it under a roof and behind a short chain-link fence so that it doesn't roll away.

Rolling snowbanks down to size.

Live Free Until the Whole Double Tax Thing Gets Ironed Out

The town of Pittsburg in New Hampshire's North Country is jammed up between the state's boundary with Maine and its border with Canada. Stretching as it does from border to border, the town's first big claim to fame is that it is big: At 300,000 acres, or 282.3 square miles, it's reported to be the largest township in the United States.

Its second claim to fame is that Pittsburg was once its own country. That's right, from 1832 to 1835, the Republic of Indian Stream (named after a small river that runs through town) was an independent constitutional republic consisting of about 300 citizens. Just in case you're wondering, they had good reason for declaring independence: double taxation. Because of ambiguity in the language of the Treaty of Paris of 1783, which established the boundary between the United States and Canada, both countries claimed Pittsburg and so both felt inclined to tax Pittsburg. The Republic of Indian Stream voted to be annexed by the United States in 1835, the U.S. militia came to town, and the boundary dispute was resolved in favor of the States.

World War II Comes to the Great North Woods

Stark

It was the height of World War II when German prisoners of war landed in the little logging town of Stark and didn't get the warmest of receptions. Their captors told them that the barbed wire fence around their prison camp wasn't so much to keep them inside as it was to keep ferocious bears and half-mad, gun-toting French-Canadians out. Locals came just to stare. Even the children of Stark taunted the POWs by singing patriotic songs out the windows of their school bus as they passed.

But by the end of the war, unlikely friendships and even romances blossomed between the Germans and the locals. Allen Koop, Dartmouth professor and author of a book about the prison camp called *Stark Decency,* recalled a Stark old-timer telling him, "Those Germans were the best thing that ever happened to Stark."

At the time, the Brown Company in Berlin was in desperate need of workers to meet its wartime wood pulp production quota, so Uncle Sam sent about 250 German POWs to work in Stark as loggers. Under the guidance of civilian foremen, the Germans spent long days harvesting pulpwood in five-man crews using axes, handsaws, and horses. Over the hard months spent working together, Brown Company employees and German POWs became friends, not only because they shared a common goal of making their weekly quotas, but also because many of the Germans were themselves anti-Nazi, so from the outset felt more like allies than enemies.

To visit the site of Stark's POW camp, head 2 miles east out of town on Route 110 and watch for a historical marker on the right. Not much remains of the camp save for the concrete footings of the watchtowers and some chimney stones.

Rhode Island Curiosities

We love Rhode *Island.*

That's the short version. The rest of this chapter is the long version, but Rhode Island is the state we love, and who we are. Yes, it's true that we ended up moving to Massachusetts a few years ago, but we're Rhode Islanders. We don't jump when we hear "Massachusetts" on the news, but we listen to any story about Rhode Island with piqued interest. Meeting someone else from Massachusetts while traveling is pleasant, but if we meet someone from Rhode Island, we get excited and start asking whom they know.

None of this is to knock Massachusetts. It's a fine state, but it's not Rhode Island. Rhode Island is home. Sometimes, when we'd start writing profiles on things we remember from our childhood, we'd get lost in nostalgia. We remember images, feelings of excitement. And Rhode Island is still home to us—always will be. Whenever the car crosses into Rhode Island while on a long trip, we reflexively raise our arms in triumph. I'm almost shedding a tear writing this, and we're not given to excess emotion.

Why does Rhode Island inspire this unique kind of loyalty? Well, it's small. Small enough that everyone knows everyone, because the whole state feels like a big town. In a sense it is, because everyone lives roughly as close to each other as they would in a town in some big state. That's the advantage of a small state; we're all just a short drive away from Providence.

Believe me, that fact made writing this a whole lot easier. If you're going to go back and forth across a state fifty times to research for a book, Rhode Island is the best one to pick. (I'm sure glad I didn't grow up in Texas.) This will also come in handy for you if you decide to go visiting some of the locations. They're all a short drive from each other. And heck, you could take a day to walk through downtown Providence and catch a dozen of them.

Did we mention Rhode Island was small? We divide it into five counties, but there is no county government. There are more than three dozen municipalities with their own local government. There are also neighborhoods and villages within the municipalities, and a wonderful array of Indian names that give you an idea of Rhode Island's history. Narragansett, Pawtucket, Chepachet, Quonset, Apponaug, Misquamicut . . . hard to spell, but fun to say. And our language isn't just Indian. We drink "cabinets" and eat "gaggers," called "milk shakes" and "hot dogs" by the rest of the less civilized world.

Rhode Island is full of treasures. We have the first Baptist church in America, and the first street in the country to use gaslights. And yes, we have the quahog, though there's no town named that in spite of what Family Guy *may have led you to believe. Some of the more well-known treasures have been left out of this book, because you already know about them. Then again, it would be impossible for me to write about Rhode Island and not include certain things like the Big Blue Bug, even though everyone already knows about it.*

Still, many of the people and places you'll read about should be new to you. There's a workshop filled with bizarre giant living puppets, just down the street from a disappearing diner. There's Chinese food with a side of either jazz or Jews, depending on your preference. There are people who build rock sculptures and eat bugs. And if you live in Rhode Island, they're all just a short drive away.

So what are you waiting for? Start reading, and get going!

★ ★

Wiener Takes All

Nothing says Rhode Island quite like New York System. In spite of the name, New York System wieners are only available in Rhode Island. While not exactly haute cuisine, Rhode Islanders often find themselves hungering for a few delectable wieners from this glorious grease-ridden institution. New York System wiener shops are all over Rhode Island, open late, and generally provide food for a buck.

New York System began back in 1927 when Gust Pappas came over from Greece. He had a little wiener cart and decided to name it "New York System" to honor New York City, having come through Ellis Island. The cart eventually became a shop on 424 Smith Street, which

Every time I look at this photo,
I get hungry.

has stayed in the Pappas family for three generations, passing through Gust's son, Ernie, and now resting in the hands of Ernie's son, Gus. In addition to ownership of the wiener shop, Gus Pappas has inherited the Secret Recipe for New York System meat sauce, which is what truly makes a NY System wiener what it is.

Despite the fact that the Smith Street shop was the first, today the most popular spot for New York System wieners is probably the Olneyville, East Providence, location at 20 Plainfield Street (401–621–9500; www.olneyvillenysystem.com). They've been serving wieners since 1946, and perhaps most importantly, they're open until 2:00 a.m. every day of the week for your late-night wiener cravings.

Not Just Club Soda

Ever wonder what the heck club soda means?

Do they mean that you should take a bottle of soda and beat someone over the head with it?

We wouldn't drink anything with a name like that. Nosireebob, we'd rather drink a soda made in Rhode Island for nearly a century—Yacht Club Soda. That's the name of the company, not the flavor of the soda. And they tell you what kind of club it is right up front: a yacht club.

Yacht Club Soda has been a Rhode Island production since 1915, microbrewing their own old-fashioned soda in delicious flavors like sarsaparilla and birch beer. And the recipes have stayed the same. Owner William Sgambato, won't reveal those recipes. But he will say that, just like when they first started making soda, the main ingredients are artesian well water, cane sugar, and vanilla extract. He knows—he tastes each batch himself.

The Sgambatos have been working at Yacht Club Soda since 1935, when Bill was a young boy of thirteen. But it wasn't until 1961 that Bill and his father bought the company. Bill's sons, Mike and John, took over running the company a few years ago, and they continue to make the microbrewed soda in the same traditional way.

They also use traditional equipment: The newest machine is the bottle washer, made in 1948. Yes, they need a bottle washer, because they still use glass bottles.

The heyday of Yacht Club Soda was more than half a century ago, but recently they have made a push to start distributing once again. Although their North Providence factory floor may be no larger than an apartment, the taste of Yacht Club Soda is known throughout Rhode Island. Anyone who has lived in the state for a couple decades likely has fond memories of the sweet and lightly carbonated soda.

In a Single Bound

Faster than a speeding bullet. More powerful than a locomotive. It's a bird. It's a plane. It's . . . a rumor.

Yes, the son of Kal-El was almost invincible, aside from his crippling weakness to Kryptonite. But rumor refuses to die, which is what lends an extra air of mystery and importance to the already impressive Superman Building at 50 Kennedy Plaza in downtown Providence. The Superman Building is more properly named the Bank of America Building, which was previously the Fleet Bank Tower, and before that the Industrial Trust Tower. While banks come and go, Superman is forever, and Providence residents have called this building the Superman Building since the 1950s.

The reason? With its art deco design and impressive tower, it bears more than a passing resemblance to the *Daily Planet* Building featured in the 1950s Superman television series. And rumor, that most powerful of forces, had it that the *Daily Planet* Building itself was based on this prodigious part of Providence's skyline.

If you were going to pay homage to a building, this isn't a bad one to pick. It was built in 1927 by Walker & Gillette of New York and George Frederick Hall of Providence as the Industrial Trust Tower. At 26 floors and 428 feet, it was not only the tallest building in Rhode Island, but the tallest in all of New England when it was built.

So was it really the basis for the *Daily Planet* Building in which Superman's alter ego worked? Probably not. While some people believe that the Industrial Trust Tower was where Clark Kent really went to work, some New Yorkers claim that their *Daily News* Building was the real inspiration. And Ohio residents insist that the Ohio Bell Building in Cleveland is the model while folks in St. Louis have their own Superman Building. The cartoonist responsible for the design denied that any one building was the source of his inspiration. So there's no proof whatsoever that Providence's Superman Building was the real deal.

However, it cannot be denied that it does look very, very similar. And for this reason, Rhode Islanders continue to call it the Superman Building, even if it probably wasn't the *Daily Planet*.

It's a bird. It's a plane. It's the Superman Building.

★ ★

All You Need Is Lovecraft

There is perhaps no Rhode Islander better known outside of Rhode Island and less known in it than the late H. P. Lovecraft. The H. P. stands for Howard Phillips who, as H. P. Lovecraft has, probably influenced modern horror more than anyone. Everyone from Stephen King to Clive Barker cites Lovecraft as a big influence. Yet in spite of his worldwide fame, if you ask a random Rhode Islander what they think of H. P. Lovecraft, there's a 50 percent chance that their response will be "Who?"

H. P. Lovecraft was born on August 20, 1890, in Providence, and his childhood provided a lot of background for a horror writer. When H. P. was three years old, his father suffered a nervous breakdown and was put in a sanitarium, where he died. Whether nature or nurture, it seemed to run in the family, for Lovecraft's mother also suffered a nervous breakdown years later, for which she too would be institutionalized until her death. Lovecraft avoided that fate by having his nervous breakdown early, at the age of eighteen. The downside was that this breakdown forced him to leave high school, and he never returned to get his diploma.

Lovecraft more than made up for it. Reading and writing from a young age, his interest in science (as well as strange and macabre fiction) had already bloomed before he reached puberty. He was writing journals of astronomy and the like for his friends, and soon took up writing columns in various local newspapers. He eventually began writing short stories, and briefly married a woman named Sonia Greene. Then she had to be put in a sanitarium.

Lovecraft left Sonia in 1926, returning to his beloved Providence after two years in New York (which he called "a Babel of sound and filth").

He spent the rest of his life in Providence, prolifically communicating with the outside world through letters: Some have estimated that Lovecraft wrote nearly 100,000 letters, in volume far outpacing his fiction. However, it was after his final return to Providence that Lovecraft proceeded to write his most well-known fiction, including "At the

Mountains of Madness" and the cult classic "The Call of Cthulhu." Many of his stories took place in the imaginary town of Arkham, which he based on Providence. Lovecraft died of cancer in 1937, and was sadly never quite famous during his lifetime.

However, such is his posthumous popularity that, although his name was carved onto the family monument in Providence's Swan Point Cemetery when he died, in 1977 a group of fans bought him his own headstone. On it, they inscribed not only his name and dates, but a powerful statement from one of his many, many personal letters: "i am providence."

Every year, fans gather to read a eulogy of Lovecraft's life. Some say that the spirit of Lovecraft himself still haunts these annual gatherings, because fans have reported everything from winds and snows that seemed timed to punctuate a reading, to a murder of crows that arrived to observe and caw for a key part of the proceedings. If you'd like to attend the next H. P. Lovecraft Commemorative Service, you can call the H. P. Lovecraft Commemorative Activities Committee at (401) 732–4870 for details.

To visit the gravestone of H. P. Lovecraft, you can find it in Lot 5 at Swan Point Cemetery, 585 Blackstone Boulevard (401–272–1314). But note that taking photos of any of the headstones in this cemetery is not permitted, and that rule is strictly enforced.

The Old Ball Game

If you ask the average Joe on the street who won baseball's first World Series, he won't know, because it was more than a century ago. If you ask the average baseball fan, he'll tell you that it was Boston, back in 1903. But if you ask an expert who really knows baseball, he'll tell you that baseball's first World Series championship was won by the Providence Grays, in 1884.

It wasn't technically called the World Series, because the term hadn't been coined yet, but the Grays' victory over the New York Metropolitans sealed their undisputed reputation as the world champions of baseball for that year. After their 1885 season, the Grays

★ ★

disbanded, and by the late twentieth century, it seemed as if baseball's first world champions and the game's history in Providence would soon be forgotten.

Enter Tim Norton. In 1998 Norton attended a baseball historian's lecture about the Providence Grays, and that same year saw an article about vintage baseball, where players follow nineteenth-century rules. This sparked a desire to resurrect the Providence Grays as a vintage baseball team for a game against a New York vintage team, to honor the Grays' victory in 1884. Norton managed to gather enough people to field a team, and like many a Hollywood film, his ragtag band challenged the much more experienced New York team, all for the love for baseball.

But this time, the ragtag band of rookies were utterly defeated by the New York veterans. But having finally re-created the glory of the Providence Grays, he wasn't about to stop. As pitcher and outfielder, Norton led the Grays through more than a hundred vintage baseball games. Vintage baseball is similar to modern baseball, but some of the big differences are painfully obvious. The players do not protect themselves with such modern fripperies as "gloves" or "helmets." So fielding a ball once it comes off the bat can be painful. The bats are heavier than modern bats. And going further than most vintage teams, the Grays dress in wool uniforms, guaranteeing that any victory they earn comes not only with blood and tears, but with plenty of sweat.

The Providence Grays play to win, but they play mainly for the love of the game. Instead of receiving millions like major-league ballplayers, the Grays actually pay to play baseball. But it's totally worth it. If you attend a game played by the Providence Grays, you'll see a game with gentlemanly manners and a single baseball used for the whole game.

Also unlike the modern version, watching a game is free. You'll find the schedule on their Web site at www.providencegrays.org. Norton stopped playing in 2004, but remains as president. If you think you're man enough to join up with the Grays, drop an e-mail to Tim Norton at provgrays@yahoo.com.

There's No Place Like Dome

While the Big Blue Bug is probably Rhode Island's most famous landmark, the State House runs a close second. It sits on Smith Hill in Providence, and although recent nearby construction made it less visible from afar than it once was, it's still a beautiful sight to behold. The building was built between 1895 and 1901 and looks like a miniature version of the U.S. Capitol. The Rhode Island State House consists of 327,000 cubic feet of white Georgia marble, as well as a few million bricks and well over a thousand tons of iron beams. But the real prize of the Rhode Island State House is the dome.

The statue is called the Independent Man, but he's pretty dependent on the dome for support.

The glorious dome is topped by a large statue of The Independent Man, a quarter-ton bronze statue covered in gold leaf that symbolizes the independent spirit that led to the founding of Rhode Island. At one point the dome was one of the top three unsupported domes in the world and still weighs in as the fourth-largest unsupported marble dome in the world. (The first three are St. Peter's Basilica in Rome, the Minnesota State Capitol, and the Taj Mahal, in that order.)

The dome is 50 feet in diameter at its widest, which is impressive for a dome whose marble blocks are held together by nothing but tension and gravity. Of course, big domes don't come cheap. Building the State House costed more than $3 million in 1900 dollars; that would be closer to $70 million today.

Inside the dome is a mural called *The Four Freedoms,* which depicts four scenes from the state's history. In addition to the mural, around the inside of the dome is carved a quote from Tacitus that reads "rara temporum felicitas ubi sentire quae velis et quae sentias dicere licet." Roughly translated, this means "Rare felicity of the times when it is permitted to think as you like and say what you think." Lower your eyes further and you see four medallions depicting Education, Justice, Literature, and Commerce. Look down even further, to the ground itself, and the middle of the rotunda holds the State Seal of Rhode Island.

Self-guided tours are available Monday thru Friday from 9:00 a.m. to 3:00 p.m. To schedule a tour visit www.sec.state.ri.us. or call the Secretary of State's office at (401) 222-2357.

You Are What You Eat

If it's true that you can judge a person by what he or she eats, then the best place to truly learn about the human race is none other than the Culinary Museum and Archives at Johnson and Wales University on Harborside Boulevard (401–598–2805). It is America's biggest museum devoted to the history of the culinary and hospitality industries, which makes sense, as Johnson and Wales is the country's biggest university

★ ★

The hall of outmoded cookware.

devoted to the culinary and hospitality industries. The museum has even been called "the Smithsonian of the food service industry." But while enrolling at the university will cost you roughly $20,000 a year, getting into the museum to learn all about the culinary industry will only cost you $7.00, $4.00 if you're a college student.

The collection includes literally hundreds of thousands of pieces of culinary history, even if you miss out on 50,000 cookbooks here or there, you'll hardly notice. If you try to see all the public collections, you'll already have bitten off more than you can chew. The huge museum contains everything from information on the New England tavern to a prodigious collection of kitchen gadgets through the ages. Food may go bad after a few weeks, but cooking tools from millennia past are still worth seeing. There is even an exhibit on diners that includes the famed Worcester Diner car, showing how the diner got its start in Rhode Island.

But visitors hunger for the presidential collection, with exhibits like History of the First Stomach and America the Bountiful that, combined, cover pretty much all the space between presidents and food. This includes campaigns (Hoover's slogan in 1928 was "a chicken in every pot"), presidential menus (Eisenhower cooked his own pancakes), dinner invitations, and even thank-you letters to constituents who sent turkeys.

Interestingly, the Culinary Archives and Museum was not originally a museum. When founded in 1979, it was a library containing a few thousand rare cookbooks. But ten years later, chef Louis Szathmary (of Chicago's famous restaurant The Bakery) donated thousands of items from his personal collection. In fact, they have not finished unpacking, cataloging, and storing all of the donations to this day. Several of the items in the museum are still unlabeled, so if you decide to visit, you'd be advised to take a guided tour from one of the students. And twenty years from now, your tour guide may be a famous chef.

Constant State of Mockery

Actually, Charlie Hall's Ocean State Follies specialize in constant mockery of state. This group of performers puts on shows that lampoon everything about Rhode Island from political scandals and current controversies to regional accents and notable figures. They dress up as big-haired girls named Cheryl and Rhonda from Cranston, pronouncing Creeeeeeeanston with the nasal twang typical of that region. They sing parody songs ranging from the commercial snippet ("I want my Buddy back," to the tune of Chili's "I want my baby back ribs," referring to former mayor Buddy Cianci, who was convicted and jailed), to the classic musicals ("East Side Story," about the east side of Providence), to the popular songs (Simon and Garfunkel surely never intended you to hear "Are you going to Scarborough Beach? Seaweed, gum, gold chains, and moussed hairs . . . ").

★ ★

If it sounds like most of their material wouldn't be as funny if you don't live in Rhode Island, that's because it's true. If youse don't live here, youse might miss a lot of the jokes. But don't sweat: There are enough jokes in there that even if you miss 20 percent of them, you'll still have a good time. And not only is the patter between songs accessible to anyone, but they have a special segment explaining "Roe Dylandese" (or as they call it, "Rhodonics") to any unfortunate out-of-stater. After all, langwich is the key to humah.

Charlie Hall as former governor Bruce Sundlun, who became infamous for complaining about plasticware.

People across the country make fun of Rhode Island all the time, usually asking if it's part of New York. But the Follies make fun of Rhode Island in a much more detailed and entertaining manner.

And lest you think humorist Charlie Hall doesn't love the state he so mercilessly mocks, he also wrote the lyrics for "Rhode Island's It for Me," a serious and beautiful piece which has become the official state song. But usually he's still making fun of the state, because that's what he's best at.

Really, if you live in Rhode Island, you ought to see the Ocean State Follies at least once. Conveniently, you can plan this by visiting their Web site, www.oceanstatefollies.com.

★ ★

Bug Bites

David Gracer has the food bug. And he'd like you to have some food bugs too. Gracer is the man behind Insects Are Food, and is trying to bring the eating of insects back into the common culture. More specifically, he'd like to bring entomophagy (eating insects) into American culture, since many other countries around the world already eat insects, especially throughout Asia and Africa. Even fancy European menus used to feature insects, but they have become less popular in the last few centuries. Still, as America goes culturally, so goes the world, and thus Dave Gracer has a clear mission to show them the light—even if that light has a few dead bugs that got stuck in it.

David Gracer of Insects Are Food.
Not just a fly-by-night operation—
he also has cicadas.

Gracer gives shows at various nature centers and schools to introduce people to the wonderful world of insect eating. He generally gives a talk, leads a walk to catch a few things, holds a question-and-answer session, and then offers up some tasty bugs. Half of the audience is usually kids, who Gracer hopes will learn to discover things for themselves. Convincing Americans to ignore their cultural conditioning isn't easy. There's definitely an "ick" factor, explains Gracer, which causes most Americans to recoil and say "Ewwwwwww!" at the idea of eating bugs. But insects have good pharmacological properties, lots of protein, and are probably more environmentally friendly to eat than whatever you're eating now. In fact, if eating insects was something seen regularly on TV, there's little doubt that people would consider it normal.

Perhaps this is why one of Gracer's dreams is to have insects as a steady diet for a full month. It would be similar to the movie *Super Size Me*, about a man eating nothing but McDonald's for a month, only much healthier. "I wanted to find a sufficient variety of insects and culinary techniques to make them the centerpiece of my meal for thirty days," says Gracer. Sadly, finding a variety of insects is trickier than you might expect. For example, crickets and mealworms are easy enough to get at pet stores, as long as you don't announce what you want them for. Many places won't sell insects to people who say they plan to eat them, but are happy to sell them if they presume you're feeding them to your pets.

Surprisingly, Gracer was somewhat of a finicky eater as a child. He was an environmentalist and went wild mushroom hunting, but certainly did not grow up eating bugs (at least not on purpose). In 1999 a friend of his gave him some flavored mealworm snacks. Gracer, though not impressed by the taste, was intrigued. After attending a presentation by insect advocate David Gordon, Gracer was converted. He got some images from a show in New York and began doing his own presentations. It started at the Entomological Society of America meeting in spring 2003, and although he only does a few shows a year at present, he hopes to do more.

On the home front, Gracer has a freezer that is completely stuffed with various boxes and bags of frozen insects. He was even kind enough to fry me up some cicadas, crickets, and water bugs—the first two making a tasty snack, the latter tasting like salty fruit. Gracer's favorite insect to eat is the katydid. His wife, alas, dislikes eating insects, but also dislikes crab. People allergic to shellfish tend to also be allergic to insects, because the two have a lot of similarities; hence the name of his company, Insects Are Food. However, insists Gracer, "Crickets eat much better than lobsters."

If you'd like to learn more about eating insects, and aren't too afraid to try, drop David Gracer a line at info@insectsarefood.com or visit his Web site at www.insectsarefood.com. Best of all, you don't even have to pretend it's for your pet.

From Russia, With Love

Quick, where's the only place in North America that you can see a former Soviet cruise missile submarine in all its glory? No, it isn't Moscow, Idaho. It's Collier Point Park in Providence, home to the *Juliett-484*, a 300-foot Russian submarine now converted into a museum. Yes, complete with giant red star, a soviet sub now sits in Providence, open for to tour. And people are just Russian to get in.

Oddly, the people that brought the *Juliett-484* to Providence were the folks from the USS *Saratoga* Museum Foundation, based around the USS *Saratoga*. Why odd? Back when it was in service, Russian submarines of the Juliett class tended to target U.S. Navy ships, especially the USS *Saratoga*. Anyway, the *Juliett-484* was built in a Gorky Russian shipyard in 1963 and launched in 1965. Nobody can say exactly what it did, because the mission logs are still secret. But they tended to target cities in the eastern United States, until the advent of ballistic missiles relegated the Juliett to anti-ship duties.

The *Juliett-484* is open but there are a few rules: First, you must wear shoes because sandals aren't allowed. Second, you must pass through a fake submarine hatch before boarding the actual submarine, just like an army drill. And third, you must pay the admission fee. Thankfully, this is only a few bucks, which isn't too bad. The Russian Sub Museum is open on weekends; go to www.juliett484.org/juliett/index.html or call (401) 521–3600 for more information.

Come one, come all, comrade, to the (red-) star attraction.

Come Hell and High Water

First, in 1938 came the Great New England Hurricane. These winds came up from Florida and caught everyone in New England—especially everyone in Rhode Island—completely by surprise. Prior to that, there hadn't been a big hurricane in Rhode Island since 1815. But the 120-miles-per-hour winds came right at the time of high tide, causing waters to rise 13 feet above normal and doing $100 million in property damage just in Rhode Island.

Then in 1954 Hurricane Carol, with winds of 100 mph, wreaked havoc once again in the form of flooding throughout Providence. Anyone who remembers either of these no doubt remembers the water. But the best way to understand how high the floodwaters came is to visit Providence today, where two plaques on the side of the former Amica Building at 10 Weybosset Street (now just called 10 Weybosset) in the middle of the city gives a real sense of history.

The top plaque reads DURING THE HURRICANE AND FLOOD OF SEPTEMBER 21, 1938, THE WATERS ROSE TO THIS LEVEL. The bottom plaque reads DURING THE HURRICANE AND FLOOD OF AUGUST 31, 1954, THE WATERS ROSE TO THIS LEVEL.

Your hair might have stayed dry in the 1954 flood, but the 1938 floodwaters rose higher.

Hearty Vegetation

Roger Williams, the man who founded Rhode Island, was buried in 1684 in his own backyard. In 1860 his remains were dug up to be moved to a family crypt in the North Burial Ground, but what they found was very surprising: The coffin was in scraps and pieces, and the apple tree that was next to his grave had grown down through the coffin into Roger Williams himself. The roots of the tree had grown right through the spot where his head would have rested, and then into his chest. The apple tree had consumed the founder of Rhode Island, essentially using him as fertilizer. It can be said, in more ways than one, he is truly part of what made Rhode Island what it is today.

The few bits of bones that could be salvaged were reburied, eventually to be moved once again in 1936 to their current location on Prospect Hill. But far more interesting is the tree root itself, which to some degree even took the shape of Roger Williams. This root was saved, and is currently guarded by the Rhode Island Historical Society at the John Brown House Museum at 52 Power Street (401–273–7507).

The Jig Is Up

Some people think that directing traffic is the most boring thing in the world. But people who have seen Officer Tony LePore, aka "The Dancing Cop," often think that few things are more exciting than directing traffic. Because the Dancing Cop, as you might expect, dances and madly gesticulates in order to tell the cars when to go. His white-gloved hands spin in circles and curve in waves just like the rest of his body, to the delight of Rhode Islanders since 1984.

Tony LePore became Officer LePore in the early 1970s when he joined the Providence Police Department. After nine years on night duty and two medals of valor, he switched to day duty, which included directing traffic at the corner of Dorrance and Westminster Streets. Two years of normal traffic direction quickly proved boring, so one day in 1984, Officer LePore decided to add a little pizzazz with some

★ ★

elaborate hand movements and spinning. "The little boy in me just came out," says LePore, who had been a bit of a class clown in his youth.

He quickly won statewide fame, and since public reaction was so positive, his bosses had no problem with it. LePore continued adding more moves to his traffic-directing repertoire until he retired in 1988. But the public wanted more dancin' to the beat, on the beat, and newspapers began asking, whatever happened to the Dancing Cop? Finally, in the early 1990s, Providence mayor Buddy Cianci asked LePore if he would come back and direct traffic during the holiday season. LePore agreed, was re-sworn in as a part-time officer, and directed traffic at a few intersections across Providence in the way that only he can. Naturally, the public was thrilled.

So if you're driving through Providence in December and you see a police officer directing traffic with a pirouette, you'll know it's none other than the Dancing Cop.

And now Tony has his own Web site (www.providencedancingcop .com) where you can read about Tony's life, view Tony's scrapbook, and buy Tony's Dancing Cop T-shirts, caps, dolls and Dancing Cop Deputy pins.

Cuckoo for Cocoa Dust
Central Falls

Nowadays, the place in America known for chocolate is Hershey, Pennsylvania. But a few hundred years ago, Central Falls was the big chocolate place. Back in 1780 Sylvanus Brown built a dam across the Blackstone River, and thus was founded a mill that was known as the Chocolate Mill. The Chocolate Mill didn't just make chocolate, it also made tools. But tools are boring, and you can't eat them. More importantly, many mills made tools, but chocolate was one of the first luxury items being produced in the area. The mill ground cacao beans into cocoa, because apparently grinding things swaps their vowels.

Regardless, having a chocolate mill was so exciting that the whole area became known as Chocolateville. A man named Wheat was the

big manufacturer of chocolate at the time, probably surprising everyone who thought he'd be grinding flour, not cocoa. Chocolateville was
a hopping town, and the location right on the river meant that a lot of
mills sprung up there—so many, in fact, that it became the country's
most densely populated city. Most historians argue that the mills are
what brought the people, but chocolate has its own siren song. The
Chocolate Mill continued crushing cacao beans in the name of Chocolateville until the 1820s, when the name was changed to Central Falls.

But Chocolateville remembers its history. Now, nearly two centuries
later, Garrison Confections, a gourmet chocolate manufacturer, moved
its factory from Providence to Central Falls. The factory lets them take
tons of processed chocolate and turn it into many gourmet chocolates.
But that isn't thinking big enough for Andrew Shotts, award-winning
chocolatier and owner of Garrison Confections. He plans to build a
huge factory for processing raw cacao beans into cocoa, just like the
Chocolate Mill of days gone by.

Vampire Hunter
Cranston

Most vampire hunters only exist in movies or on TV. But Cranston's
Michael Bell has spent years hunting vampires all over New England.
Granted, he doesn't come across many living vampires these days,
but as one of New England's premier folklore experts, he tracks their
stories and histories very carefully.

Michael has an MA in Folklore and Mythology and a PhD in Folklore, so his schooling is no myth. But his biggest attraction to folklore
was his biggest attraction—his wife. She was teaching high school
English and using folklore to interest her students in reading, which
caused Michael to shift his focus. They've now been married for more
than forty years, and while his wife has long since changed careers,
Michael stuck with folklore.

In fact, when the Rhode Island Historical Society needs to know
something about folklore, they tend to turn to Michael Bell. He has
spearheaded a number of programs to help preserve Rhode Island's

folklore, with help from other similarly interested people, and has a large collection of pictures and recordings which he plans to make into a public archive.

Meanwhile, Michael has collected all of the vampire stories he has heard into a volume called *Food for the Dead: On the Trail of New England's Vampires*. The title comes from an old quote about vampires killing people without leaving their graves, such that the living become food for the dead. The book includes his favorite tales, such as the story of famed Rhode Island vampire Mercy Brown, including a report that he heard from someone who heard it from an eyewitness.

Rhode Island is a small enough state that I doubt any vampires could remain anonymous here for long. But if there were any vampires about, be confident that Michael Bell is tracking them down.

Big Head, Big Ideas
Cranston

Despite being the man behind Big Head Studio, Scott Bonelli's cranium is of a fairly average size—but what's in that cranium is probably dangerous. Bonelli was in theater design for many years, ever since he was sixteen. He kept building props and tried to master as many trades as possible. After sixteen years of building theater props, he amassed plenty of tradesmanship, but his breakthrough came when famed designer Michael McGarty asked him to build a gigantic fiberglass head. Originally it was just planned as a model, but it was decided that a 14-foot head needed to be built, and Bonelli won the bid. The gigantic foam sculpture cost roughly $10,000, was covered in nine gallons of liquid latex, and towered over the production it was used for. In case you're curious, it was named Dave.

Anyway, that 14-foot behemoth noggin is the reason for the name Big Head Studio. But perhaps unsurprisingly, most of Bonelli's projects do not involve building humongous heads. Some involve very tiny skulls, such as the Siamese twin skull he crafted for use in sideshows. In fact, Bonelli produces a number of sideshow artifacts that combine the real and the fake, to the point where it's hard to tell where one ends and the other begins. His conjoined baby piglet fetuses in a jar are real piglet fetuses, but may not have started conjoined. The necklace on display from the Fugawe tribe is made from real pieces of bone, but the Fugawe tribe is just an old joke. His human skullcaps and mercury-preserved human hands may have fake histories, but the pieces are real.

Polly want a two-headed skull and collection of macabre sideshow props?

Still, Big Head Studio isn't all sideshow props. After covering a 14-foot head in gallons of liquid latex, Bonelli found he preferred painting smaller and more animate canvases, so now paints live bodies on Thursday nights. To think, when most artists say they're going to paint a nude model, they mean something different.

★ ★

Whether you want more information about painting pretty things, viewing sideshow grotesqueries, or building colossal braincases, you can reach Scott Bonelli at scott@bigheadstudio.com or (401) 465–6829 or visit the Web site at www.bigheadstudio.com. Just don't tell him how cool his sideshow oddities are—we wouldn't want him to get a big head.

Del-icious
Cranston

Some people say, when life gives you lemons, make lemonade. But Rhode Islanders know that when life gives you lemons, you should make Del's instead. What's Del's? Why, a popular brand of frozen lemonade and the quintessential summer drink in Rhode Island. Actually,

Nothing says summer like frozen lemonade.

popular doesn't quite do it justice. Del's is to frozen lemonade what Band-Aids are to adhesive bandages and Jell-O is to gelatin. Sure, other brands are out there, but Del's is the one everyone knows, so any other frozen lemonade is likely to be called Del's as well. So what is frozen lemonade? It's a cross between lemonade, lemon sorbet, and lemon slush, basically consisting of lemons, crushed ice, sugar, and two scoops of good-tasting magic.

Del's is practically synonymous with summer in Rhode Island. Trucks and carts of Del's are everywhere, from the parks to the zoo to the sports fields. The state's favorite filmmakers, the Farrelly Brothers, have showed people drinking Del's in their movies, like *There's Something About Mary* and *Me, Myself & Irene,* to capture the feeling of summer in Rhode Island. When it came time to vote for Rhode Island's state drink, Del's was narrowly defeated by coffee milk. But if the vote had taken place on a hot summer's day, it's likely that the results would have been the other way around.

Del's traces its history to a man named DeLucia in Naples, Italy in 1840, when DeLucia stored winter snow in caves, insulated with straw, and in summer mixed the snow with sugar and fresh lemon juice. His son, Franco DeLucia, came to America at the turn of the twentieth century and brought the recipe with him. Unfortunately, between rationing during World War II and the work required to hand-crank the lemonade, selling it was a tricky proposition. Franco's son Angelo created a machine that automatically produced the frozen lemonade, so in 1948 the two of them opened a Del's Frozen Lemonade stand on Oaklawn Avenue in Cranston, next to the bowling alley they owned.

Today Bruce DeLucia is president of the company, and there are more than forty franchises, less than half of which are in Rhode Island. Del's has expanded through New England to sell products in some thirty-six states, reaching as far as Japan. Del's may have been served at the 1996 Summer Olympics in Atlanta, but the best place to get it is still Rhode Island. There are other flavors like watermelon and cherry, but the original lemon remains the best. If you want to make some yourself, you can order some mix online at www.dels.com.

★ ★

Mightier Than the Sword
Lincoln

The A. T. Cross Company, Lincoln's famous pen factory, was created in 1846 and is America's first manufacturer of upscale writing instruments. They also claim to be the last independent manufacturer of fine writing instruments in the country. And all of their pens are still made right in Rhode Island.

The company has accumulated nearly two dozen patents for various pen and pencil technologies over the years, usually for prototypes of today's commonly used pens. For example, Cross developed the propel-repel pencil and the Stylographic pen, which although they have been outmoded by the mechanical pencil and the ballpoint pen, were quite clever in their time.

Richard Cross founded the company in Providence, making upscale gold and silver casings for wooden pencils. He passed the company on to his son A. T., who then sold it to an employee named Boss in 1916 (and no, there was never a boss there named Employee). The Boss family remains the boss family to this day. What's the result of having a company run by a former employee? A boss who lets any employee reject a product if it looks faulty. You know what they say: You can cross your boss, and you can boss your Cross, but don't cross the Boss who's the boss of Cross.

Milk in Your Coffee? Coffee in Your Milk!
Lincoln

If coffee isn't your cup of tea, or even your cup of coffee, you may be pleasantly surprised when you try coffee milk. Of course, if you're from Rhode Island, it's no surprise at all: You've been drinking the stuff for years. After all, it's part of the culture. Coffee milk is one of the standard options along with regular milk and chocolate milk. They have it in all the stores. They have it at the Dunkin' Donuts on every corner. They even have it in school cafeterias.

And yet, most out-of-staters are entirely unfamiliar with this delectable mix of milk and coffee syrup. But one supposes that's inevitable when Lincoln, Rhode Island, plays host to essentially the only company in the world that produces coffee syrup: Autocrat.

Rhode Island's state drink. A swallow will tell you.

Autocrat coffee has been around since the 1890s, but it was only in 1940 that the company started making coffee syrup. And though for decades there was competition brewing in the coffee syrup business from a company called Eclipse, Autocrat acquired them in 1991 to become the sole coffee syrup supplier of the land. So what's the only thing better than being the sole supplier of the nectar of the gods?

Having coffee milk named the state drink of Rhode Island. It's that kind of thing that makes former Rhode Islanders the world over feel a patriotic duty to buy coffee syrup so they can raise a glass of Rhode Island's state drink to honor the motherland. If that desire takes over you, or even if you're just a benighted soul who wants to taste glory, you can order coffee syrup by giving Autocrat a buzz at 1–800–AUTOCRAT.

You Say You Want a Revolution

Pawtucket

What's that? You thought the American Industrial Revolution started in some big state with tons of factories? Now wait just a cotton-pickin' minute. Because there's one man who can be credited with starting the Industrial Revolution in America, and that man is Samuel Slater. Slater went to Pawtucket in 1793 where he built the first mechanized factory and textile mill in the country, and called it, surprisingly enough, Slater Mill.

Slater Mill was the first mass-production textile mill in America, harnessing waterpower to produce cotton yarn. Slater didn't stop with his first mill; once he had a few dozen employees, he began building around the mill. Adding housing allowed him to attract families, which was handy, as many of his employees were children, since their smaller hands tended to be useful for small adjustments where adult hands might be too big. See? Handy.

He went on to buy land farther down the river and build another mill in a place he called Slatersville. There he not only built housing, but a company store, schools, and even churches. Once all of his workers lived in the town he created, he could pay them with company credit (usable at the company store) rather than cash. So, along with the Industrial Revolution, Slater brought the first company town to America. Anyway, back at the site of the first Slater Mill, another mill was eventually built in 1810, named the Wilkinson Mill. This was a somewhat larger mill that boasted stone walls less flammable than the Slater Mill and a machine shop on the bottom floor that made parts for the

★ ★

Slater Mill: Home of the Industrial Revolution.

mill (and parts for Slater Mill and others) to run. Both the Wilkinson Mill and the Slater Mill remain at the same site to this day, and have working machinery that you can view. Slater Mill is open to the public seven days a week, from May through September. The staff dresses in period costumes, which makes touring the mill much more interactive. They'll demonstrate the finest in eighteenth- and nineteenth-century technology, and occasionally let you turn a crank as well, if you're nice.

In addition to the Wilkinson and Slater Mills, the Slater Mill site includes the Sylvanus Brown House, which offers a look at home life during the olden days. To take a guided tour of all three of these old buildings only costs $10 per adult, but save a dollar by printing out a coupon from their Web site at www.slatermill.org. The Slater Mill site is at 67 Roosevelt Avenue in Pawtucket. For more information call (401) 725–8638.

★ ★

Hot Potato
Pawtucket

Idaho may be the state most famous for potatoes, but Rhode Island is the state that thought of sticking eyes in the potatoes. Okay, potatoes already have eyes. But we added ears, a nose, a mouth, and voilà— Mr. Potato Head, a collection of facial features to make your spud into more than just a common tater. This beloved children's toy was invented by George Lerner in the late 1940s and sold to Rhode Island- ers Henry and Merril Hassenfeld of Hassenfeld Brothers, later shortened to Hasbro. They released Mr. Potato Head to the public in 1952, and it became an overnight success—earning more than $4 million for Hasbro within its first year alone. Part of this may have been due to the fact that it was the first toy ever to be sold through national television advertising, but the genius of the idea cannot be denied.

In Soviet Russia, Potato cooks you!

Originally, it was just a box of face parts designed to be stuck into a potato, but as the Irish know, you can't always depend on having a potato around. So, in 1964, Hasbro began packaging a plastic potato with the kit. In 1974 the plastic potato was horribly changed, not only doubling in size, but also no longer allowing would-be Picassos to put noses in the eye sockets. In 1987 they finally realized the error of their ways, and began producing plastic potatoes that were a friend of creativity once more. The range of accessories has dwindled over the years, with the most notable disappearance being the pipe, after much lobbying from the American Cancer Society.

Sadly, many of the life-size potatoes have since moved on, so you may never see figures like Spud Light or the Surfer Spud, but some of them are still around. And nothing's better than a 6-foot potato holding food. If you want to see Mr. Potato Head for yourself, you'll find him outside Hasbro's main office at 1027 Newport Avenue, Pawtucket.

Egg Rolls and Drum Rolls

Woonsocket

Fish and bicycles. Peanut butter and pickles. Toasters and frogs. If these all seem like natural pairings to you, then you won't be at all surprised that one of Rhode Island's most well-known restaurants is famous for its combination of Chinese food and jazz. Chan's Fine Oriental Dining, at 267 Main Street in Woonsocket, serves up moo shu pork with a side order of blues (which is odd, because China is more famous for being red). Though the restaurant has been around since 1905, the Chan family didn't take ownership until 1965. And while they have won awards for having the best Chinese food in Rhode Island, the real excitement at Chan's is the jazz.

Since the 1970s jazz artists from all over the world have played at Chan's, from Roomful of Blues to the great Dizzy Gillespie. Once the music started becoming as much of a draw as the food, Chan decided to expand the restaurant into a full-fledged jazz club. Live jazz is available at Chan's every weekend, and many people have begun to come to Chan's Fine Oriental Cuisine without any intent of sampling the cuisine. This is a shame, as their menu has everything from pupu platters to these shrimp in a delicious black bean sauce . . . but we digress. Those who are not interested in the culinary menu will be glad to know that the entertainment menu has been expanded as well. In addition to jazz, the club now features blues, folk, cabaret, and even comedy performances. The only downside? An hour after you hear the jazz, you'll be hungry for more.

For those who prefer their Chinese food with something other than Muzak.

They're open daily, but if you're planning to go on a jazz night, you'd best make a reservation by calling (401) 765–1900. To see who's playing, visit their Web site: www.chanseggrollsandjazz.com.

Side by Each
Woonsocket

Rhode Island has a dialect. There are accents, there are dropped r's, and there are words like bubblah that few other states use. But even within Rhode Island, there is Woonsocket. Woonsocket, in fact, is probably best known for the bizarre speech patterns that prevailed there during the twentieth century. Phrases like "side by each" instead of "side by side," or "Throw me down the stairs my coat" instead of "Throw my coat down the stairs to me." This is because the population of Woonsocket is largely French or French-Canadian. How French? Well, let's just say that some people call it la ville la plus française aux États-Unis, which in case you didn't notice, is French. Oh, also, it means "the French-est city in the United States."

After the Industrial Revolution, textile mills popped up in the area. Communities of immigrants formed around the mill, villages formed out of those communities, and Woonsocket grew out of those villages. The number of French-speaking immigrants was so overwhelming that most of the non-French immigrant workers who moved there ended up learning French.

And that's why Woonsocket is known for people saying things like "Drive slow your car" or "I'm taking a walk, me." Sadly, as the generations go by, this speech pattern is starting to disappear. While it used to be that everyone in the region talked like this, these days only the older residents of the city say things like "I live on top of my sister." Even though more than 46 percent of the population identified themselves as French or French-Canadian in the 2000 Census, the younger generation is now more likely to talk with common American slang than with the Woonsocket dialect of their grandparents. But many of the grandparents are still there, so if you visit Woonsocket, you're still likely to be able to hear the famous Woonsocket phraseology for another few years.

After all, it is la ville la plus française aux États-Unis (peut-être sauf Louisiana).

Measuring Up

When it comes to systems of measurements, Rhode Island shines. For decades, newscasters and reporters around the country have been using the RhodeIsland as a unit of measurement. When talking about a small foreign country, the anchor will explain that it's twice the size of Rhode Island. Martian craters being explored are reported to be forty-three times the size of Rhode Island. Comparing things to Rhode Island is simply the best way for our country to understand large areas. All that remains is for our government to admit that since we're not converting to metric, we need to adopt the RhodeIsland as an official unit of measurement.

In spite of the fact that this has yet to occur, Rhode Island continues to be used as the benchmark for large things across the globe. Meteorites, forest fires, newly discovered moon craters—all of them are dutifully reported in terms of their size relative to Rhode Island. An iceberg 1,500 square miles large is not something the world can understand. An iceberg the size of Rhode Island is. Even other states (such as Texas) are often described in terms of how many times the size of Rhode Island they are.

Some states may take pride in being many times larger than Rhode Island, but it should be obvious to any impartial observer that the state most revered is the one everyone else feels the need to compare themselves to.

Duel Purpose

These days, if two people have a dispute, they usually hire lawyers and settle it in court. Centuries ago, people would sometimes duel instead, which was a lot less messy. Duels started to fade in popularity in the 1800s, when most states passed laws against them. Basically, the laws stated that a duel still counted as murder if you killed the other person, with the result that even if you won, you lost. (See how lawyers make things messier?)

But while most other states in the area had anti-duel laws on the books, Rhode Island had no such regulations (just one more way that Rogue's Island earned its name). Interestingly, of the five duels ever recorded in the state of Rhode Island, not a single one of them involved an actual resident of the state. Rather, parties in contention from other states traveled to Rhode Island to settle their differences without being arrested.

Ironically, none of them would have been arrested for murder anyway, because nobody was ever killed. The first duel ever recorded in the state took place in March 1806. James Henderson Eliot believed that William Austin had written an article insulting his father. Both men traveled from Massachusetts to shoot it out, and Austin walked away wounded.

The last recorded duel in Rhode Island took place in October 1835 between two New Yorkers—a state much more well-known for angry people. And they had more reason than ever to be angry after the duel: Both walked away merely wounded. Eventually, Rhode Island would also ban dueling, and people would no more travel from out of state to attempt to kill each other.

Driving You Crazy

People in every state complain about the other drivers. In Rhode Island, however, our complaints have legitimacy: Rhode Island officially has the worst drivers in America. In 2005 GMAC Insurance took a nationwide survey to test drivers' knowledge of basic car safety and road rules. Out of fifty states, Rhode Island placed fiftieth. The average score for a Rhode Islander taking the test was 77 percent, only a few points above failure.

A fluke, you say? Well, a similar national survey was taken in 2006, and Rhode Island once again managed to place fiftieth, with an average score that had dropped to just over 75 percent. More than one-fourth of Rhode Islanders surveyed failed the test entirely.

Ship of Fools

Jamestown

Only a fool would attempt to build a ship out of half a car, a sofa, and a lot of underwear. And only a complete fool would attempt to sail such a boat in a race. No wonder, then, that the Jamestown Yacht Club's annual silly sailing event is called the Fools' Rules Regatta.

The rules are simple: build a ship, on the beach, constructed entirely out of things that aren't manufactured for marine use. Boats must be constructed from random items people might have in their homes, like beer cans, a bathtub, and a sail stitched together from burlap sacks. The vessels must be propelled entirely by wind. And whoever builds the boat is the crew.

People have tried to launch everything from water coolers to lawn chairs tied to balloons. Though the course is only 500 yards long, many of the craft don't make it. In addition to the winner, there are three special awards: the Most Ingenious Design award; the Worst Example of Naval Architecture award; and the Judges' Award, given to the boat and crew with the best overall theme, which usually involves costumes.

Building your own boat is just ducky.

The nonsense all starts at the Town Beach at East Ferry, Jamestown, where a cannon signals participants to begin building. Two hours later, the races begin. The event only occurs once a year, but it's definitely worth seeing. You'd be a fool to miss it. For more information visit the Jamestown Yacht Club Web site at www.jyc.org or call (401) 423–1492.

★ ★

Touro Touro Touro

Newport

When it comes to religion, Rhode Island has a history of being a bit offbeat. After all, the state was founded by Roger Williams when he was asked to leave the Puritan colony of Massachusetts. Thus he founded Rhode Island with a strong belief in separation of church and state. And while Rhode Island is the most Catholic state in America, it's also the home of Touro Synagogue, the country's oldest. And not just anywhere in Rhode Island, but in Newport, in a county with only a few hundred Jews. And if that still doesn't make Touro Synagogue seem unlikely enough, then consider that Touro is a Sephardic synagogue despite the fact that most of the members are Ashkenazi (European descent).

God's original residence. Well, one of them.

It began in 1658 when a few Jewish families came to Newport and founded a congregation named Yeshuat Israel (literally "Salvation of Israel"). The building has been on the same spot ever since, but it wasn't until Isaac Touro came to Newport from Amsterdam to serve as the congregation's cantor and rabbi that the synagogue was dedicated—in December 1763.

Touro Synagogue was captured by the British in 1776 and used as a hospital, which prevented it from being burned. Still, the most famous thing about Touro is probably its letter from George Washington. In 1790 Moses Seixas, warden of Yeshuat Israel, wrote to George Washington to confirm that the new government would allow the Jews their freedom of religion. Seixas wrote to say he saw the government as "one which to bigotry gives no sanction, to persecution no assistance," and blessed Washington.

Washington wrote back with his own blessings, and confirmed that his government would guarantee religious freedom by repeating Seixas's own words: "Happily the Government of the United States, which gives to bigotry no sanction, to persecution no assistance requires only that they who live under its protection should demean themselves as good citizens, in giving it on all occasions their effectual support."

If you would like more information, you can contact the Touro Synagogue Foundation at (401) 847–4794 or visit www.tourosynagogue.org.

That's Your Theory

Newport

The Old Stone Mill is definitely one of Rhode Island's great historical buildings. Known as the Viking Stone Mill or Norse Tower, this giant cylindrical stone building stands in Newport's Touro Park. The tower is 24 feet high, with arches on the bottom and square holes on the top. The construction has largely withstood the test of time, and the tower is a beautiful sight to behold, clearly a relic of a previous age. The thing is, nobody knows what age it comes from or who built it.

Some say the tower was built by Vikings a millennium ago. And there is some evidence to suggest that the tower may have been a Viking church. Not only does the shape of the building itself resemble the early church buildings in Scandinavia, but the Viking Stone Mill also happens to be perfectly oriented to the points of the compass, as were all Scandinavian churches at that time.

Then again, it could have been built by Governor Benedict Arnold, the great-grandfather of the more infamous Benedict Arnold, who left a will upon his death in 1677 that referred to a "stone built windmill," which he is said to have constructed. And the Old Stone Mill does resemble the mills of England, where Arnold was born. In 1848 the mortar of various city buildings, including Governor Arnold's tomb and a stone house on Spring Street dating from 1639, were compared to mortar from the tower and found to be "identical in quality and character."

The Old Stone Mill: We're not sure how it got there, but we're glad to have it just the same.

★ ★

Viking-theory supporters insist that while Governor Arnold may have converted this building into a windmill, it was still initially constructed by the Vikings in their colony called "Vinland." After all, why else would Longfellow have written a poem ("The Skeleton in Armor") about a Viking who sailed to Vinland to build a stone tower for his beloved? Unfortunately, the Viking theory has lost some credence since carbon-14 dating samples have pegged the mortar as no older than the fifteenth century.

Today, the reigning theory is that of the colonials. An archaeological dig uncovered grinding stones that supported the gristmill theory, as well as a footprint that seems to have been made by a colonial shoe. For this reason, the plaque now at the tower reads as follows: OLD STONE MILL / BUILT PROBABLY ABOUT 1660 / BY BENEDICT ARNOLD / FIRST GOVERNOR OF RHODE ISLAND / UNDER THE CHARTER OF 1643 / REFERRED TO IN HIS WILL AS / "MY STONE BUILT WINDMILL" / LEGEND ASCRIBED ITS ERECTION TO THE / NORSEMEN DURING THEIR SUPPOSED / VISIT ABOUT 1000 A.D.

Touro Park is on Bellvue Avenue in the center of Newport.

Old-Style Tavern

Newport

If you're looking for a good old tavern, you won't find one gooder or older than the White Horse Tavern in Newport. It opened back in 1687 and is believed to be the oldest operating tavern in the country. It began as the meeting place for the colony's general assembly and city council, because even in the seventeenth century, politicians wanted good food that they could charge to the public. Aside from good food, the tavern was known for being owned by William Mayes, the famous pirate. His father owned the tavern before him, but it was the young Mayes who got the liquor license in 1702.

A few decades later, Jonathan Nichols took over as innkeeper and named the tavern the White Horse. It was converted to a boardinghouse in 1901, but the Preservation Society of Newport County acquired it in 1954, restored it and opened it as a restaurant, which it is to this day.

★ ★

The White Horse Tavern can be found at 26 Marlborough Street in Newport. Call (401) 849–3600 or visit www.whitehorsetavern.com for more information.

A Beacon of History

Block Island

No, it's not part of New York. Block Island is part of Rhode Island, and is surrounded by dangerous shoals. How dangerous? Well, dangerous enough to cause so many shipwrecks that in the nineteenth century, people called it the "stumbling block" of the coast. Clearly, a lighthouse was necessary, and after the northern lighthouse was built in 1829, a federal Grant built the Southeast Light in 1875. And by federal Grant, we're talking about President Ulysses S., who signed the order to build the lighthouse, which, at the time, contained the most powerful lens available: a first-order Fresnel lens costing $10,000 (that's 200 bills with Grant's picture on them). This was tacked on to a 52-foot-high Victorian Gothic station to become the tallest light on the New England coast. Grant himself even came down to visit.

In 1928 the station was electrified. Ten years later it was temporarily un-electrified when a big hurricane took its toll on the lighthouse. In addition to the destruction of the oil house, radio beacon, and numerous windows, all the power went out. But with such dangerous shoals off the coast, the Southeast Light could not rest, so the lighthouse keepers turned the lens by hand until power could be restored.

When the lighthouse was built in 1875, it was a full 300 feet away from the Mohegan Bluffs. But by 1990 the lighthouse was only 55 feet from the edge of the ever-eroding bluff, and the Coast Guard decided to deactivate it and replace it with a steel tower and automated signal beacon. But the historic lighthouse had its fans, who couldn't bear to see it destroyed. A group of volunteers called the Block Island Southeast Lighthouse Foundation raised $2 million to pay for the lighthouse to be relocated 300 feet from the new edge of the cliffs.

In 1993 it was time to move the lighthouse. The Army Corps of Engineers used thirty-eight hydraulic lifts and countless tons of steel rails and cable, and within a few months actually managed to move the lighthouse to a new location 300 feet from the edge of the cliff. The Southeast Light was reactivated a year later.

To get more information about tours, or chat about the glory of Fresnel lenses, call the Block Island Southeast Lighthouse Foundation at (401) 466–5009. You can also visit the Web site at www.lighthouse.cc/blockisoutheast.

Good Old-Fashioned Powwow
Charlestown

The Narragansett Indians know how to party. And they know how to have a meeting. The secret to both? Doing them at once. The Narragansett Annual Meeting, aka the Narragansett Powwow, has been running annually for more than 330 years and is the oldest powwow in the country. The word powwow itself derived from the Narragansett powwaw, which means "spiritual leader." Nowadays a powwow describes any of the big meetings that Native American tribes might have, when they join together for traditional singing and dancing. Powwows generally start with a grand entry, where everyone in the ceremony files in before they get down to singing and dancing.

The annual Narragansett Powwow has a bit of serious business, like the song of honor, the cleansing of the circle, presentation of the peace pipe, and prayer. After that, there's some serious fun in the form of traditional singing and dancing, which, though entertaining, is taken quite seriously. And then there's the fun fun, with children dancing, food, and vendors of all sorts of traditional Native American crafts. For more information visit www.narragansett-tribe.org.

Have Mercy!
Exeter

If one of your family members was sick with tuberculosis, what would you think is the most likely cause? If you answered, "A vampiric other family member returning from the dead to drain their lifeforce," then

★ ★

you got the same answer that George T. Brown came up with in the
1890s. His wife, Mary, died in 1883 and his eldest daughter, Mary
Olive, died a few years later. In 1892 his other daughter, Mercy, died
and his son, Edwin, became sick. George T. Brown, as any good father
would, wanted to find a cure.

The grave of Mercy Brown, vampire.
Hopefully she's dead . . .

Medical science in the 1890s wasn't quite as advanced as it is today,
and superstition reigned supreme. George believed one of his dead
family members was returning as a vampire to cause Edwin's illness,
and got people to help him exhume the bodies of his family for examination. Sure enough, Mercy's body was not nearly as decomposed as

that of her mother or sister, which was clearly because she was a vampire and not at all related to the fact that she had only been dead a few months instead of four years. Her chest was cut open and liquid blood was found in her heart, which was taken as the final proof needed that Mercy Brown was a vampire and the cause of the tuberculosis—not only in Edwin, but in other sick people in the community as well.

Naturally, once you've found the heart of a tuberculosis-causing vampire, you have to burn it. The *Providence Journal,* a very forward-thinking newspaper, had an editorial at the time condemning the practice of exhuming bodies to burn their hearts. But George was undeterred, and after burning Mercy's heart, mixed the ashes with water to make a drink for Edwin. Nineteenth-century lore said that drinking the vampire's heart would remove the curse. Modern science says eating dead people isn't too healthy, and indeed Edwin died soon after.

Nonetheless, Mercy Brown remains as one of the most famous non-Transylvanian vampires ever. Her gravestone is in the Chestnut Hill Cemetery behind the Chestnut Hill Baptist Church on Route 102 in Exeter.

Some say that Mercy Brown still walks through the graveyard—watching, waiting, and sometimes whispering or whimpering. Also watching and waiting is Mercy's descendent Lewis Peck, especially around Halloween, to deter anyone who would vandalize the grave site. So between the vampire ghost and the vampire heir, we recommend that if you do visit the grave of Mercy Brown, be respectful. Nobody wants an angry vampire.

Build and Sting
North Kingstown

The Seabees are the U.S. Navy's construction battalion, and the two things they're good at are building and fighting. Originally, the navy used soldiers for fighting and civilians to build things, such as bases on various Pacific Islands. But since things were being built in the middle of a war, civilian construction crews could find themselves in a tight spot. International law declared that civilians couldn't be armed and resist enemy forces, or they could be executed as guerrillas. So the construction crew building the base on Wake Island had no protection when the Japanese came and killed some of them and took the rest of them prisoner, forcing them into years of labor and eventually executing them anyway.

This brought home the idea that Americans building bases needed to be in the military. And so in January 1942 the First Construction Detachment left from Quonset Point in Rhode Island. Once it had gathered nearly 300 men from a few other locations, it was deployed to build a fuel tank farm in Bora Bora. In September of that year, the Seabees went to Guadalcanal for their first work in a combat zone, building an airfield under heavy fire from both the Japanese and the horrible weather. After that the Seabees were at the forefront of every island invasion, paving the way for the troops that would follow. The secret of their success? Experience. While most soldiers were young men barely out of their teens, the average Seabee age was thirty-seven at the time the unit was founded. These were men with experience, who had all chosen to leave their careers voluntarily to fight, and build, for their country.

And what could better represent this than a big statue of an angry bee wielding tools and a machine gun? At the Quonset Point Naval Base where the Seabees were born worked a man named Frank J. Iafrate, who would draw sketches of the officers who came to his office to study construction designs. One of those officers was assigned to the First Construction Detachment and asked Iafrate to draw a cartoony insignia that could represent the unit. Iafrate's first thought was the beaver, but some quick research showed that beavers turn tail and run when confronted with danger. Iafrate settled on the bee, who works diligently until you interrupt his work, at which point he stings you until you learn to leave him alone. As an added bonus, construction battalion is abbreviated as CB, pronounced sea bee. Get it?

Thus, the Seabee was born, and on March 5, 1942, the construction battalion was officially given the name Seabees, and the bee insignia was approved. And Rhode Island is where they were born. And thus Iafrate built the Seabee statue that stands in front of the Seabee Museum, at the site of the former U.S. Naval Construction Battalion Center.

The Fighting Seabees. You can forget about getting any honey.

In spite of their dangerous work, most people wouldn't have heard of them if not for John Wayne's 1944 movie, *The Fighting Seabees*. The movie created good buzz about the Seabees, which is good, because it took the sting out of being mostly underappreciated before then. Meanwhile, if you want to see a giant bee with a machine gun and construction tools, then just drive on down to the Seabee Museum (401–294–7233) at 21 Iafrate Way in Davisville, North Kingstown.

★ ★

Job of the Hut

North Kingstown

Back in World War II, the navy needed a cheap, lightweight, and portable shelter that was easy to transport and assemble. So their Bureau of Yards and Docks turned to the George A. Fuller construction company in New York, with a request for an incredibly quick turnaround time: The shelters had to be designed and readied for production and manufactured all within a month. These bizarre little structures are now known as Quonset huts, because they were invented at Quonset Point in North Kingstown back in 1941.

The Quonset hut may not be pretty, but it helped us win the war.

The Quonset hut is thought by many to be a Native American invention, which isn't quite true, at least not directly. The name sounds Native American, because Quonset is an Algonquian word, and the huts themselves bear a more-than-passing resemblance to Iroquois longhouses that were used as council lodges.

However, the main basis for the Quonset hut was the British Nissen hut from the First World War. The key difference between the Nissen hut and the Quonset hut is the arched design of the Quonset, which offers not only less wasted space, but more structural strength. These monsters of corrugated sheet metal were commonly 20 feet wide and 48 feet long, weighing six tons. And an eight-man crew could assemble one the same day it arrived. This allowed the soldiers to build operational bases much faster than was previously possible, which was essential for fighting World War II. I mean, if it wasn't essential, they wouldn't have built more than 150,000 of them. Seriously. There were a few 40-by-100-foot giant Quonset huts used as warehouses, but the bulk were 20-by-48-foot.

After the war, most of the Quonset huts were sold to the public as surplus for $1,000 apiece. During a time when housing was at a premium, a 20-by-48-foot shelter for a thousand bucks was a pretty good deal. Many universities used Quonset huts to help with housing shortages. Naturally, farmers found them useful, and pretty soon Quonset huts were in use everywhere across America.

Steam Room
East Greenwich

Bob Merriam comes from a family that knows about New England's industrial past. Like his father before him, Bob went to Harvard's engineering school and worked as an engineer. He taught engineering at Swarthmore, and everybody in his family loves industrial history. Bob felt Rhode Island's industrial history was being ignored, so with the help of some like-minded friends and a little engine-uity, he started the New England Wireless and Steam Museum to preserve and honor the engineering achievements of the past.

Now more than forty years later, the East Greenwich museum has five buildings, including a classic New England meeting hall and the world's oldest surviving radio station. Walter Massie of Providence built this wireless radio station for Point Judith back in 1907. In 1912 a judge declared that Guglielmo Marconi (who, coincidentally, was born the same year as Massie) had the patent, so Massie's station was declared illegal. It was later slated to be torn down, but the owner donated the building, and Massie's son donated his father's equipment. Thus the wireless radio station now survives, and is on the National Register of Historic Places.

Of course, there are plenty of steam engines here as well: engines made by Armington & Sims, a Providence manufacturer that made the engines used by Thomas Edison; Hartford, Connecticut's original generator from 1883, which still works so well that Bob can disconnect the museum from the national power grid and light the whole building with it.

The operation is run by volunteers, so don't drop by without calling to schedule an appointment: (401) 885–0545. If you really love steam engines, you'll want to attend their annual Great Yankee Steam-Up. Details can be found at http://newsm.org.

Thomas Edison used just such an engine. Bright idea.

Anchors Away

Most children who grew up in East Greenwich the past thirty years have climbed atop the mighty anchor in the middle of Academy Field at 111 Pierce Street. But few of them know where it came from—we didn't, and we'd been sitting atop that anchor for years.

The anchor was loaned to East Greenwich by the federal government in 1977 to celebrate the 300th anniversary of the town's founding in 1677. Why just a loan? Well, the government may one day decide they want it back, so the loan is renewed every ten years. Meanwhile, it serves as a perfect symbol of the town and state. Not only is the anchor featured on the state flag, but on the East Greenwich coat of arms as well. So until the government becomes stern and ships off our anchor, it remains used for sea voyages of the imaginary kind.

When you're young, it looks like a giant metal goose. Honestly.

The Pipes, the Pipes Are Calling

Warwick

Imagine you hear spooky noises coming from the pipes in your house late one night, noises so scary and ghostlike that you aren't sure whether to call a plumber or some paranormal investigators. Luckily, if you call Grant Wilson and Jason Hawes, you get both. Jason and Grant have been plumbers in Warwick for many years, but they also founded The Atlantic Paranormal Society (TAPS) to investigate supernatural disturbances. Haven't heard of TAPS? Well, perhaps you know them as the Ghost Hunters.

Yes, those Ghost Hunters, the ones with a show on the Sci-Fi Channel. They're more famous now that they have a TV show, but they haven't given up plumbing. Though flush with success, they're level-headed enough to know that TV celebrity can quickly vanish down the toilet, whereas plumbing is a job that Jason calls "recession-proof."

Other believers soon joined, and TAPS continued to grow. Jason and Grant have acquired a lot of fancy equipment over the years, from infrared cameras to EMF meters, which they use to detect and document evidence of the paranormal. They tend to investigate at night because spirits that emit light or sound are easier to detect at night, because most reports of supernatural activity occur at night, but mainly because during the day they're fixing pipes.

They now have TAPS branches across the country, and their show is watched by nearly two million people. If you have supernatural problems, visit their Web site at www.the-atlantic-paranormal-society.com.

The Great Gaspee
Warwick

Everybody's heard of the Boston Tea Party. But when it comes to really sticking it to the British, Rhode Island did it first and better.

In June 1772 Captain Lindsey was taking the sloop *Hannah* from Newport to Providence. To stop smuggling (which included at least half of the ships in Rhode Island at the time), the area was patrolled by the HMS *Gaspee*, commanded by a Lieutenant Dudingston. The *Gaspee* chased Captain Lindsey, who lured the *Gaspee* into shallows near Warwick where it ran aground. With the *Gaspee* stuck on a sandbar, Lindsey went to tell the good news to John Brown, who sent Abraham Whipple to capture the ship.

While Whipple's men tried to board the *Gaspee*, Dudington resisted and was shot and killed by a man named Joseph Bucklin. This was the first British casualty by firearm in the American Revolution. Having shot the commander, the Rhode Islanders set fire to the ship. King George offered a hefty reward for the guilty parties, but a plague of amnesia seemed to come over all Rhode Island.

As stones of memoriam go, we're actually not too sad that the *Gaspee* is gone.

Because many had forgotten, the Gaspee Days Committee was formed in 1965. Gaspee Days are celebrated each June to commemorate the real start of the Revolution. With colonial costumes, food, and even a reenactment of the boat-burning itself, Gaspee Days are much more fun than some tea party. Visit www.gaspee.com or call (401) 781–1772 if you have a burning desire for more details.

6

Vermont Curiosities

In and around the Arctic Circle, a condition called "permafrost" causes a mixture of underground moisture and soil to freeze into a concrete-like mass—sturdy enough (until recently, anyway) to support highways and three-story buildings, winter and summer, year after year. In Vermont, a bit south and slightly milder, we're lucky enough not to have such a climate. Instead, dozens of microclimates produce a winter moisture and soil combination that freezes much more randomly, causing sharp upthrusts particularly noticeable on secondary roads. Motorists quickly adapt, however, especially when alerted by road signs reading frost heaves ahead!

This brings us to Vermont's only professional basketball team: Here's to the Frost Heaves! Any state serious enough of purpose to name an athletic team in honor of indigenous geological phenomena rather than mammals of prey earns points for originality. The team's tag line challenges upcoming opponents by evoking the origins of its name: "We're gonna be the bump in their road."

Vermont was born original. Pressured by New Hampshire to the east, by New York to the west, and by Massachusetts to the south to give up more and more land as colonies were being formed back in the 1700s, it declined membership as one of the first thirteen United States, deciding instead to go its own way as a sovereign nation. It finally joined the union in 1791, under more favorable terms.

* *

Fifty years later, Rev. (and historian) Hosea Beckley noted in The History of Vermont *that Vermonters "are not ashamed to be seen going to Boston in caps made of their own mountain fur; in striped woolens manufactured within their own dwellings; in vehicles constructed by themselves; and drawn by horses of their own raising." Residents today who come from Vermont families going back five, six, and seven generations are known for this same iconoclastic spirit. Newcomers who see something about the state and its people that makes them want to live here too, soon adapt to it—either totally or partially. Those who don't adapt usually don't stay. (Total disclosure: I'm in my second decade as a Vermonter, meaning that I'll never shed the label "Flatlander," which adheres to all inhabitants who don't yet have four generations of ancestors "in the ground." My wife, born in Alaska, at least has a face-saving comeback. I grew up in Illinois, where the highest point in my former county is Bald Mound, at 739 feet. Not much I can do about it now.)*

The Trail That Inspired the Appalachian Trail

If you want to get a feel for Vermont's geography, geology, topography, flora, and fauna, here's a walk you might consider. The downside is that you'll need to set aside four to six weeks to complete it, if you want to earn "end-to-ender" status. This is the Long Trail, which follows the spine of the Green Mountains for 272 miles, from Massachusetts to Quebec.

But let's say you don't have six weeks, or need more information before you make a commitment. The Green Mountain Club, which protects and maintains the trail, has created a way to test-drive the Long Trail and learn more about the experience. Visit its headquarters, talk to staff members, look over the trail guides and maps, and conquer the Short Trail, a half-mile loop and microcosm of the total experience. Now you're ready for any number of day hikes, as well.

The Long Trail shares a route with the younger Appalachian Trail until the two part company just north of Sherburne Center, about 100 miles north of the Massachusetts border.

This "footpath in the wilderness" occurred to Vermont outdoorsman James P. Taylor nearly a century ago as he waited for the fog to lift during a hike on Stratton Mountain. To get things moving Taylor, assistant headmaster of Vermont Academy, founded the Green Mountain Club (GMC) in 1910 and was its first president. Over the next twenty years, a 272-mile path was cleared, hitting just about every summit along the way, from Consultation Peak near the Massachusetts border to Mount Carleton, just south of the Canadian border. Today seventy huts and shelters 8 to 10 miles apart provide overnight cover and a dry place to prepare meals.

During its history the GMC has vigorously worked to preserve the wilderness character of the Long Trail. When a scenic highway the

Vermont Weather Extremes

The coldest temperature ever recorded in Vermont was 50 degrees below zero Fahrenheit in Bloomfield, Essex County, on December 30, 1933. The warmest was 105 degrees Fahrenheit in Vernon in the southeast corner of the state, on July 4, 1911. The greatest amount of snow from a single storm—50 inches in three days—fell on Readsboro in Bennington County on March 2–5, 1947. The greatest snowfall total for a single season was 318.6 inches (26½ feet) in 1970–71.

Trivia

Vermont—Most Rural State in the Nation

The definition of "rural" depends upon the number of people who reside in places with fewer than 2,500 people. Because most of the 255 cities, towns, and gores in which Vermonters live have fewer than 2,500 residents, the state is by definition rural. Services and elected officials usually follow these local boundaries. Unlike most states, in which counties are the unit used to determine rural and urban populations, Vermont's fourteen counties are organized only to provide law enforcement and judicial services. No other governmental services exist at the county level.

length of the Green Mountain Range was proposed in the mid 1930s, the club mounted a spirited enough opposition to cause its rejection in a statewide referendum. A planned missile communications facility on Mount Mansfield in 1958 met the same fate. The GMC has conserved more than 25,000 acres of Long Trail lands, many of which have been added to Vermont's state forests. More than 800 volunteers aid GMC staffers in keeping an eye on trails and making repairs when needed.

The club is about 4 miles south of Stowe on the west side of Route 100. Take the next right entrance at the sign for the 1836 Cabins and Evergreen Gardens just before the GMC office. Hours vary by season. No admission charged. For more information visit www.greenmountainclub.org or call (802) 244–7037.

What's a Petroglyph, You Ask?
Bellows Falls

Walking east for about 30 feet on the south side of Bellows Falls' Vilas Bridge, you'll see, just above the waterline, two fading yellow paint stripes about 10 feet apart, each indicating the location of eight to twelve faces carved into the rock. Depending on which researcher you talk to they are thought to be prehistoric Indian carvings 2,000 or more years old, or only 300 years old but possibly commemorating a battle with settlers in the early 1700s.

Spotting the petroglyphs is not easy. The view from Vilas Bridge is preferable to following the sign on the north side of Bridge Street, which directs viewers down an abandoned railroad spur on the south side of the street. Needless to say, wearing high heels or sandals could be hazardous to your health.

If you are driving north on U.S. Route 5, turn right on Westminster Street, and right again 2 blocks farther on Bridge Street. Park in one of the spaces in front of the Bellows Falls Post Office. Or drive east another 100 yards, turning right into the abandoned railroad spur opposite the Indian Carvings sign. Note: The carvings are often under-water during spring runoff in March and April.

A Relic in Its Own Right

Bellows Falls

The Miss Bellows Falls Diner, built in the late 1920s by the Worcester Lunch Car Company, is Vermont's only surviving barrel-roofed diner. The restaurant, moved to Bellows Falls from Massachusetts in 1942, features porcelain panels and railroad-style windows on its exterior and its original marble counter, tile floor, and oak and chrome highlights.

Miss Bellows Falls Diner is on Westminster Street. Going north, it's on the left 1 block beyond the clock tower. (Breakfast is excellent. I hear lunch isn't bad, either.) For more information visit the Web site at www.missbellowsfallsdiner.com.

Listed in the National Registry of Historic Places, the Miss Bellows Falls Diner in a former life was called Frankie and Johnny's.

★ ★

Hetty Green, Richest Woman in the World
Bellows Falls

Adjusted for twenty-first-century dollars, Hetty Green is the richest American woman in history. Her fortune when she died in 1916 was estimated at $100 million, which in today's dollars is more than $2.5 billion—more than Oprah. Yet Hetty is remembered more for her eccentricities than for her millions.

Hetty Green's tough negotiating tactics earned her the nickname "Witch of Wall Street." They also made her the richest woman in the world.

Hetty Howland Robinson was born in New Bedford, Massachusetts, in 1834. Her father and grandfather owned a large whaling fleet. At age six she could read the day's financial papers; at eight she opened her first savings account. When her father died, he left Hetty $7.5 million, much of which she invested in railroads and real estate.

In her early thirties Hetty met and married Edward Green, a wealthy silk and tea trader who had spent twenty years in the Orient. They had two children, Ned and Sylvia, and moved to Edward's family home in Bellows Falls. Hetty did not change the penny-pinching ways she developed as a child: She walked blocks to buy broken cookies in bulk, returned her berry boxes for a nickel, and once spent hours looking for a two-cent stamp. Though most of her eccentric behavior was viewed as harmless, she once refused to pay a doctor to treat Ned's knee, dislocated in a sledding accident with the damage exacerbated a year later when he was hit by a wagon pulled by a Saint Bernard. When treatment at free clinics failed, Ned's leg was amputated.

Hetty and Edward divorced after Edward's business investments went sour. When Hetty Green died at age eight-one, she left her entire estate to her two children. Sylvia gave the rundown Green family home to the town of Bellows Falls. The site, at the corner of Westminster and Church Streets, is now occupied by a bank, a municipal parking lot, and Hetty Green Park.

Directly across School Street from Hetty Green Park is Immanuel Episcopal Church and its adjacent cemetery at the end of Church Street, where Hetty and other members of her family are buried. Her 8-foot-high obelisk monument is in the lower cemetery just off the sidewalk, between two tall trees and halfway from either entrance.

First Canal in the United States
Bellows Falls

The Erie Canal is the best known, but the first canal system that realized the dream of mass transportation of goods easily within the continent began in Vermont. The Erie Canal was opened in 1825 and was called the engineering marvel of the nineteenth century. But if you go into Bellows Falls, you'll see the plaque that appears above a bridge over the first canal, designed and built by Samuel Morey, of Fairlee.

★ ★

"BELLOWS FALLS CANAL

HERE FIRST CANAL IN UNITED STATES WAS BUILT IN 1802.
THE BRITISH-OWNED COMPANY WHICH WAS CHARTERED TO
RENDER THE CONNECTICUT RIVER NAVIGABLE HERE IN 1791
WAS TEN YEARS BUILDING THE NINE LOCKS AND DAM
AROUND THE GREAT FALLS, 52-FEET HIGH."

In the early 1800s, boats loaded with lumber
and produce avoided the Connecticut River's
52-foot-deep gorge by passing through eight
locks on the Bellows Falls Canal.

After the first railroad came through Bellows Falls in 1849, river
traffic declined sharply, and the canal has been used ever since for
water power only. More than 200 years later, the canal is chugging
away, although it is somewhat deeper and wider.

The Bellows Falls Canal plaque is near the bridge on Bridge Street,
100 yards or so west of the directional sign for the Indian Carvings.

★ ★

Fort Dummer, Vermont's First Nontribal Settlement

Brattleboro

After crossing the Vermont-Massachusetts border from the south on Interstate 91, your first landmark, up on the right, will be the entrance to Fort Dummer State Park. These days, Vermont residents have little need for a fort to protect their turf.

Back in the eighteenth century, though, matters were a bit more serious. Fort Dummer was built in 1724 along the banks of the Connecticut River to protect what was then a Massachusetts colony from invasions by the French and Indians. The Salmon Hole Massacre of 1748, for example, was one of hundreds of skirmishes that took place during King George's War, from 1744–48.

Early one May morning, eighty soldiers led by Captain Eleazer Melvin, of Northfield, Massachusetts, were three weeks into a scouting expedition from Fort Dummer. They stopped at the headwaters of the West River, in Londonderry, believing they had outrun their French and Indian pursuers. Stripping off their packs, they stopped to rest a bit and shoot a few salmon for breakfast. Two French soldiers and nine Indians who had been close behind them heard the shots and quickly located their adversaries. They opened fire from behind logs and trees, killing six soldiers. While killing but six of a group of eighty stretches the definition of massacre a bit, you must admit that a confrontation named the "Salmon Hole Massacre" sure has an intriguing ring to it.

Trivia

The 162,000 cows living on Vermont farms are said to produce more than 2.6 billion pounds of milk a year—or more than 16,000 pounds per cow. We'll do the math: That's forty-four pounds per cow per day.

Today's park overlooks the site of Fort Dummer, which was flooded when the Vernon Dam was built in 1908. The fort is now underwater, near a lumber company on the Vermont side of the river. The campground, located in the southern foothills of the Green Mountains, includes fifty-one tent/trailer sites and ten lean-to sites along with hot showers but no trailer hookups. Also in the park are a picnic area and hiking trails.

From I-91, take exit 1. Go 1/10 mile north on U.S. Route 5A, and then go ½ mile east on Fairground Road, and finally 1 mile south on Main Street and Old Guilford Road. For more information visit www.vtstateparks.com/htm/fortdummer.cfm.

Indian British Yankee Go Home!
Dummerston

In 1892, at the age of twenty-seven, poet and novelist Rudyard Kipling married an American girl and moved from London to Dummerston, just north of Brattleboro. Kipling was internationally famous when he married Caroline Balestier, whose recently deceased brother had been Kipling's good friend. The couple built a grand house with a distant view of New Hampshire's Mount Monadnock, near Carrie's parents' home. Kipling, who was a British subject born in India, named his new home Naulakha, Hindi for "precious jewel."

In just a few months, Kipling began receiving more mail in Dummerston than the largest business in nearby Brattleboro. U.S. Postmaster General Wilson authorized a special post office (to this day, it is said, the only one ever created for an individual) to handle the author's letters and packages. "Waite, Vermont" was located in the home of Kipling's neighbor, Anna Waite, who was also appointed postmaster. The Waite postmark has been prized by philatelists for more than a century.

Kipling loved his time in Vermont, and at Naulakha over the next four years, he wrote the *Jungle Book* and *Captains Courageous* and began work on *Kim* and the *Just So Stories*.

Eventually, Kipling's dream life became a nightmare. Carrie had a serious falling-out with her other brother, Beatty, who was described

★ ★

variously as a "feckless alcoholic" and unmatched in "sheer boorish-ness." A lurid lawsuit, trial, and much negative publicity followed the muscular Beatty's threat to "kick the god-damned soul" out of the much smaller and slightly built Kipling. After four years in America, the Kipling family returned to England.

Back home Kipling told his friends: "There are only two places in the world where I want to live—Bombay and Brattleboro. And I can't live in either."

Rudyard Kipling named his house in Vermont "Naulakha," from the title of a book he wrote with American friend Wolcott Balestier—whose sister he later married.

Naulakha was the Landmark Trust's first property in North America, which means you and up to seven other Kipling fans can rent it and stay where the great author himself once lived. Up to eight guests may stay at Naulakha, which includes four bedrooms (three twin, one double); three bathrooms; full kitchen; washer, dryer, and dishwasher. Dogs are allowed. Until recently, all bookings had to be made through the Office of the Landmark Trust in England: Shottesbrooke, Maidenhead, Berkshire SL6 3SW, United Kingdom, tel. 011 44 1628 825925; fax. 011 44 1628 825417. Now, however, you can save the overseas call and reach the Landmark Trust USA office at (802) 254–6868.

The Kipling home is located north of Brattleboro, off I-91 at exit 3. Turn south on U.S. Route 5 at the traffic circle, right on Black Mountain Road, and right again to 707 Kipling Road. Visit www.landmark trustusa.org/index.html for more information about renting Naulakha and also about the history and renovation of the home.

Taste Delights from a School Bus in a Meadow
Putney

If you drive into Curtis's Barbecue most any day between 10 a.m. and dusk, look to the right. You'll see smoke curling above a meat pit as rows of rising gray beams meet the sunshine. Right away you know

Just out of sight beyond the bus (right) is the grill tended by Curtis, where seven days a week, seven months a year, he works to justify his "Ninth Wonder of the World" renown.

Birth of Snow-boarding

Most people agree that the sport of snow-boarding began in the eastern half of the United States, specifically in Vermont. There are claims from the Mount Baker area of Washington, and even from Breckenridge, Massachusetts, but Stratton Mountain near Bondville gets most of the votes. Stratton Mountain has been home to the U.S. Open Snowboarding Championships for more than twenty years and opened its lifts and trails to snowboarding in 1983.

When snowboarding pioneer Bud Keene was asked by Vermont Sports Online why Vermont has produced so many outstanding snowboarders, he said: "There are more halfpipes along Route 100 than in most other places in the U.S. And then there's the eastern mindset—riding in bad weather, in adverse conditions, riding on ice. . . . Tradition also plays a role. This is the birth of snowboarding and it makes for a small ecosystem back here."

Stratton Mountain Resort is located on the highest peak in southern Vermont, 20 miles from Manchester. It is the largest resort in the region. If you visit, a twelve-passenger gondola will take you from the resort to the peak of 3,936-foot Stratton Mountain.

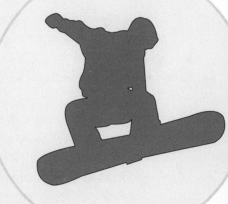

From 1-91, take exit 2, and then on Route 30 drive approximately 30 miles north to Bondville. Stratton Mountain Resort is 4 miles from Bondville. For more information visit www.stratton.com, or call (800) 787–2886.

★ ★

Moonlight in Vermont

The classic and haunting ballad "Moonlight in Vermont" was written by two non-Vermonters. John Blackburn, who wrote the lyrics, taught drama for two years at Bennington College. He teamed with composer Karl Suessdorf when both worked in Los Angeles during World War II.

Composer Johnny Mercer liked the melody and brought it to vocalist Margaret Whiting in 1945. It created little splash, but when Whiting rerecorded the song ten years later, it made the top ten. It was subsequently recorded by such artists as Frank Sinatra, Ella Fitzgerald, Billie Holliday, Ray Charles, and Willie Nelson. In 1985 Vermont's legislature decreed a "Moonlight in Vermont Day," and Whiting made her first trip to the state to sing the song before a joint session of the legislature.

In the late 1990s this same legislature rejected "Moonlight in Vermont" as the official state song, partly, it was said, because it was too difficult for the average person to sing.

something special is afoot. The entrance sign reads: ninth wonder of the world. That sounds about right.

With a long-handled fork, Curtis Tuff deftly moves five-pound slabs of pork ribs and half chickens to warmer or cooler spots on his 5-foot-by-10-foot grill, depending on their degree of doneness. Behind Curtis in this three-acre meadow are two blue school buses where orders are filled, including side dishes such as baked potatoes, coleslaw, corn on the cob, and baked beans. Says *Gourmet* magazine's roadside reporter Michael Stern: "The ribs are cooked so the meat pulls off in big, succulent strips that virtually burst with piggy flavor and the perfume of smoke." Both spicy and mild homemade sauces are at the ready.

In a state better known for cheese and maple syrup, ribs are the last food you'd expect. Yet Curtis has been at this site since 1968, going through twenty-one cords of hardwood or more every season (at least five of which he splits himself). He put two daughters through Vermont Academy and Mount Ida College, one of whom, with her husband, recently opened a branch restaurant in Chester, Vermont.

From I-91, take exit 4 and go north on U.S. Route 5 for less than half a mile. Curtis's Barbecue is on the right, just before the service station. Curtis's is open April through October, Thursday–Sunday, 10:00 a.m. to dusk. For more information visit www.curtisbbqvt.com or call (802) 387–5474.

The Grandma Moses Museum Heist

Bennington

Here's how it went down: Anna Mary Robertson Moses began to paint seriously at age seventy-six, and in 1939 a New York art collector saw samples of her work displayed in a Hoosick Falls, New York, drugstore, 5 miles from her home in Eagle Bridge. This led to a one-woman show in 1940 and established Grandma Moses, as she was called, as a fixture in the history of American art.

Margaret Carr and Ruth Garner, sisters who ran a florist shop in Rose Valley, Pennsylvania, just outside Philadelphia, met Grandma Moses in 1952. Over the next few years, they paid her several visits, usually buying one or more paintings, either by the artist or her son, Forrest King Moses. Eventually they became friends, talking by phone twice a year, sending gifts, and occasionally visiting Grandma Moses at her home in Eagle Bridge, where she occasionally gave them a painting they admired.

On December 13, 1961, Grandma Moses died at the age of 101. She left her sister-friends a sofa and other memorabilia to commemorate their friendship. When Margaret Carr died in 1984, she bequeathed seven of the artist's paintings to the Bennington Museum, plus the sofa, letters, clippings, and other gifts they had received over the years.

In 1972, the New York schoolhouse attended by Grandma Moses was moved to the Bennington Museum. It explores her work.

Mrs. Carr had made meticulous arrangements to ship the paintings and other materials to the museum. The shipment never arrived. At different times investigators from the Pennsylvania State Police, the FBI, and the Galerie St. Etienne in New York City all went to Mrs. Carr's home in Rose Valley and found the two Forrest Moses paintings, the sofa, and memorabilia. The seven Grandma Moses paintings had disappeared. All leads in the case dead-ended right there, and that's how the matter stood for the next fourteen years.

Curator Jamie Franklin filled in the story from there. "On February 9, 1998, the seven paintings arrived at the Bennington Museum in two wooden crates addressed to Director Steve Miller from a commercial shipping company in Quakerstown, Pennsylvania," said Franklin. "A cryptic note on purple mimeograph paper was signed 'Ring Sar,' and attempts to trace the source of both the shipment and the shippers were unsuccessful."

All of the information the shippers provided the shipping company turned out to be false. Best guess is that the heist was perpetrated by a person or persons who had known Margaret Carr, as well as about the will, including the paintings' final destination. Because the paintings were kept in excellent condition, the guess is that the thieves were not interested in making a profit, but simply enjoyed the artist's work.

The Bennington Museum holds the largest collection of art by Grandma Moses. Great-grandson Will Moses is continuing the family folk art tradition at the Mt. Nebo Gallery, in Eagle Bridge, New York.

The Bennington Museum is in downtown Bennington at 75 Main Street (Route 9). The museum is open 10:00 a.m. to 5:00 p.m., with days of the week varying by season. See www.benningtonmuseum.org for the best information or call (802) 447–1571.

The One, the Only Covered Bridge Museum

Bennington

It is a magical experience to go across a covered bridge for the first time, especially if you take a few minutes to examine the level of craftsmanship that went into its construction. The Vermont Covered Bridge Museum gives you an opportunity for this and provides 3-D models, dioramas, and a working covered bridge railroad layout to show in realistic detail what these bridges could do and how they did it. You can even sit at one of two computer workstations to build and test your own covered bridge design.

The original purpose of the covered bridge was not to keep travelers from nasty weather. Its enclosing roof protected the timbers from weathering, which prolonged the life of the bridge. Nevertheless, this natural shelter was also used as a gathering place or picnic location. Covered bridges also were considered to be great boxing rings. It is said that Norwich University moved from Norwich to Northfield, Vermont, in an attempt to stop boxing matches on the Ledyard Bridge between its students and those of Dartmouth College.

Here's the skinny on the cost of crossing a Vermont river in the 1800s, when a covered bridge was between you and the other side

★ ★

The Covered Bridge Museum is an exact replica of a town lattice bridge. It is connected—psychically and physically—to the Bennington Center for the Natural and Cultural Arts.

("A brief darkness leading from the light to light," as Henry Wadsworth Longfellow put it a bit more lyrically):

1800s COVERED BRIDGE BILL OF FARE

A man on foot	1 cent
A man on horseback	4 cents
A one-horse carriage	10 cents
A carriage drawn by more than one horse	20 cents
Cattle	1 cent (driver free)
Sheep or swine	½ cent (driver free)

The Vermont Covered Bridge Museum is located at 44 Gypsy Lane at Route 9 in Bennington and is part of the Bennington Center for the Arts. The museum is open 10:00 a.m. to 5:00 p.m., Tuesday–Sunday. Check out www.benningtoncenterforthearts.org/CBMHome.htm for a wide variety of information, or call (802) 442-7158.

A Black Veterans' Museum in the Nation's Whitest State

Pownal

A scant one-half of one percent of Vermont's population consists of African Americans. Yet the state is the location of the nation's only museum devoted to the heroism and military exploits of black soldiers, sailors, and marines.

Founder Bruce Bird is neither black nor a veteran; he is someone who saw a major part of American history hardly addressed. "I've been studying military history for fifty-five years, and thinking about a museum since the 1980s. Then about five years ago, it occurred to me that 1.2 million African Americans served in the military during World War II, and that nobody was talking about it, other than through an occasional book," Bird said. "So if I'm going to do a museum, why not that, because no one else is doing it."

Why Vermont? "Because I was born here."

As to the exhibits:

"The Tuskegee Airmen

Founder and curator Bruce Bird has filled a gap in our nation's history by highlighting the exploits of more than one million Black World War II veterans who served with distinction.

(332nd Fighter Group) are really the royalty of the black servicemen in World War II," says Bruce, so it is no wonder an exhibit dedicated to them makes up one of the highlights of the museum. From 1942 through 1946, nearly 1,000 pilots received commissions and pilot wings at Tuskegee Army Airfield. Many thousands more bombardiers, navigators, and gunnery crews were trained at other air bases across the country. Because of the rampant racism and bigotry of the time, these men fought two wars—one against a military enemy overseas, and the other against bigotry both at home and abroad. Even so, they compiled an outstanding record. In more than 200 missions over Germany, not a single bomber was lost to enemy fighters.

"But there were an awful lot of other people doing other things who got absolutely no recognition anywhere, and they suffered as much and died just as dead as anybody else," says Bruce. To commemorate these men and women, and hundreds of thousands more, Bird has assembled their photos, artifacts, and dramatic narratives in what used to be Pownal's Oak Hill School, which dates back to the nineteenth century. He is also on call from schools and community groups to speak about the museum and this period in our history.

The museum is on Oak Hill School Road, which is off of Vermont Route 7, 8.5 miles south of Bennington. Drive west on the road $\frac{1}{10}$ mile and the museum will be on your right at 179 Oak Hill School Road. The museum is open Monday–Thursday, 10:00 a.m. to 5:00 p.m. year-round. Admission is charged. For more information visit www.blackww2museum.org, or call (802) 823–5519.

"I Had a Lover's Quarrel with the World"
Shaftsbury

Robert Frost's headstone inscription succinctly summarizes the great disparity between his professional successes and personal tragedies over a lifetime of nearly eighty-nine years. His first moneymaking poem was published when he was twenty, he was the first writer to be awarded four Pulitzer Prizes, he lectured internationally, and in 1961 the Vermont legislature named him the poet laureate of Vermont.

On the other hand, Frost's father died when the poet was eleven (leaving the family with $8 after expenses), Frost's first son died at age four (and his mother six months later), his fourth daughter died three days after birth, his sister was committed to an insane asylum and later

Robert Frost moved from New Hampshire to Vermont in 1920. One reason: On the eighty acres of farmland, he could grow "a thousand apple trees of some unforbidden variety."

died there, his second daughter died a day after her first daughter was born, and his second son committed suicide.

The Robert Frost Stone House Museum in Shaftsbury contains galleries in the house where Frost both lived and wrote some of his best poetry. One of his most famous poems, "Stopping by Woods on a Snowy Evening," was composed on a sweltering June morning at his dining room table. Other Stone House exhibits include the J. J. Lankes Gallery, featuring woodcuts of Frost's favorite illustrator, and the bookshop offering books, recordings, and posters. Frost's grave is located nearby in Old Bennington.

From Main Street in Bennington, go north on U.S. Route 7 to exit 2, Shaftsbury. At end of ramp, turn right onto Vermont Route 7A and go north. Go ¾ mile past Hiland Hall School. The museum is on the left side, at 121 Historic Route 7A. The Stone House Museum is open

Escaping Vermont Winters without Moving a Muscle

Volume IV of the *Bulletin of the New York Public Library* lists ten separate disputes between New York and Vermont from 1780 until 1899 to fix the precise location of Vermont's western boundary. For example, in 1814 that line was moved westward some 50 feet from the border established two years earlier. According to Warren S. Patrick, one Rupert farmer affected by this particular surveyor's decision realized that his house and land were now entirely in the state of New York. "Thank God," he said to his wife. "I don't think I could stand another Vermont winter."

from May to November, 10:00 a.m. to 5:00 p.m., Tuesday through Sunday. For more information visit www.frostfriends.org or call (802) 447–6200.

Phineas Gage—He Needed This Job like a Hole in the Head
Cavendish

Bolted to a rock on Pleasant Street is a plaque commemorating "The Gage Accident." It was placed there in 1998, 150 years after a story that goes like this:

On September 13, 1848, Phineas P. Gage, a twenty-five-year-old Rutland & Burlington Railroad construction foreman, was setting dynamite charges to remove rock impeding the railroad's expansion across Vermont. He would drill a narrow hole in the rock and fill it halfway with blasting powder. Next came a fuse, and finally the powder was covered with protective sand and tamped down. Gage customarily signaled one of his men to pour in the sand before he tamped it down, with a rod designed for him by a local blacksmith. On this afternoon, however, he gestured for his partner to put in the sand and then was distracted by another worker. When he looked back and rammed his thirteen-pound tamping rod into the hole, he failed to see that his partner had not yet added the sand. His rod struck rock, created a spark, and whammo!

A tremendous blast propelled the 3-foot, 7-inch rod through Gage's left cheekbone, exiting the top of his skull at high speed, and landing, covered with blood and brains, more than 100 feet behind him. When his fellow workers reached the stunned Gage, they were amazed to see that he was not only alive but conscious. They carried him to an ox-drawn cart, which took him the three-quarters of a mile back to Cavendish. He was erect and got up the steps to the Adams Hotel with just a little assistance. According to neurobiologist Antonio Damasio,

Imagine what poor Phineas thought when these x-rays came in. Oh, right. X-rays hadn't been invented yet. (These pictures are from a "prepared cranium.")

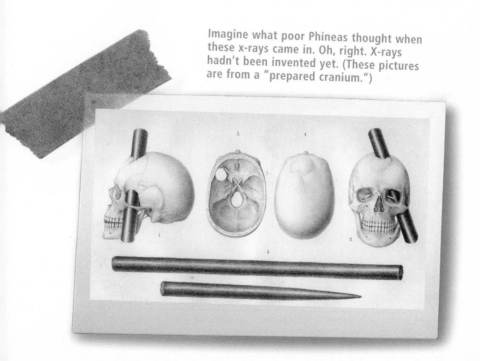

in his book *Descartes' Error,* when the doctor arrived at Adams Hotel, Gage was seated on the front porch and greeted him by saying, "Doctor, here is business enough for you."

He was under the doctor's care for ten weeks and then discharged to his home in Lebanon, New Hampshire. Within two months he had completely recovered: He could walk, speak, and was pain free.

But it was soon clear that the Phineas Gage who went back to work was a different man. The hardworking, responsible, and popular Phineas was now, as his doctor wrote, ". . . fitful, irreverent, indulging in the grossest profanity . . . pertinaciously obstinate, yet capricious and vacillating. . . . [H]is mind was radically changed, so decidedly that his friends and acquaintances said he was 'no longer Gage.'"

Phineas was fired from his job in 1850 and spent about a year as a sideshow attraction at P. T. Barnum's New York museum, displaying his scars—and the tamping iron that caused them—to anyone willing to pay for the privilege. His health began to fail in 1859, and he moved to San Francisco to live with his mother. In 1860 he began to have epileptic seizures and died a few months later at the age of forty-two, buried with the rod that damaged him.

In 1990 an autopsy on Gage's exhumed body by Drs. Antonio and Hanna Damasio confirmed that the ruinous damage to the frontal lobes by the rod is what caused Gage's antisocial behavior, and that the seizures leading to his death were accident-related as well. Both his skull and the rod are part of a permanent exhibition at Harvard Medical School's Warren Anatomical Museum in Boston, Massachusetts.

In 1998, at the 150th commemoration of the tragic explosion, Phineas's rod was brought by armed guard from Harvard to Cavendish for the ceremony.

To reach Cavendish, take exit 8 on I-91. Go west on Route 131 for 13 miles. The memorial plaque is in an empty lot at the corner of Route 131 and Pleasant Street. For more information and pictures, go to www.roadsideamerica.com/story/10858.

★ ★

America's Oldest Flour Company Is Not Showing Its Age

Norwich

As soon as you hit the front door, you know that the folks at King Arthur Flour have things under control—in a nice way.

The company was born in 1790 as the Sands, Taylor, and Wood Company, selling flour by the barrel off Long Wharf in Boston. It changed its name to King Arthur Flour after the owners saw a performance of *King Arthur and the Knights of the Round Table*.

All King Arthur flours have been free of bleach or chemicals of any kind for more than 200 years, which alone would qualify this company as a curiosity. Three of its eight flours are 100 percent organic. The company also sells a line of baking equipment, ingredients, mixes, and fresh-baked goods both in the store and through its Baker's Catalogue.

Among the gazillion other specialties and recipes, some going back more than 200 years, pizza definitely is on King Arthur Flour's radar—including recipes. Monitor its URL to see.

The bakery produces up to 400 loaves of bread on a weekday, 600 on a weekend day, and a team of eight bakers crank out the product in shifts of two. In addition, the company maintains a hotline staffed by eight seasoned bakers who answer 61,000 calls and e-mails a year from bakers with problems. Rebecca Faill, a cooking-school graduate and former caterer, has heard it all, from a woman trying to duplicate her neighbor's award-winning pie to a monk fine-tuning a bread recipe for his monastery.

King Arthur's Flour is a gray building with red trim located on U.S. Route 5, ½ mile south of I-91 exit 13, on the left just past the car dealership. The Baker's Store is located at 135 Route 5 South, Norwich, Vermont. Store hours are Monday through Saturday, 8:30 a.m. to 6:00 p.m. and Sunday, 8:30 a.m. to 4:00 p.m. Read more about King Arthur Flour and its many services on www.kingarthurflour.com or call (802) 649–3361.

The President Coolidge Summer Home—Just above His Store
Plymouth Notch

Bill Jenney, regional historic site administrator at the birthplace and boyhood home of Calvin Coolidge, recounts the night that the presidential guard was changed: "In August of 1923, when Vice President Coolidge happened to be up here visiting his family, word came that President Warren Harding had died. [Coolidge] had to be sworn in immediately, and the only available official was his father, who was also the local notary public. Actually, there was a second ceremony with a federal judge back in Washington, because there was some debate as to whether a state official could swear in a federal officer. That Coolidge was sworn in by his father in the family homestead, in the middle of the night, by the light of a kerosene lamp, played quite well in the presidential campaign for the 1924 election, when he . . . won with the highest plurality then known."

John Calvin Coolidge Jr. was born on July 4, 1872, within yards of the room in which his father swore him in as president. He graduated from Amherst College with honors and entered law and politics in

The Coolidge birthplace bedroom looks exactly as it did on July 4, 1872, when Calvin Coolidge was born. The chamber pot rests at lower right.

Northampton, Massachusetts. Some think that because Coolidge was an accidental president, he had little taste for the top office. But slowly and methodically, he went up the Republican political ladder, from councilman in Northampton to governor of Massachusetts. His forceful intervention in the Boston police strike of 1919 propelled him to national attention, and President Warren G. Harding named him as his running mate in the 1920 election. Twenty-nine months later, Harding died of a heart attack at age fifty-seven.

The small Vermont hill town of Plymouth Notch is virtually unchanged from the days during which President Coolidge ran his summer White House here in the dance hall above his father's general store. His entire staff consisted of a secretary and a stenographer. The last summer before his reelection the staff was augmented by a Secret Service detail of eighteen, because of death threats. That summer he

★ ★

also was recovering from the death of his son, also Calvin Jr., whose infected blister from playing tennis at the White House courts with his brother John led to blood poisoning. Coolidge declined to run for a second term on his own, believing that his one year in office after Harding's death should count as a full term.

The homes of Coolidge's family and neighbors on the site are carefully preserved, as are the village church, general store, and cheese factory—still making cheese using the original 1890 recipe. Also on-site are a visitors' center, two museum stores, two walking trails, a restaurant, and a picnic area. To visit the steep, hillside cemetery where Calvin Coolidge rests with seven generations of his family, turn right out of the visitors' parking area onto Route 100A, and turn left onto Lynds Hill Road, about 100 yards south.

The President Calvin Coolidge State Historic Site is located 6 miles south of U.S. Route 4 on State Route 100A. The site is open from the last weekend in May until mid October, daily 9:30 a.m. to 5:00 p.m. For more specific information and to see a list of events, go to www .historicvermont.org/coolidge or call (802) 672–3773.

Quechee Gorge, Vermont's "Little Grand Canyon"
Quechee

As a matter of scale, minuscule is probably more accurate a word than little, if Quechee Gorge and the Grand Canyon are being used in the same sentence. As a part of 600-acre Quechee Gorge State Park, it is still the most spectacular river gorge in Vermont. Just east of Quechee Village, the Ottauquechee River turns south and plunges into the narrow, rocky cleft of Quechee Gorge—165 feet deep and more than a mile long. Quechee Gorge is what remains of a waterfall that carved its way north over thousands of years, eroding tough metamorphic rock until the formidable barrier was cut clean through.

Enter the path along the gorge just north of the east side of the U.S. Route 4 bridge. To the right is a picnic area, and a quarter mile farther is the old Dewey Wool Mill, no longer in operation, and the

At right can be seen the result of erosion so massive it moved the Outtauquechee River waterfall far enough north to create Quechee Gorge.

waterfall that made it work. Walking back under the bridge will take you to the gorge outlook, but be careful. This walk is strenuous.

About 1,500 feet before the bridge (on the left going toward Woodstock) is Quechee Gorge State Park Campground.

Quechee Gorge can be reached by taking exit 1 on Interstate 89 toward Woodstock, and then going 7 miles southeast on U.S. Route 4. Admission is free. An annual highlight is the Quechee Gorge Hot Air Balloon Festival on Father's Day weekend. Thousands attend, so if you're interested, make reservations early. For more information visit the park's Web site at www.vtstateparks.com/htm/quechee.cfm.

★ ★

How the Simpsons Chose Vermont

Springfield

Here was the competition: Oregon, Illinois, Massachusetts, Colorado, Nebraska, Missouri, Louisiana, Florida, New Jersey, Michigan, Ohio, Kentucky, and Tennessee. Illinois was a close second; Florida was last. Vermont got the job done.

What made the difference? Each entrant submitted a three- to five-minute film, showcasing its community's "Simpsons Spirit." Twentieth Century–Fox provided interested parties with key filmmaking tools, including a digital video camera, *The Simpsons Movie* posters, and enough "Simpson-yellow" paint to last Homer through several nuclear meltdowns.

Yet Springfield, Vermont, won despite not even being invited to compete at first. Springfield found out at the eleventh hour and wasn't even able to start production on its video until two weeks before the

Simpsons creator and executive producer Matt Groening poses in Springfield with his creations at the premiere of *The Simpsons Movie*—his other reason to visit Vermont in 2007.

deadline. Final score: Vermont 1; Tennessee, Ohio, Oregon, and every-body else 0. In a futile attempt to prove that Hollywood has a heart, each of the other thirteen Springfields had a screening of its own, the night before *The Simpsons Movie* hit theaters nationwide in late July 2007. And lest you think otherwise, this big-screen premiere was the real reason for all this folderol in the first place.

Just about anyone in Springfield will be happy to answer your Simp-sons questions, or anything else about the town. Just ask. Take I-91 exit 7 west into town on Route 11.

Birth of the Vermont Nation
Windsor

The first constitution of the "Free and Independent State of Vermont" was adopted on July 8, 1777, less than a year after the signing of the Declaration of Independence, at Elijah West's Tavern, in Windsor. The present state of Vermont was occupied by New Hampshire, New York, and Massachusetts for much of the eighteenth century. These were not benevolent neighbors. Vermont residents fumed at the large fees New York laid on them just for transferring title to their lands, for example.

For this and other reasons, they decided to form their own republic and wrote a constitution modeled after Benjamin Franklin's for the State of Pennsylvania. The Vermont framers went further, however. Their constitution was the first to prohibit slavery, and the first to grant voting rights without regard to property ownership or specific income.

At about the time the Constitution was being finalized, British forces attacked and captured the fort complex of Ticonderoga, just across Lake Champlain. The British pursued the retreating American forces and met General Arthur St. Clair's rearguard at Hubbardton on July 7. Even though 1,000 Americans, including Ethan Allen and a band of 200 Green Mountain Men, successfully delayed the British advance, many residents on the west side of the Green Mountains had to run for their lives. Word of these alarming events reached Wind-sor on July 8, and the constitution was voted on—accompanied by a violent thunderstorm—just before the convention disbanded.

★ ★

In Windsor in 1777, delegates of the new Republic of Vermont drafted a constitution even more progressive than the U.S. Constitution signed ten years later in Philadelphia.

Vermont's Old Constitution House is a restoration of Elijah West's Tavern, which was nearby. The land for the new location was donated by the family of William Evarts, who served as secretary of state for President Rutherford B. Hayes and was chief counsel for the defense in the impeachment trial of President Andrew Johnson.

It is located at 16 Main Street at the northern end of the village of Windsor on U.S. Route 5, accessible from exits 8 and 9 on I-91. The museum is open to the public 11:00 a.m. to 5:00 p.m. on Saturday and Sunday from late May through mid October. For more information call (802) 672–3773 or visit www.historicvermont.org/constitution.

Matthew Lyon—Elected to Congress from Jail

Fair Haven

The village green plaque pictured here just hints at Matthew Lyon's remarkable life and his contributions to early Vermont. Here's a bit more of the story.

After attending school and beginning to learn the printing trade in his native Ireland, Matthew Lyon sailed to America as an indentured servant at age fifteen. He first worked on a farm in Woodbury, Connecticut, and then moved to Wallingford, Vermont, where he gained his independence. During the Revolution, Lyon was commissioned as a lieutenant with Ethan Allen and the Green Mountain Boys and helped capture Fort Ticonderoga.

To clarify the plaque's wording (compressed because of limited space), Lyon was jailed for violating the Sedition Act, true. But that act was declared unconstitutional a year later.

Lyon became wealthy after the Revolutionary War by learning how to make paper from wood pulp. He founded the village of Fair Haven and created the *Fair Haven Gazette,* a weekly for which he served as both editor and publisher. The *Gazette* gave Lyon a chance to express his strong pro-Jefferson views at the expense of John Adams, whom he viewed as a monarchist.

Lyon's influence helped elect him to Congress in 1796, where he wielded even more influence, even if by somewhat unconventional methods. On one occasion he spat on Federalist congressman Roger Griswold for insults against him having to do with his anti-Adams position. Griswold attacked him with his cane, but Lyon was able to get to the House fireplace, where he grabbed a poker and gave Griswold a nasty pasting.

In 1798 Lyon was convicted and sentenced to four months in jail for violating the Sedition Act, signed by President Adams and making it unlawful for an American to defame a president. Even so, he easily won reelection despite sitting out the election in jail. A year later the Sedition Act was declared unconstitutional, and in 1800 Matthew Lyon cast the deciding presidential vote for his hero, Thomas Jefferson, in a runoff after an electoral college deadlock.

Lyon, his wife, and twelve children then moved to Kentucky, where he successfully ran for Congress once more. When Lyon moved again to Arkansas, he failed in his bid to become a congressman from a third state. He was elected but died before he could take a seat there.

Fair Haven is 12 miles west of Rutland on U.S. Route 4. Take exit 2 south to get to the center of town. For more information please visit www.fairhavenvt.org.

Giant Elephants . . . Once Roamed . . . in Vermont
Mount Holly

Depending on whose opinion you accept, the woolly mammoth began grazing about 11,000 years ago, several thousand years after the ice retreated and grasslands reestablished themselves in the meadows of what is now Vermont. These large mammals chewed grass and leaves with eight-pound molars. It takes a heap o' fuel to keep a five-ton woolly mammoth happy—or ambulatory, at the very least.

A Swiss zoologist named Louis Agassiz proved to be instrumental in our understanding of what life was like in the Ice Age, among other things. In 1848, two years after he came to the United States—Harvard professorship in hand—Agassiz received tangible validation of a part of his theory. Workmen in Mount Holly, building a railroad from Bellows Falls to Rutland, uncovered the remains of a woolly mammoth from what were the mud layers of an ancient swamp, 11 feet below the surface. Most of the bones were taken by the workmen, but, as written in the *Vermont Semi-Weekly Record* in September 5, 1865, "the most perfect tusk was secured by Prof. Zadock Thompson and is lodged in the State Cabinet at Montpelier. This tusk was 80 inches long and four inches in diameter. The molar tooth, now in the possession of Prof. Agassiz, weighs eight pounds and presents a grinding surface of eight

Fossil finds greatly aided late paleontologists in establishing written history.

Second-Generation Trailmaster

When Scott Fletcher was drafted into the Air Force in 1969, he gave his year-old Evinrude snowmobile to his parents and told them to keep it warm for him. By the time he returned home in 1973, Scott's parents had become avid snowmobilers. His dad had traded in the Evinrude for a new sled and was named trailmaster for the Rockingham Abenaki Snowmobile Club two years earlier. Scott had a lot of catching up to do.

Scott's parents, long-distance riders, once drove their snowmobiles up to their camp in Morgan, Vermont, north of Seymour Lake (the largest totally within the state's borders) near the Canadian border. This was a 240-mile, two-day drive, which included a motel stay in Randolph or thereabouts.

Today Scott is trailmaster for the Abenaki Club, and his grooming days go back to the early 1970s, when grooming devices were not as advanced as they are today. "We used to drag bedsprings—you name it," says Scott. He and his wife, Maureen, are looking forward to the day when they can regularly make the round-trip Scott's mother and father traveled years ago. "That's going to have to wait until I retire," says Scott, who has worked at the Grafton Cheese Company for forty-one years, and for thirty-five of them has been head cheese maker. "We'd like to make that trip now, but there's a bit too much traffic on the weekends, and we're too busy to go up in the middle of the week."

inches long and four broad. A plaster cast of it is on exhibition with the tusk at our State Cabinet."

Seventeen years later, near Brattleboro about 30 miles to the south, laborer James Morse was similarly mucking about on Daniel Pratt's

* *

farm and found the tusk of a young mammoth, about half the size of the Mount Holly specimen. The *Vermont Semi-Weekly Record* duly recorded this event as well: "The workman on discovering it took a piece to Mr. Pratt, remarking as he handed it to him, that he had found a curious piece of wood. Mr. Pratt on looking at it discovered its true nature."

The fossil tusk of the young woolly mammoth can be seen on the third floor of the Brooks Memorial Library (near the elevator), at 324 Main Street, Brattleboro. Call (802) 254–5290 or visit www.brooks.lib .vt.us for more information. A plaster cast of the full-sized mammoth molar can be seen at the Perkins Geology Museum, University of Vermont, 180 Colchester Avenue, Burlington. Call (802) 656–8694 or visit www.uvm.edu/perkins for additional information. (What happened to the original tusk is a mystery.)

Help . . . the Bridge Is Sinking!
Brookfield

In the early 1800s inhabitants of Brookfield could cross the ice in the winter, but they could not drive carriages over the pond in the summer. To drive around the pond took too much time. In 1820 the townspeople created a bridge of logs to connect the two sides. Each year water-soaked logs were replaced with new ones until 1884, when Orlando Ralph devised a bridge that rested on tarred kerosene barrels that floated on the water. In 1978 the wooden barrels were replaced with plastic containers filled with Styrofoam. The Sunset Lake Floating Bridge is supported by those floating barrels, we're told, because the lake is too deep for traditional pilings.

Well, you arrive at 8:00 a.m., for example. You're looking at that bronze plaque, just above you on the right telling you about the bridge's history. No traffic, either coming your way or behind you, to witness your cowardice. Ahead, you see what are probably the planks of a wooden bridge, but they're half a foot beneath the blackness of what could be a 500-foot-deep lake. Index finger ready to hit 911 on your mobile?

For Brookfield residents, crossing the bridge is transportation. For everyone else, the first time is an adrenaline rush.

Actually, the 150-yard-or-so voyage is painless and fun. You may even want to go back and forth a couple of times, traffic permitting. You can also fish off the bridge or swim near it, in addition to driving your car over it. Your tires will get wet, but the bridge will get you safely across. No trucks, though.

From I-89 South, take exit 4. On Route 66, go east 1 mile to Randolph Center, and turn north. One mile farther, where Route 66 makes a sharp right, go left onto Ridge Road. Drive 6 miles to Route 65, and turn left. Sunset Lake Bridge is 200 feet on the left. For more information see www.central-vt.com/web/floating.

Morey's Steamboat—Was Fulton a Fraud?
Fairlee

Most history books credit Robert Fulton's *Clermont* with making the first successful steamboat trip in 1807. True, Fulton's Hudson River voyage from New York City to Albany was the first commercial steamboat service in the world.

Gould's History of River Navigation, however, describes the voyage not as a success, but as a disaster. "The rudder had so little power that the vessel could hardly be managed. The spray from the wheels dashed over the passengers." The skippers of other river craft took advantage of the *Clermont*'s unwieldiness, and cut in front of her to save time.

But here's the kicker: The *Clermont* was not the first, but the twelfth steamboat to be built and become a part of river traffic in the nineteenth century.

In 1792, fifteen years earlier, Fairlee, Vermont, inventor Samuel Morey built a steamboat with a paddle-wheel in the prow. One Sunday he and an assistant, John Mann, made their first trip across the Connecticut River and back from Orford, New Hampshire, to Fairlee. A few years later, Morey constructed a new and improved version, with paddle-wheels on each side for more speed and better stability. He sailed from Bradenton, New Jersey, to Philadelphia on the Delaware River, where his newly christened *Aunt Sally* was publicly exhibited.

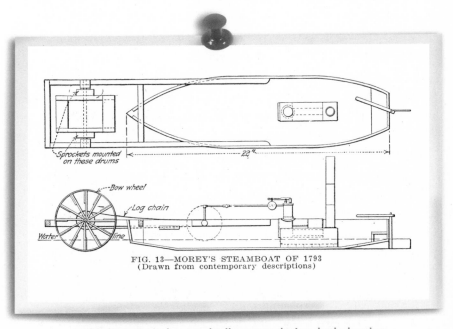

FIG. 13—MOREY'S STEAMBOAT OF 1793
(Drawn from contemporary descriptions)

If Fulton started out so badly—poor design, bad planning, internal bickering—why did he come off so well in the history books? Simple: He managed to strike the best financial deal.

Fulton and Morey were aware of each other's efforts as early as 1793, and the race was on for the funding that would assure commercial success.

Enter Robert R. Livingston, chancellor of New York State, a wealthy entrepreneur, and an inventor as well. Before meeting Fulton, Livingston took a ride in Morey's steamboat and offered to back him in a joint venture, but Morey refused when Livingston insisted on too large a percentage of the proceeds. Livingston then went to Fulton, and the deal that resulted is what eventually made its way into the history books. When Morey heard about it, he is said to have scuttled the *Aunt Sally* in what is now Lake Morey.

Fairlee is located off Exit 15 on I-91 north; www.ctrivertravel.net/fairlee.htm.

Walking the Nation's Smallest Capital
Montpelier

Just a few miles south of exit 8 on I-89, the tableau of green valleys, farms, and hills spread out below make a highway warrior feel more like a Piper Cub pilot on the last approach before putting down. On your right is the city of Montpelier, home of fewer than 8,000 souls, with the population swelling to nearly 8,200 when the legislature is in session (representatives plus assistants, press, lobbyists, and assorted hangers-on). Just off the exit you can see the golden dome. Now there's proof you're in a capital city.

If the legislature isn't in session, you'll have a good shot at a parking spot near the capitol. If so, walk in the front door and take a tour if you'd like. When you're ready, walk out the other side to a trail that leads straight to 185-acre Hubbard Park. Here you'll find wooded stands of oak, beech, pine, and hemlock, dotted with picnic areas, a pond, hiking trails, and a 54-foot stone observation tower.

For capitol tour information visit www.vtstatehouse.org or call (802) 828–0386; for more information about the smallest capital, visit www.montpelier-vt.org.

Structure a self-guided tour of the most walkable town around, by time available, interests, or as your mood suggests. Plan your route on a downtown bench over a cup of coffee.

A Touch of Swedish Lapland in Vermont

Stowe

The Kaffi Reykjavik Ice Bar, in Reykjavik, Iceland, gets its raw materials from Vatnajökull, the largest ice cap in Europe. The Icehotel in Swedish Lapland cuts ice blocks for its walls and bar stools from the frozen Torne River, 750 miles north of Stockholm. Fortunately, Rusty Nail Bar and Grill general manager Ken Walters found an ice furniture source in Pennsylvania for his Stowe, Vermont, establishment—the only frozen saloon in the Northeast, so far as he knows.

Ken's inspiration was Quebec's thirty-six-room Ice Hotel, but his objectives were considerably more modest: a congenial space for customers to cool down and share a cold (make that ice-cold) drink after an afternoon on the slopes and ski trails. Even so, it takes twenty-two tons of ice every year to construct the Rusty Nail's 800-square-foot Ice

Since we last visited the Rusty Nail, the Ice Bar has seen hard times—but only temporarily, we hope. Last winter's warmth washed it out, but we're thinking it'll be back. Call first.

Bar, including 8-foot walls, tall ice tables, and the 25-foot-long bar itself. The space has opened on Christmas week every year for the past few years and draws enthusiastic—and curious—traffic from more than 100 miles away.

Ice bartender Kate Wise has heard it all from tourists some might call skeptical; others, clueless:

"What is that bar really made of?"

"Is it the same temperature here as it is outside?"

"How do you keep an ice bar going in the summer?"

The last one is easy. "Come back in August and see," she says.

Even though Kate and the rest of the ice bartenders are outfitted with toasty jackets, hats, gloves, and boots to reduce the discomfort level, it isn't nearly as pleasant for them as wearing tee shirts while schmoozing with customers at 72 degrees—in August, for example, when that curious customer returns to learn the warm-weather fate of New England's only ice bar.

✶ ✶

Take Route 108 (Mountain Road) out of Stowe, and the Rusty Nail Bar and Grill is located at 1190 Mountain Road. Open at 3:00 p.m. daily, weather permitting. Visit www.rustynailicebar.com or call (802) 253–6245 for more information.

High School Dropout Transforms College Education
Strafford

A goodly number of this country's 105 land grant colleges and universities—Iowa State, Cornell University, the University of Vermont, and Washington State University among them—have a Morrill Hall on campus. Largely this is because if it weren't for Senator Justin Smith Morrill, those institutions would not exist. In 1862 President Abraham Lincoln signed the Morrill Land-Grant Colleges Act, written and fought for by Senator Morrill for the previous seven years. This act allocated funds from the sales of public lands to support new colleges that taught agriculture, engineering, business, and home economics. It opened the door for poor and minority students to pursue a college education.

Justin Morrill grew up in Strafford, Vermont, and eagerly looked forward to attending college, but his family was too poor to send him. He left school for good at age fifteen. His interest in architecture, horticulture, and politics, though, was intense enough for him to become learned in all three. After seventeen years as a merchant and seven as a farmer, Morrill was elected to the Congress, and eventually the U.S. Senate, serving in one body or another for nearly fifty years. Today more than 25 million graduates have Senator Morrill to thank for their college education.

The Gothic Revival homestead and farm complex in Strafford (Vermont's first National Historic Landmark) was designed by Justin Morrill and built for him in 1848. The house is furnished with original and family pieces. Interpretive exhibits are located in several of the barns and outbuildings.

From Route 132 in South Strafford, take the Justin Smith Morrill Highway and go 2 miles to the Strafford Village. The homestead is located on the right-hand side of the road on the north end of the village. The homestead is open from Memorial Day to Columbus Day, Saturday and Sunday 11:00 a.m. to 5:00 p.m. For more information visit www.morrillhomestead.org.

RIP, Bovinity Divinity

Waterbury

Up an imposing hill and beyond a much less imposing parking lot, a white picket fence surrounds a grove of beech trees. In these peaceful confines you'll find Ben & Jerry's Flavor Graveyard, a repository for ill-named or ill-conceived ice cream concoctions that have failed the test of consumer approval. I was looking for a headstone that commemorated a real doozy, perhaps a Garlic Lamb Fat Fudge Swirl or a Carrot Tomato Vegan Delight. Instead I spy a dead flavor I would have graded a definite keeper: Maine Blueberry Ice Cream. What could have happened? Was it too down home? Too ordinary? No. Too seasonal. From the inscription I learn that when summer faded, this flavor's sales did as well.

But here's an envelope pusher even I could have predicted: Tennessee Mud had Loser stamped on its one-pint carton from at least two directions. Bourbon lovers looking for a taste treat reminding them of a favored beverage—and perhaps a wee buzz?—turned up their noses. Parents fearing residual traces of alcohol likely were driven to the safer scoops of Howard Johnson's 31 Flavors, or a local ice creamery. (The ingredients were said to include a taste of "Jack Daniel's Old No. 7 Tennessee Sour Mash Whiskey," a contention the B&J public relations department, after several phone calls, would neither confirm nor deny.) The epitaph says it all:

THE BOTTLE IS EMPTY,
THE CUP AND THE GLASS.
MUD WITH JACK DANIEL'S
WAS NOT MEANT TO LAST.

1988–1989

Cocoanut Cream Pie Low-Fat Ice Cream, Honey Apple Raisin Chocolate Cookie, KaBerry KABOOM!, Lemon Peppermint Carob Chip, Makin' Whoopee Pie, Ooey Gooey Cake Low-Fat Frozen Yogurt, Peanuts! Popcorn!, Peppermint Schtick . . . Had enough?

Discovering other flavors that deserved capital punishment, you may be as glad as I was to hear that Economic Crunch, Honey I'm Home, and Bovinity Divinity have gotten their just desserts.

The Flavor Graveyard is on the grounds of Ben & Jerry's Waterbury factory, the company's flagship manufacturing plant. Ben & Jerry's happens to be one of the nation's best companies in terms of social responsibility, their mission reading, in part: "Initiating ways to improve the quality of life locally, nationally, and internationally." Even after being absorbed by corporate giant Unilever, B&J has been able to retain and act on its long-held progressive values.

Take I-89 exit 10 and go north on Route 100 North. The factory is up a mile on the left. Tours at the Waterbury factory are conducted seven days a week year-round, except for Thanksgiving, Christmas, and New Year's Day. Hours vary by season. For more information call (802) 882–1240, extension 2285.

Vermont's Sheep Heyday

In Vermont's sheep heyday Addison County counted 373 sheep per square mile. This Vermont County raised more sheep and produced more wool, in proportion to its size and population, than any other county in the United States. The Vermont sheep industry allowed a burgeoning wool-processing industry to arise here as well. Carding mills, which first appeared in Vermont in the 1790s, combed raw wool to prepare it for spinning. Fulling mills washed and sized the woof fiber, or woolen cloth.

The Great Bristol Outhouse Race
Bristol

Let's say you're in Bristol next Fourth of July and want to take part in the festivities. One possibility is the traditional Outhouse Race, run just before the parade, in which competing outhouse contestants race one another to a finish line. The outhouses are on wheels, and the teams consist of one member sitting on the seat and two runners outside it, either pushing or pulling their vehicle of necessity. (Outhouse decoration rules require a door—"for privacy, of course.") Members of the crowd can bet on their favorite entrant in a heat by buying tickets of the color assigned to that entrant and for that heat. All tickets are numbered and double, so the purchaser gets one half and the seller retains the other half.

Betting on your favorite entrant, though, takes a bit of concentration. Following is the first part of a description of a "Sample Race," as prepared by the officials:

"Suppose in the first heat that the entrants are teams W, X, Y, and Z. Team W has been assigned the red ticket color, team X has been assigned the blue ticket color, team Y has been assigned the orange ticket color, and team Z has been assigned the yellow ticket color. You wish to bet that team X will win this heat. You then buy a blue ticket from a seller, who is a member of the Bristol Rotary Club and is wearing a sandwich board listing the names of the entrants for this first heat and the ticket color assigned to each. This information is also posted at the registration desk and announced over the public address system. There is generally no shortage of ticket sellers. The first heat is run, and team Y is declared the winner. Team Y was assigned the orange color, which means that your blue ticket can be properly discarded, along with all the other blue tickets, red tickets and yellow tickets sold for the first heat."

An annual Bristol ritual before the Fourth of July parade is the Outhouse Race, fiercely fought contests among the three-person teams—two running outside and one on the seat.

The hypothetical results of subsequent heats are just as thoroughly described. Fortunately, a fifteen- to twenty-minute interlude between heats will give wagering spectators a chance to clear their heads. Our advice: If you'd like either to run the race or bet on it, read the rules, race explanation, and sample race description online well before you arrive. To download an entry form go to www.addisoncounty.com and in the search box type "outhouse race."

A Museum of Treasures, Both Seen and Unseen
Ferrisburgh

You might think that visitors to the Lake Champlain Maritime Museum interested in underwater exhibits but without scuba certification (roughly 98 percent of the U.S. population) would miss out completely. Not so. Beginning in 2004, the utilization of remotely operated underwater vehicles (ROVs) began allowing all visitors an opportunity to see the shipwrecks.

Executive director and cofounder Art Cohn is quick to define the museum's mission as "preserving and sharing the history and archaeology of the region, and the study and management of underwater cultural resources." According to Cohn, the exhibit that most thoroughly embodies this mission, as well as the museum's ongoing work, is the one featuring the canal schooner *General Butler*.

"It's a perfect example of underwater resource management," says Cohn. "The 88-foot wooden remains of a canal boat located in Burlington harbor . . . has been a major focus of our research… It has the blue-collar, day-to-day commerce these boats represented. It has the canal era, a major focus of our study. And it's got underwater resource management all over it." A full-sized replica in the museum is modeled from detailed archaeological measurements.

Sunk in a violent storm in December 1876, the *General Butler* was discovered in 1980. Here is its story, taken from contemporary eyewitness and press accounts: William Montgomery was captaining the *General Butler* (named after a Massachusetts lawyer and Civil War hero) one Saturday in December when heavy gales drove the vessel toward the Burlington breakwater. *General Butler* was carrying a load of Isle La Motte marble for delivery to the Burlington Marble Works. Also on board were a deckhand, Montgomery's teenage daughter Cora and her schoolgirl friend, and a quarry operator from Isle La Motte.

The power of the storm was too much for the aging schooner, and the vessel began to drift southward. The deckhand threw over the storm anchor in a vain attempt to keep the vessel from crashing into the breakwater's stone-filled cribs. Meanwhile, Captain Montgomery chained a spare tiller bar onto the ship's steering gear. He then ordered the anchor line severed with an axe and attempted to round the southern end of the breakwater; *General Butler* instead smashed into the breakwater.

The twelve-bolt helmet was used by deep-sea divers from the 1830s to the 1970s, until it was replaced by SCUBA equipment. Try one on at the Lake Champlain Maritime Museum!

The passengers and crew were able to leap free of the wreck-
age onto the breakwater. The captain was last to leave the ship and
barely made it to safety after jumping at the crest of a large wave. The
General Butler sank immediately. Stranded on the open breakwater,
whipped by fierce winds and driving snow, the canal boat's refugees
might have died were it not for James Wakefield and his son, Jack. The
two untied a small government lighthouse boat and rowed out to the
breakwater. Captain Montgomery lifted his daughter and her friend
into James Wakefield's arms and then clambered aboard himself after
the deckhand and the quarry operator had jumped into the bobbing
rowboat.

Today, the boat rests in 40 feet of water at the south end of Burlington's breakwater. You'll be able to imagine for yourself what it was
like aboard an 1862-class canal boat by climbing the gangplank of
the schooner *Lois McClure,* in residence at the museum's Basin Harbor
facility during the summer and used as a periodic teaching tool in Vermont and New York schools and communities.

Another era of underwater resource management goes back a
century earlier, to the Revolutionary War. During the Battle of Valcour
Bay on Lake Champlain in 1776, with half the ships and firepower of
the foe, General Benedict Arnold led a naval force against the British.
Although Arnold lost what is considered the first battle fought by the
U.S. Navy, he delayed the British forces by a full year, which led to
their defeat at Saratoga in 1777. During the course of Arnold's nighttime retreat after a day of devastating losses on both sides, the British
caught up to his diminished fleet near Crown Point, on the New York
side of the lake. Arnold's Ship made it to shore, where it was set afire
before the crew escaped.

The museum's Valcour Bay Research Project involves systematically
mapping the submerged battlefield left behind at Valcour Island. So
far, several hundred artifacts have been mapped in place while a small
selection of exhibit-quality artifacts have been recovered. The *Philadelphia II* is an exact, full-size reproduction of one of Benedict Arnold's

gunboats. The original *Philadelphia* was located and recovered in 1935. It is currently on display at the Smithsonian Institution. An important related project under way is a management plan for the *Spitfire*, the last unaccounted-for gunboat from Benedict Arnold's fleet.

Follow U.S. Route 4 to Route 22A, and drive north 40 miles to Vergennes. Turn left on Panton Road, and go 1 mile. Then turn right on Basin Harbor Road, and go 6 miles to the museum on right, at 4472 Basin Harbor Road. The museum is open late May through late October, 10:00 a.m. to 5:00 p.m. daily. To get an idea of the host of activities the maritime museum provides, inquire about visiting the *Lois McClure,* or find out general information, visit www.lcmm.org, or call (802) 475–2022.

Vermont's Underground Railroad

Ferrisburgh

On a ninety-acre site on U.S. Route 7 in Ferrisburgh is the Rokeby Museum, a National Historic Landmark judged to be the best documented stop on the Underground Railway. In the decades leading up to the Civil War, Rowland T. Robinson and his wife, Rachel, harbored dozens of fugitive slaves at their farm and provided them with the employment and education that would prepare them to start new lives in the North.

The Robinsons were devout Quakers who believed that slavery was a sin to be opposed by every acceptable means. The thousands of letters in the family's collection reveal exactly what the escaped slaves went through as they risked severe punishment or worse to escape their lives of slavery. Some of these letters offer illuminating case studies of specific individuals, lending identities to their customary anonymity.

Farther south—in a slave border state like Maryland or a free border state like Pennsylvania—runaway slaves had to travel with utmost caution until they reached Massachusetts, at least. The following letter excerpt was compiled by Rokeby Museum director Jane Williamson.

★ ★

Oliver Johnson was a Vermonter and newspaper editor who helped a number of fugitive slaves. In 1837 Johnson wrote Rowland Robinson from Jenner Township in Pennsylvania. A runaway he found, a man named Simon, was wanted for a sizable reward.

"When he came here, he was destitute of clothing, and unable to proceed," wrote Johnson. "William C. Griffith, the son of a friend, who has often rendered assistance to runaways, kindly offered to keep him until spring. . . . It is not considered safe for him to remain here after winter has gone by, as search will no doubt be made for him.

"He is 28 years old," Johnson continued, "and appeared to me to be an honest, likely man. . . . I was so well pleased with his appearance that I could not help thinking he would be a good man for you to hire. Mr. Griffith says that he is very trustworthy, of a kind disposition, and knows how to do almost all kinds of farm work. He is used to teaming,

In the Robinson house, now known as the Rokeby Museum, dozens of slaves found refuge and were prepared for productive lives of freedom from the 1830s through the Civil War.

★ ★

and is very good to manage horses. He says that he could beat any man in the neighborhood where he lived at mowing, cradling, or pitching."

In its day Rokeby was one of the most prosperous farms in the Champlain Valley, and an ideal transitional destination for slaves preparing themselves for lives as free men and women.

On-site are the main house and most of the original outbuildings, plus hiking trails over more than fifty acres of farmland and orchards. The house may be seen by guided tour in groups limited to twelve. Tours last forty-five minutes.

On U.S. Route 7, 2 miles south of the North Ferrisburgh village center, watch for the historic site marker and front entrance sign on the east side of the road. The museum is open from mid May to mid October. House tours are offered three times a day, Thursday through Sunday, but the rest of the farm and museum are open to self-guided tours. For more information visit www.rokeby.org or call (802) 877–3406.

When Superlatives Clash

Vergennes

Vergennes lays claim to at least two significant superlatives, each printed on one of the welcome signs at the outskirts of the city. Entering from the west, Vergennes is "the smallest city in Vermont." Entering from the east, it is "the oldest city in Vermont."

Depending on the context, both statements hold water. Because there are only nine cities in the state, by Vermont's technical definition of a city, Vergennes's status as oldest is easy to establish. It bests the charter date of the next oldest city by seventy-seven years. The "smallest city" ranking, though, is more of a problem, primarily because nearly every one of those scrambling for the title has thought of ways to skew the definition to better press its case.

In terms of population, Vergennes is a lock. Fifteen hundred fewer people live there than in Newport. In terms of actual square footage, things get murky. Saint Albans appears to have the edge over

★ ★

Vergennes, 2.0 square miles to 2.5. Winooski is even smaller at 1.5 square miles. Winooski has been aggressive in challenging Vergennes for the "smallest" title.

We take this information to Mel Hawley, Vergennes's zoning administrator and former city manager. Mel acknowledges that Winooski had the edge in square miles, but only because Vergennes had resurveyed its boundaries and was therefore honest enough to admit that it was larger than its original charter stipulated.

"If you read our charter," says Mel, "Vergennes is 400 rods by 480 rods. Doing the math, that's a mile and a quarter by a mile and a half. Multiplying 1.25 by 1.5 you get 1.875 square miles. If you look at our tax maps, though, which we did a few years ago, we're taxing on the basis of 1,600 acres. When you do the conversion, Vergennes is 2.5 square miles."

So Vergennes has capitulated to Winooski? "I didn't say that," Mel replies. "Winooski has 6,600 people. That makes us the smallest city in Vermont by far."

Vergennes is located on Route 22A, 25 miles south of Burlington. For more information visit www.vergennes.org.

Bragging rights are a big deal in Vermont. One is for "smallest city."

The Forked Stick Society

Good dowsers are known for their ability to find sources of underground water. The best dowsers are known for their ability to find lost items, track criminals, locate missing persons, and seek guidance of a more spiritual nature. Since its founding in 1958, in Danville, Vermont, the focus of the American Society of Dowsers has expanded from simply seeking water to include many uses and practices of dowsing. (For more information visit the American Society of Dowser's Web site at www.dowsers.org.)

—Chris Burns, *The Vermont Encyclopedia*

The Audience Is in Vermont; the Performers Are in Canada
Derby Line

That would be the Haskell Opera House, with one minor qualification: As you will see by the black borderline when you visit, there actually are a few seats on the Canadian side. For fourteen seasons, QNEK (Quebec Northeast Kingdom) Productions has staged lively and varied musicals, revues, comedies, children's shows, and plays, all acted by its resident theater company.

Downstairs is the Haskell Free Library. Proceeds from the opera house assure that it is really free. "No rentals; no membership fees," says librarian Mary Roy. "We do have fines [for overdue books], though. A whopping two cents a day." (The librarians accept either U.S. or Canadian currency, on the grounds that things will pretty much even out at the end of the month.) By the way, a look at the black borderline on the library reading room floor will quickly tell you why

★ ★

this building is sometimes called "the only U.S. library with no books; the only Canadian theater with no stage."

Modeled after the now defunct Boston Opera House, the neoclassical building was built to straddle the international border between Derby Line and what is now Stanstead, Quebec. American sawmill owner Carlos Haskell and his Canadian wife, Martha Stewart Haskell, wanted it to be used by people in both countries.

Take exit 29 on Interstate 91; turn left over the bridge, go down the hill, and stop at the largest brick building in town, visible on the right, at 93 Caswell Avenue. The library is open year-round, Tuesday, Wednesday, and Friday, 10:00 a.m. to 5:00 p.m., and Thursday, 10:00 a.m. to 8:00 p.m. For more information visit www.haskellopera.org, or call the library at (802) 873–3022. The opera house's season runs from April to October. For concert tickets or information, call QNEK productions at (802) 334–2216 or visit www.qnek.com.

Did you guess that the line on the floor is an international boundary? Does the arrow help? (That's why we're here.)

★ ★

Trivia

Somebody had to photograph the first snowflake: quoted from the exhibit plaque at Saint Johnsbury's Fairbanks Museum. Wilson "Snowflake" Bentley was a Vermont treasure, as unique as the snow crystals he captured as microphotographs. A self-educated farmer from Jericho, he invented the process of microphotography using a microscope and camera. He went on to capture over 5,000 images of snow crystals from 1885 until his death in 1931. In addition, he studied formations of frost, dew, and raindrops in great detail. He also conducted some of the first research in cloud physics.

ECHO . . . ECHO . . . ECHO . . . Lake Aquarium and Science Center

Burlington

Just before you set foot in ECHO, a fine mist sprayed between slabs of lake slate bathes the air on both sides of the two-story glass entrance. We saw dancing rainbows, but that can't always happen, can it? Even if not, it sure is a good mood-setter.

This estimable establishment is called "ECHO Lake Aquarium and Science Center at the Leahy Center for Lake Champlain." ECHO stands for Ecology, Culture, History, and Opportunity—a mouthful that is also quite accurate. It is named in honor of Vermont's U.S. Senator Patrick Leahy and his wife, Marcelle. Senator Leahy raised $7.5 million—over half the building's total cost—from three federal agencies to build the waterfront center.

"All of the content and all of exhibits work together," says Julie Silverman. "In 1995 we took over an old naval reserve building that

★ ★

Look at that cute little guy saying "come
on in!" One passerby was heard to say as
she looked at the window painting: "I think
the drawing is fabulous. It just looks airy
and inviting."

was on this site. We stayed there for six years until plans for the new
building were in place. Two years later, in 2003, we moved in.

"Anything we could salvage from the old building, we did. The
boards we're standing on are Douglas fir timbers from the old building, replaned, remilled, and put in as decking." This example of recla-
mation is but one of dozens of ecological decisions that led to ECHO
being the first Vermont building certified by the U.S. Green Building
Council the year it opened. Other criteria for this rating include energy
use and renewal, environmental impact, and waste management and
recycling.

Julie sums up the philosophy behind the many attractions at ECHO, including the more than seventy species of live fish, amphibians, and reptiles. "We are very much place based," she says. "Most of the content and exhibits are about the Lake Champlain basin. We give people an opportunity to see species they would never see otherwise—the sturgeon, for example, because that type of historic animal has been around as long as the dinosaurs."

According to Julie, that information usually elicits one of two follow-up questions, particularly from school groups: "That lives in Lake Champlain?" or "That fish is as old as a dinosaur?"

"Yes," of course, is the answer to the first question. As to the second, guides proclaim, usually on a daily basis, "No, we're not talking about that particular sturgeon. We're saying the sturgeon species has been around as long as the dinosaurs!"

Enter Burlington on U.S. Route 2, which becomes Main Street. Turn north onto Battery Street. Drive 1 block and take a left at the light onto College Street. ECHO is located at the bottom of College Street on the waterfront. Hours vary by season and special exhibits change frequently, so check ahead. For more information visit www.echovermont.org or call (877) ECHOFUN (877–324–6386).

Is He One of Us, or Not?

Fairfield

If twenty-first president Chester A. Arthur were alive today, he'd have a little 'splainin' to do.

"Sir," one might ask, "were you legally entitled to become president? You say you were born in Fairfield, Vermont. Yet no birth certificate has been found to indicate that you were not in fact born just over the border in Canada."

Or "Sir, you said throughout your lifetime that you were born in 1829, but the year inscribed on your gravestone is 1830."

Or even "Sir, it is said that you secluded yourself in the White House for two and one-half months after President James A. Garfield was shot and before he died. It is said the reason for this is that you knew many people thought you had something to do with his assassination. What do you say in answer to this charge, sir?"

President Arthur could be asked still other questions: Why no vice president? Why no first lady? (Actually, that last of these is easily answered. Arthur's wife, Nell, died of pneumonia less than two years before he became president.) President Arthur did ask his sister to assume some social duties and help him care for the youngest of his two children, who was then eleven. He also had installed a stained glass window in Saint John's Episcopal Church, across the street from the White House, in memory of his wife. The memorial window, which exists today, was lit at night so the president could look at it.

Before he entered politics, Chester Arthur was principal of North Pownal Academy, in the southeast corner of Vermont. Later, as a politician, he was often accused of cronyism. In his powerful position as collector of the Port of New York, for example, he hired many more

President Chester A. Arthur's modest birthplace in Fairfield.

Alburg's Binational Customs House

In 1781 the Vermont legislature granted to Ira Allen and sixty-four associates the only town in Grand Isle County that was not a Lake Champlain island. This was Alburg, a peninsula connected by bridges to the other island towns. In those days smuggling was known to occur across the Canadian border, especially during Prohibition. Since then the U.S. and Canadian governments have collaborated to build a common customs house along the U.S.–Canada boundary line in Alburg. It is the only customs house operated and maintained by both countries on the entire international border.

employees than were needed, most of them loyal Republican Party workers. As both vice president and president, however, he established a reputation for independence. Although his party vigorously opposed civil service reform, he asked for and received legislation that established a Civil Service Commission.

Shortly after he became president, Chester A. Arthur discovered that he suffered from a fatal kidney disease. He died in 1886 at the age of fifty-seven, a year and one-half after leaving office.

To visit the Chester A. Arthur birthplace, on U.S. Route 7, after coming to Fairfield, go north approximately 1 mile and bear right at the fork. Continue 5 miles to the historic site. The road will turn to gravel. The site is open July 4 through mid October on Saturday and Sunday, 11:00 a.m. to 5:00 p.m. Donations are appreciated. For more information visit www.historicvermont.org/sites/html/arthur.html or call (802) 828–3051.

★ ★

No Place for the Devil in the Old Round Church

Richmond

Right. No corners equals no place for the Devil to hide. That's one theory, anyway, accounting for churches built in this manner. Richmond's
Old Round Church doesn't really qualify, because it consists of sixteen
sides, which still, of course, leaves corners, albeit pretty skimpy ones.

The Old Round Church was built in 1813 as a nondenominational
meetinghouse, with the town's Baptists, Universalists, Congregational-
ists, and Methodists all sharing the facilities, and all serving as propri-
etors. The land was donated by a tavern keeper and a storekeeper, and
the church construction costs came to $2,305.42—all raised by the
sale of pews.

**Some say the Round Church has sixteen sides because
builder William Rhodes had seventeen workers—one
for each side, and the last for the belfry.**

This church held up for 160 years, when it was closed by state
officials as unsafe for public use. In 1976 the church was turned over
to the Richmond Historical Society for restoration. Five years and

$180,000 later, the church was opened again and has remained so. A second restoration now under way will add a new cedar shingle roof, sprinkler system, handrails to the balcony stairwells, and a paint job inside and out.

From I-89, take exit 11 and drive east to the center of Richmond Village on U.S. Route 2. At the four corners, turn right and take Bridge Street south. The Old Round Church is on the left, just across the Winooski River, less than 1 mile from the village. The church is open to the public during the summer and fall foliage seasons, 10:00 a.m. to 4:00 p.m. daily. For more information, including a virtual tour, visit www.oldroundchurch.com.

The Museum That Sugar Built

Shelburne

Shelburne Museum is the creation of Electra Havemeyer Webb, whose father inherited the American Sugar Refinery Company from his father and renamed it the Domino Sugar Company. Henry O. Havemeyer was able to leave Electra enough money for any collectible she coveted. Electra's father and mother also passed on to her their own strong collecting habits. Electra knew exactly what she wanted, and from the museum's founding in 1947 until she died in 1960, she had collected some 80,000 items, including valuable impressionist art by Monet, Manet, and Degas she had chosen from her parents' collection. Today the museum is estimated to include 150,000 items.

Let's sample the curiosities. Probably most dramatic is the *Ticonderoga,* a hundred-year-old side-paddle-wheel passenger steamboat—the last to operate commercially on Lake Champlain. This National Historic Landmark was still in service and about to be scrapped when historian Ralph N. Hill's crusade to "Save the *Ti*" led him to Electra Havemeyer Webb. She bought it as an excursion boat in 1951, but when that enterprise failed, she decided to move the ship overland 2 miles to the museum, a monumental task on its own.

One building added to the collection after Electra's death is difficult to miss. The Round Barn probably will be the first building you

Here's the scene Arnold Graton looked on helplessly from the second helicopter as the silo was being lowered.

see after entering the museum grounds. Built 50 miles away in East Passumpsic, Vermont, in 1901, late in 1985 it was dismantled, plank by numbered-and-lettered plank and transported to Shelburne by a convoy of flatbed trucks.

That was the simple part. A 9,000-pound wooden silo, the core of the barn, was judged to be too fragile to make the trip by truck. An airlift was funded by grants from Pratt & Whitney and the Sikorsky companies, and on March 11, 1986, a Skycrane helicopter made the journey from East Passumpsic to Shelburne.

★ ★

By coincidence the Pratt & Whitney employee who suggested using a Skycrane was the barn builder's granddaughter. Bernice Quimby, a thirty-seven-year employee of United Technologies Pratt & Whitney Division, grew up less than a mile from the barn. Her carpenter grandfather, Fred "Silo" Quimby, had built three round barns. The one in East Passumpsic, donated to the museum by its owners, was the last one standing.

In aggregate, the variety of exhibits in the museum's buildings will gratify the broadest of tastes. Electra's personal preferences ran to folk art, which, as she defined it, is the work of untaught men and women who made useful things beautiful. This describes most of the Shelburne's exhibits, including the quilts, art, weathervanes, textiles, furniture, tools, toys, vehicles, and glass walking sticks. To make the best use of your time, take advantage of the museum's two-day admittance with a full-price admission.

From I-89 north, take the South Burlington exit. Go south on U.S. Route 7 for 7 miles, to the village of Shelburne, and look for the sign on the right. The museum is open daily, 10:00 am to 5:00 pm, mid May through October. For more information go to www.shelburne museum.org or call (802) 985–3346.

Shelburne Farms: Two miles from the museum, at Harbor and Bay Roads, is Shelburne Farms, built by Dr. William Steward Webb and his wife, Lila, Electra's in-laws. Today the 1889 mansion serves as a twenty-five-bedroom inn and is surrounded by a 1,000-acre farm now run by two Webb grandsons as a nonprofit organization dedicated to agricultural conservation and education. For more information visit www.shelburnefarms.org or call (802) 985–8686.

Reverence—A Dream Come True, Big Time
South Burlington

Driving north along I-89 between exits 12 and 13, look for an unexpected sight on your right: the tails of two whales, 13 feet long, diving into a sea of grass. The inspiration for Jim Sardonis's striking 1989 sculpture was a dream. "I was standing on a beach," says Jim, "and

★ ★

Sardonis's *Reverence* was inspired by
the 1998 Alaska oil spill.

these two whale tails came up, with the water pouring off. And I woke
up thinking this would make a great sculpture. At first I thought of
a fountain setting, but it soon evolved into using the ground as an
imaginary ocean surface, and allowing people to get right up to it and
feel the scale a little bit more. After being commissioned to create the
sculpture, I went out on a couple of whale watches to observe hump-
backs. It was very inspiring."

The two whales, which took Jim nine months to complete, were
made from thirty-six tons of Impala black granite imported from South
Africa. The two finished pieces total roughly ten tons and are anchored
by stainless steel pins in a 5-foot-deep concrete foundation. Each tail
consists of two pieces joined just below the flukes.

★ ★

While Jim was working on the whale tails, which he had named *Pas de deux,* the Exxon *Valdez* oil spill in Alaska made headlines world-wide. Jim decided to use his work to raise people's consciousness about environmental issues. As a result he renamed his work *Reverence* and has completed a number of sculptures in this vein, among them those of several extinct species—passenger pigeons and great auks, for example.

From I-89 exit 12, take a right at the end of the ramp, then right again at the first light. Drive 2 to 3 miles past a couple of shopping centers to the Technology Sculpture Park sign on the left. Turn left, drive halfway around the circular drive, and park. Walk across the field toward I-89. The sculpture is on the highest point of surrounding land.

For more of Jim's work visit www.sardonis.com.

index

index

index

index

index

index

index